Canadian
Words & Sayings

OTHER BOOKS BY BILL CASSELMAN
from McARTHUR & COMPANY

Casselman's Canadian Words

Casselmania

Canadian Garden Words

Canadian Food Words

Canadian Sayings

Canadian Sayings 2

Canadian Sayings 3

What's in a Canadian Name?

As The Canoe Tips:
Comic Scenes from Canadian Life

Canadian
Words & Sayings

Bill Casselman

McArthur & Company
Toronto

First published in Canada in 2006 by
McArthur & Company
322 King St. West, Suite 402
Toronto, Ontario M5V 1J2
www.mcarthur-co.com

Library and Archives Canada Cataloguing in Publication

Casselman, Bill, 1942-
Canadian words and sayings / Bill Casselman.

ISBN 1-55278-569-6

1. Canadianisms (English). 2. English language—Etymology.
I. Title.

FC23.C364 2006 422 C2006-903096-0

Cover and Composition by *Mad Dog Design*
Printed in Canada by *Webcom*

The publisher would like to acknowledge the financial support of the Government of Canada through the Book Publishing Development Program, The Canada Council for the Arts, and the Ontario Government of Ontario through the Ontario Media Development Corporation Ontario Book Initiative.

10 9 8 7 6 5 4 3 2 1

for Judy Casselman

Fide et fortis familiam custodit.

Contents

Dedication / v

Preface / xxi

Part One: CANADIAN WORDS

The Purpose of Part One / 1

Agincourt, Ontario / 3
Alberta Chuckwagon Slang / 4
Alberta's Fort Whoop-Up / 4
Alder Trees, Canadian Beavers & Venice, Italy / 5
Apples of Canada / 10
Arbor vitae: The Canadian Origin of
this Cedar's Name / 13
Arctic Char & The Origin of the Word *Arctic* / 14
Arctic Willow Tea / 15
Athabasca / 16
Bafflegab & Gobbledygook of Canada CD / 17
Bakeapple / 34
Baked Wind Pills / 37
Balsam & Balm: Word Lore Galore / 37
Balsamroot / 44
Bangbelly / 45
Bear Foot / 46
Bear's Butter / 46

Bedlunch / 47
Bellybusters / 47
Birchbark Moose Calls? / 47
"Birdcages" of Victoria, British Columbia / 49
Blé d'Inde (Indian Corn) / 49
Blue-Blood Alley in Vancouver / 50
Bluff on the Canadian Prairies / 51
Boil-Up & A Pipe / 52
Boss Ribs of Prairie Buffalo / 52
Boucanière (Acadian Smokehouse) & Pirates! / 53
Bouillon d'Habitant (Farmer's Stew) / 54
Bourassa & Borage & Burro / 57
Brewis / 60
Brollywood, British Columbia / 64
Bryan Adams / 65
Buffalo Berry / 69
Bungee of Manitoba / 70
Butte / 71
Butter Tart / 72

Cabot: Famous Name in Canadian History / 75
Cadillac: Automobile Takes Fur Trader's Name / 79
Calgary Redeye / 80
Callaghan: A Literary Surname of Canada / 80
Camas of British Columbia / 84
Canada Bloodroot or Puccoon / 86
Canadian Prison Slang: Benny, Billy & Dunker / 88
Canadian Wild Ginger: A Pioneer Toothpaste / 88
Canola / 90
Cape Breton Pork Pies / 91
Caribou / 91
Catskinner / 93

Charlottetown / 93
Cheechako / 94
Chiard / 94
Cipaille or Sea Pie? / 95
Ciselette (Pork & Molasses Dessert Sauce) / 97
Colcannon Night in Newfoundland / 98
Coteaux of Canada / 102
Coulee / 103
Cow Chips & Bodewash / 103
Cushion Cactus Fruit of Alberta / 104

Damper Dogs & Flacoons in Newfoundland / 105
Digby Chicken / 106
"Dog Patch" in Edmonton / 106
Dollar Bill: A Canuck Buck / 107
Dolly Varden Trout / 108
Dough Gods / 109
Douglas Fir of British Columbia / 109
Duck Potato & Wapatoo: Canadian Terms for Arrowhead Plant / 110
Dulse / 111
Dumb Cake / 113
"Dutchmess" in Nova Scotia / 114

Eau Claire in Calgary / 114
Edmonchuk, Alberta? / 114
Eel Pie / 115
Eh? Did Canucks Invent Eh? / 116

Figgy Duff / 122
Firewater / 125
Fireweed Tea of the Yukon / 127

First Meridian of Manitoba / 128
Flipper Pie of Newfoundland / 129
Foule / 130
Fredericton / 131
Fricot (Acadian Stew) / 131
Frolic in New Brunswick Has Jumpy Origin / 133
Fungy / 133

Geoduck or Gooeyduck / 134
Gin Pole / 135
Gorbies of Muskoka! / 136
Gow of British Columbai Waters / 137
Grid Roads / 137
Grunt / 138

Halifax / 138
Hallelujah Point in Vancouver / 139
Ofra Harnoy: The Meanings of a Cellist's Name / 140
Haw Eaters or Manitoulin Islanders / 142
Hébert: Famous Surname of Québec / 145
Hepatica / 147
Here's a Ho! / 148
Herring-Choker in New Brunswick / 148
Hewitt of Hockey Shoots & Scores! / 149
High Muckamuck / 151
Hoodoo / 152
Hootch / 154
Hurt Pie / 155

Intervale of our Maritimes / 156
Irish Moss Pudding / 156

Jigg's Dinner / 159
Jill-Poke / 160
Jollop / 161
Juniper Tea / 161

Kahahoosa or Jack-in-the-Pulpit / 162
Kartoshnik — Doukhobors' Potatoes / 163
Kiack / 165
Kinnikinnick / 166
Kitsilano in Vancouver / 168
Krall as in "Diana of the Keyboards" / 171

Labrador Tea / 174
Lake Winnipeg Goldeye / 175
Lassy Mogs / 175
Logging Jargon of British Columbia / 176
Lucivee / 179
Lumber: Origin of a Word Important
to Canadian Economics & History / 179
Lunenburg Pudding / 184

Malpeque Oyster / 186
Mangeurs de Lard or Porkeaters / 187
Manitoulin / 188
Manitowaning / 188
Maple! The Totally Awesome Super Entry
of this Entire Book / 189
Marquis Wheat / 201
Medicare / 201
Mi'kmaq Potato or Groundnut / 203
Mina: The Cree Word for 'Berry' / 203
Mooseberry / 204

Moose Muffle Soup / 205
Mug Up / 206

Nanaimo Bar / 207
Nettle Soup / 208
Newfoundland Changes Its Name / 210
Nuisance Grounds / 214
Nunavik & Nunavut: Different Words
for Different Places / 215

Ontario Hydro / 216
Oolichan: A Fish That Ignites / 216
Ottawa / 217

"Packingtown" in Edmonton / 219
Peavey / 219
Pembina Berry / 220
Pemmican / 220
Pickerel Weed / 224
Pikelets / 225
Pipsissewa / 226
Pitcher Plant / 227
Ponask / 228
Ponnukokur / 228
Pork & Jerk / 229
Potlatch / 229
Pouding du Chômeur / 230
Poutine: The Complete & Factual Story / 233
Prairie Chicken / 236
Prairie: Origin of the Word / 238
Prairie Turnip / 242
Prickly Pear Cactus / 243

Prince Edward Island of Many Names / 244
Rampike / 246
Rappé Pie / 247
Real McCoy of Ontario:
An African-Canadian Invention / 247
Red River Bannock / 249
Richibucto Goose / 250
Rips / 250
Robin Hood Flour / 251
Rock Tripe or *Tripe de Roche* / 251
Rouleauville in Calgary / 252
Rubbaboo / 253

Salal / 254
Salmonberry or Olallie / 256
Saskatoonberry / 257
Saw-Off / 257
Saw-Whet Owl / 258
Scarborough / 258
Scotchman's Hill in Calgary / 259
Scripture Cord / 259
Scrunchins in Newfoundland and Labrador / 260
Scut on Prince Edward Island / 260
Shediacs / 261
Skidroad in Vancouver / 261
Skunk Cabbage & Me / 263
Skyr / 264
Sloven / 265
Smelt Storm / 266
Soapolallie, Soapberry, or Hooshum / 267
Sockeye Salmon: A British Columbia Word / 268
Son-Of-A-Gun-In-A-Sack / 270

Sonsy / 270
Sounds / 271
Squatum / 272
St. John's, Newfoundland / 272
Stog Your Face / 273

Tar Sands of Fort McMurray, Alberta / 273
Teddy of Shine / 275
Tilley Hat: Canada's Most Renowned Headgear / 275
Togue / 277
Toonie: Birth of a Canadian Money Word / 278
Toronto Street Slang / 290
Toronto Words & Place Names / 290
Tourtière / 294
Toutin / 294
Tree Nails of New Brunswick / 295
Trillium, a.k.a. Moose-Flower of Nova Scotia / 296

Vent-View / 297

Wangan & Wanigan / 297
Weather Rhymes of Canada / 298
Whore's Egg / 311
Why I'm Not a Word Cop: An Essay
against Nitpickers / 312
Winnipeg / 319
Winnipeg Jambuster / 320

Part Two: CANADIAN SAYINGS

1. Able to Enjoy Life / 323
2. Advice to a Person Picking Their Nose / 323
3. All is Not Well / 323
4. Anger / 324
5. Annoyance / 324
6. Athletes – Hockey versus Figure Skating / 326
7. Bad Aim / 328
8. Bad Luck / 328
9. Be Careful! / 329
10. Beaver Fever or Bush-sick / 329
11. Behind the Times / 330
12. Big & Tall / 331
13. Birth Order / 331
14. Blabbermouths / 332
15. Boondocks or Way Out in the Woods / 332
16. Boredom / 334
17. Buck Teeth / 334
18. Bumpkin or Hick / 334
19. Calm Down / 335
20. Canada Outdoors / 336
21. Canadian Acquaintance / 336
22. Canadian Advice / 336
23. Canadian Army Slang / 336
24. Canadian Coffee / 338
25. Canadian Directions / 338
26. Canadian Friendliness / 340
27. Canadian Navy Expressions / 340
28. Canadian Politicians / 340
29. Canadian Pride / 341
30. Canadian Real Estate / 341

31. Canadian Sports / 341
32. Canadiana / 342
33. Checking Up / 350
34. Children / 351
35. Children & Food / 351
36. Close / 351
37. Close Examination / 352
38. Clothes / 352
39. Coffee / 352
40. Common-Law Marriage / 353
41. Crankiness / 353
42. Craziness / 355
43. Criminal—Prairie Variety / 355
44. Crooks, Thieves & Bad Guys / 356
45. Cynical Knowledge / 356
46. Darkness / 356
47. Decisions, Decisions / 356
48. Disdain / 357
49. Drinking Alcohol / 357
50. Exaggeration / 357
51. Excess / 357
52. Excuses / 358
53. Executive Slang / 358
54. Family / 358
55. Farming / 359
56. Fat / 359
57. Fatigue / 361
58. Fixed in Their Ways / 361
59. Food / 361
60. Fussy / 366
61. Good Wishes to a Child / 367
62. Gossip / 367

63. Greetings / 367
64. Hair / 367
65. Haircuts / 368
66. Happiness / 368
67. Health / 368
68. Heat & Warmth / 369
69. Help / 369
70. Helpless or Forlorn / 369
71. How Are You? / 369
72. Hunger / 371
73. Impossibility / 371
74. Indecisiveness / 371
75. Injury / 372
76. *In Vino Veritas* / 372
77. Inside More Important Than Outside / 372
78. Intelligent / 373
79. Laziness / 373
80. Learning to Drive / 373
81. Lies / 373
82. Loser / 374
83. Luck, Dumb Luck! / 374
84. Marry His Brother? / 374
85. Men's Clothing / 374
86. Messy Dresser / 375
87. Minor Problem / 375
88. Mock Praise / 375
89. Money Problems / 376
90. Moping / 376
91. Naïveté / 376
92. Nastiness / 376
93. Neatness / 376
94. Never / 377

95. Nose Picking / 378
96. Obstruction / 378
97. Obviousness / 378
98. Old Age / 379
99. Old Age: White Hair / 381
100. Old Jokes / 382
101. Other Forms of Life / 382
102. Overcrowding / 382
103. Pessimism / 382
104. Pill-Poppers / 382
105. Poor / 383
106. Poverty in Québec / 386
107. Quantity / 387
108. Québec's Natural Bounty / 387
109. Rain / 387
110. Religious Ceremonies / 388
111. Reluctance to Accept a Thing / 388
112. Resting / 388
113. Sadness / 389
114. Searching / 389
115. Shoddiness / 389
116. Sick / 389
117. Smallness / 389
118. Snakes! / 390
119. Speed / 392
120. Sports / 392
121. Sports Failure / 392
122. Sports Victory / 393
123. Stinginess / 393
124. Stupidity / 395
125. Stuttering / 396
126. Tanned / 396

127. Tense / 397
128. Thief / 397
129. Thinness / 398
130. Threats / 398
131. Time / 399
132. Tired Out / 399
133. Toughness / 399
134. Trip Over Your Own Tongue during a Speech / 400
135. Truth / 400
136. Ugly / 400
137. Unpleasant / 401
138. Uselessness / 401
139. Weather in Canada / 401
140. Welfare & A New Origin of the Word *Pogey* / 412
141. Winning in Canada / 413
142. Wisdom / 414
143. Work / 414
144. You Can't Take It with You / 422

Final Note to Reader / 422

Preface

As its title proclaims, this is a book full of wholesome Canadian word stories and family-friendly Canadian sayings: words first, sayings second. Other books of mine have contained racy, raunchy, and off-colour items, but not this one. Uncle Billy promises purity and swears on a stack of rusty Paul Martin campaign buttons!

Part One: Canadian Words

This word collection highlights my own favourite Canadian word stories, especially chosen for the enjoyment of the whole family. These stories from Canadian history and from last night's news headlines are entertaining and surprising. You'll find out in the first section of the book why some terms that we use every day are not what they seem.

Did you know that Lake Huron is a vicious, nasty insult to our First Peoples? Look it up right now!

Canada has a fish that ignites. On our Pacific coast, the oolichan or *candlefish* is so full of oil it can be lighted at one end and used as a candle. British Columbia pioneers did just that.

The very first *Skid Row* or *Skid Road* in Canada was in Vancouver at the end of the nineteenth century. The term originated because out-of-work loggers drank in cheap saloons at the end of a road used to skid logs. Skids were greased logs used to slide rough timber to a waterway or railhead.

I ride the verbal chuckwagon in this new collection too, telling the amusing stories behind such hearty Canadian food words as *gooeyducks* and *hurt pie*. The juicy lore and tangy tales of Canadian foods that founded a nation are here: from *scrunchins* to *rubbaboo*, from *bangbelly* to *poutine*, from *Winnipeg jambusters* to *Nanaimo bars*.

I check out the origins of famous last names too. Did you know that pop singer Shania Twain bears an Ojibwa first name that means 'on my way'? Movie star Keanu Reeves has a first name that is Hawaiian for 'cool breeze.'

Part Two: Canadian Sayings

Here are 550 clean, non-blasphemous sayings featuring 156 newly published expressions. We've gathered funny sayings from every cranny of Canada. Take Alberta. Chinooks warm it; Alberta clippers (cold winds) freeze it. Eons ago, this land rumbled to the thud of monsters like the Albertosaurus, actual scientific name of a dinosaur whose bones were discovered near Drumheller. Less noisy but just as boisterous are the colourful folk sayings of Alberta. I once asked an outdoors guide in Jasper, "How's it going in Alberta these days?" He replied, "Slicker 'n a brookie!" expressing a sentiment that many proud Albertans share. Brookie is a local diminutive for brook trout. I picked up an **opposite** folk saying from a reader in the little town of Vulcan, Alberta: "I feel like a dyin' calf in a hailstorm." Down around Milk River country, a southern Alberta euphemism is still heard. A visitor asked a rancher, "Whatever happened to Fred? I heard he was doin' poorly, eh?" The rancher adjusted his hat and said, "Might say that. Fred's dead." A local euphemism for dead is "Gone to Sand Hills," "Fred's gone to the Sand Hills," the Sand Hills being the Happy Hunting Grounds for the Blood people of the sandy hill country south of Lethbridge. From Three Hills, Alberta, comes this dismissal: "He's lower than a snake's belly in a wagon rut." Consider too this Albertan put-down: "That dude from Ottawa thinks Medicine Hat is a cure for head lice."

Do all sayings belong to a distant rural past where toothless yokels in bib overalls sat around a Franklin stove, leaning back on bentwood chairs at the rear of the general store and trading wisecracks as they sip a jug of moonshiner's white lightning? No, indeed. Canadians are coining new sayings every day, to comment on current trends, modern behaviours, contemporary problems. Consider this zinger: *Ma petite ville Québécoise est tellement polluée qu'à tous les matins, le coq ne chante pas, il tousse!* "My little Quebec town is so polluted, roosters don't crow in the morning, they cough up phlegm." Gruesome? Maybe. But a reminder that David Suzuki and other friends of the Canadian environment have been telling us the truth. By the way, the translations from French are mine. If they are incorrect, don't go postal and secede from the Dominion, just give me heck and email me the correct translation.

Letters, We Get Letters

I love to receive email and snail mail from readers and here's one I want to share.

Dear Bill,

I bought your first Canadian Sayings *book for my dad and our whole family loves it. I can't wait to read the rest of your books. Your work is important and appreciated. I have one possible addition for an upcoming book: 'as useless as last year's woodpecker.' It means a severely useless thing and was heard in Street's Ridge, Nova Scotia. Hope you find this interesting and keep up the fantastic work! In the shared interest of amazing Canadian sayings and words I remain,*

Brianne Hunsley, of Halifax, Little River, New Brunswick, and Baie Verte, New Brunswick

Thank you, Brianne!

School & Classroom Ideas for Using Canadian Sayings

A Canadian folk saying can be the lively springboard for a short essay or a little theme paper. Instead of that bane of all public school topics, "How I Spent My Summer Vacation" or that other tired old topic "What I Got for Christmas," ask a class to take as a thought leader a saying like "I'm so happy, I could break out in cartwheels and roll all over myself." Ask a student for a few paragraphs about the time when you finished the day and said with a smile, "The puck is going my way." Or maybe you thought it in French, *La rondelle roule pour moi*. Perhaps it was a day of mixed blessings and you shrugged your shoulders and said, "That's life in the putty factory." Even students know that fate is fickle. It bends and turns like putty in your hands, even when it is being manufactured in the putty factory.

In a senior public school classroom, enjoyable and educational use can be made of these sayings. Class projects can include studying a few of the sayings and then getting the kids to canvass their parents for everyday folk sayings that the parents use, that the kids hear in their houses (but not the naughty ones!). This creates a good take-home project that will not bedevil the parents. The next day the students bring to the classroom for discussion the sayings they have collected at home from Mom and Dad, from Gran and Gramps, from older siblings, from uncles and aunts, or from a brief and polite canvassing of friendly neighbours. It's a project that permits the child to see her or his family as unique. The sayings could be preserved in a special folder made in art class.

At a time in our national life when pressure to become more American mounts every day, it is no small thing to remind our children that Canada is a distinct nation. We have created unique Canadian words and sayings that belong strictly to us. Both help make us Canucks, not Yanks. Kids ought to know that, as early as Grade One.

If you know Canadian sayings not included here, please email them to me. When I use your saying, you get to have your name in the next edition of *Canadian Sayings*, if you wish.

The last thought of this preface? This book on Canada's words and sayings should be in every house where people are proud to say: "That's Canadian, eh."

Bill Casselman

email: canadiansayings@mountaincable.net
website: www.billcasselman.com

PART ONE

Canadian Words

THE PURPOSE OF PART ONE

One of the goals of this collection of Canadian terms is to show students where the words we use every day—usually without thinking about them—come from and how awesome Canadian word stories are. We also want to make the big long jawbreakers in Canadian history and Canadian geography and biology easy to learn. Is that possible? You bet! The technical terms in science and learning can be fascinating. Part One of this book shows how scientific Canadian names have the easiest, homiest origins in Latin and Greek and modern European languages. They are not daunting, tongue-twisting loads of word freight and word fright. Technical terms are nothing to fear, if you take the trouble to find out where and how they arose. When you do, you will find that you remember these terms much better. No matter what grade you are in, no matter how far you plan to pursue your education, in a successful life you will always have to learn new technical terms. If you pick them up now, and discover how easy and unfrightening they are, your burden of memory work later in high school or college or university or in that second or third job will be eased greatly. Trust me. Check out the first five pages of these Canadian word stories and tell me you are not hooked.

AGINCOURT, ONTARIO

This suburban sprawl of what was once farmland north of Toronto was named after the place of a famous battle in northern France. In 1415 Henry V's longbowmen trounced a French army, allowing English Henry to lay claim to the French throne. The longbow was the chief weapon of English armies from the fourteenth century until the introduction of firearms. The French town of Agincourt bears an early Teutonic warrior name, probably *Hakenkurz* 'Short Blade' modified by French folk etymology, the modification helped by the fact that the German adjective for short *kurz* is related to the French adjective for short *court*, and that both derive from the Latin *cohors, cohortis* whose ultimate meaning is 'land enclosed, cut off, shortened like a garden plot'; compare the Latin word for garden *hortus*. That was the original meaning of the noun *court* in English, and all the many related words we now use like *courtesy*, *courtesan*, and *curtsy*. The Roman army divided a camp up into areas, named after farm enclosures, *cohortes*. A fellow soldier sharing the same enclosure was your cohort.

Less likely is the derivation that suggests that Agincourt may be a place name in early French like *Agincortis* 'feudal estate whose symbol is the blade of a sword' with the medieval Latin *cortis* 'estate, domain, town' and *agin*, a French diminutive of *ac* 'sharp edge.' While not utterly preposterous, this suggestion does not accord with common French naming rules for places.

ALBERTA CHUCKWAGON SLANG

In Alberta rangeland slang, rashers of bacon are "rattlesnakes," just as "red lead" is chuckwagon ketchup, "tent pegs" are frozen strips of beef, and fried hash stored too many days in a trail-cook's larder was called "yesterday, today, and tomorrow." See also our later entry for "Son-of-a-gun-in-a-sack."

ALBERTA'S FORT WHOOP-UP

In Canada's Old West, perhaps the most notorious den of whisky-peddlers and frontier badmen was at Fort Whoop-Up, a whisky post set up in 1869 by two American thugs from Montana Territory named John Healey and Alf Hamilton. Fort Whoop-Up was established at the confluence of the Oldman and St. Mary Rivers near the site of present-day Lethbridge, Alberta. "Keg angels" and "whisky ranchers" were other names for these merchants of illicit alcohol. The going rate was one cup of whisky for one buffalo robe, that is, a buffalo hide dressed on both sides. The firewater they peddled to First Peoples was often diluted with swamp water. As it happens, one actual recipe survives in the archives at the Glenbow Alberta Institute, a holograph in the hand of John D. Higinbotham, a pioneer Lethbridge druggist, whose note I quote:

Fort Whoop-Up Recipe for the Liquor Traded to Indians:

Alcohol 1 qt.
Black Strap Chewing Tobacco - 1 lb.
Jamaica Ginger - 1 bottle
Black Molasses - 1 quart
Water - q.s.
The whole boiled until "ripe."
A cup of the above for one buffalo hide.

The abbreviation *q.s.* is pharmacist's Latin for *quantum satis* 'however much is enough,' that is, sufficient quantity to do the job. Some job. So wide and ill was the repute of this whisky fort that the whole area around the Alberta–Montana border came to be known as "Whoop-up country." In 1874, the Northwest Mounted Police arrived, booted the whisky traders out, and converted the fort to a police outpost.

Whoop-up as a noun denoting a rousing Western party had existed before the fort was named. Whoop as a verb and hunting interjection has been in our language since Middle English. Whoop-up and its American equivalent whoop-de-doo and whoopla and whoopee are in print by the middle of the nineteenth century.

ALDER TREES, CANADIAN BEAVERS & VENICE, ITALY

What do dam-building Canadian beavers and

sixteenth-century Venice have in common? Underwater pilings made of alder wood! Beavers (*Castor canadensis*) build dams with underwater portions often composed of alder boughs, which are superbly waterproof once submerged. Beavers also use and eat aspen and birch. Venice, with its Latin motto, *Serenissima Respublica*, Most Serene Republic, is said to be held above the encroaching waves on once stout pilings made of a European species of alder, probably *Alnus glutinosa*, the Black Alder, in Canada an imported species planted as an ornamental tree. The Black Alder's young leaves are glutinose, that is, clammy, so sticky in fact that some medieval Europeans scattered alder leaves on the floors of their houses to trap fleas. In medieval France and Holland, waterproof alder wood was widely used to build sluices and troughs. The dyer's craft sees alder bark and young shoots used to make black, red, and yellow dyes.

Genus Name of the Alder Tree: *Alnus*

Family: *Betulaceae*, the birch family < *betula* Latin, birch

French: *l'aune*, older spelling *l'aulne* < *alnus* Latin, alder

Word Lore

Alder < *aler, alor* Old English. The letter *d* inserted in dialect pronunciations was fixed in manuscript English by the fourteenth century. The Latin, French, and English words for alder tree all hark back to a common Indo-European root in **al* and **el*. The people who spoke Proto-Indo-European knew some betulaceous tree like the alder. Their root appears in languages like Old Scandinavian (what Vikings spoke) *elrir*, *ölr*, in Old High German *elira*, in Modern German *Erle*, in Lithuanian *alksnis*, and in Polish *olcha*.

Canadian Alder Place Names

Humans and alders share one habitat preference. Both like to live along streams. Hence the large number of Canadian, British, and American place names that include the -alder root or an earlier version of it. The village of Aldershot, now part of Burlington, Ontario, was named after a British military base. Its name in Old English was *Alre-sceat* 'alder-hoot.' A *sceat* was a piece of land that projected or shot out into a lake or other body of water. At the town of Aldershot north of Kentville in Nova Scotia, Canadian army recruits trained at Camp Aldershot before and during World Wars I and II. The Ontario and Nova Scotian towns were both named after an army base in Hampshire, England, made famous after it was founded to train British troops sent to fight in the Crimean War between 1853 and 1856.

Other Alder Places

- Alder Point, north of Sydney Mines on Cape Breton Island, Nova Scotia
- Alderford (narrow crossing place on a river where alders grow), England

• Aldergrove, British Columbia, near Abbotsford
• Alderholt (*holt*, Old English 'woods, thicket') England
• Aldridge (in AD 1086, in the *Domesday Book*, it was listed as *Alrewic* 'alder dwelling' or 'farm')
• The Aulneau peninsula juts into Lake-of-the-Woods in northwestern Ontario.
• *Ruisseau aux Aulnes* (Alder Creek) empties into the Etchemin River southeast of Québec City.

English Surnames
Alder is a surname in Northumberland. Some instances of the surname Aldridge are from two Old English roots that mean 'farm beside alder trees' or 'ridge with alders.'

French Surnames
Aulne and Aune are both French surnames derived from an ancestor living beside alders. So too are French last names like Launay and Delaunay, as well as Aunaye, and the diminutive forms: Aunet, Alnette, Aulneau, Auneau, and Aunillon.

Other Alder Surnames
Latvian has a surname, Alksnis 'alder.' Russian has Olchin or Vólchin 'alder.' To step outside the Indo-European family, one finds a Finnish last name like Leppanen (or Leppainen) 'alder.'

German Alders & Nasty Freakazoid Goblins!
Alder tree in German is *die Erle*. The German surname *Erler* recalls a founding ancestor's home in

a grove of alders. The *Erlkönig* or Erlking was a nasty Teutonic tree goblin who lurked in dark forests. The spiteful sprite's name means 'King of the Alder,' his preferred abode. The Erlking lured children to their doom, as in the poem by Goethe, set to music by Loewe, and memorably by Schubert. "*Wer reitet so spät durch Nacht und Wind*?" Who rides so late through the night and the wind? It is a father on horseback with his son. The boy complains that the Erlking is choking him. But the father can't see the goblin, and, at the end of this gruesome song, the child ends up dead. Charming little ditty for an early-nineteenth-century evening of song in the parlour!

Species

Five of the world's thirty alder species are native to Canada. Most are shrublike rather than tree size.

Speckled Alder, widespread across Canada, is extremely important to its micro-ecosystem. Nitrogen-fixing bacteria on its root nodules make alder one of the few trees in the world that can fix nitrogen in a form plants can take in. The bacteria change gaseous nitrogen in the air into ammonia. Their high nitrogen content makes alder leaves decay quickly providing aquatic and soil nitrogen, especially useful when the tree colonizes new areas after a forest fire or after clear-cutting by lumber companies. Early-flowering alder catkins are magnets for bees. Alder seeds and flowers feed golden-winged warblers, hummingbirds, flycatchers, woodcocks, pine siskins, redpolls, and many other Canadian birds.

The Sitka Alder of British Columbia, usually shrubby, can be planted to ease soil erosion and control stream flow.

Favourite Wacko Alder Quotation

There was in English a now obsolete adjective, aldern, formed like oaken. Here is a recipe **not** to try from *The Historie of Foure-footed Beastes*, a bestiary by Edward Topsell printed in 1607, in its original spelling: "If the right eye of a Hedge-hog be fryed with the oil of Alderne or Linseed, and put in a vessel of red brasse, and afterward anoint his eyes therewith, as with an eye-salve, he shall see as well in the dark as in the light."

APPLES OF CANADA

From some of the roughly two dozen true species native to the northern temperate zone, including the crab apples, have come the thousands of hybrids and sports that produce modern eating apples. The process took centuries of selecting, grafting, and hybridizing of naturally small-fruited wild species like *Malus sylvestris* (Latin, 'of the forest'), *Malus pumila* (*pumilus* Latin adj., 'dwarf'), and *Malus prunifolia* (Latin, 'with leaves like a plum tree'). Apple trees shipped from France grew at Annapolis Royal by 1635. Our earliest settlers used apples principally to make cider.

The McIntosh Red is Canada's most famous apple. Farmer and apple-breeder John McIntosh immigrated from the Mohawk Valley to Iroquois in Upper Canada in 1796. By 1811 he was clearing land at nearby Dundela when he discovered an old orchard. One of the twenty trees bore very tasty apples. His son Allan McIntosh grafted stock of the original tree in 1835 and went into the apple business big-time. The McIntosh trees tolerated varied soils and climates. Near the site of the original tree, which died in 1910, is a plaque that says the original McIntosh tree bore apples for ninety years! Once, in England, I spoke of eating a McIntosh. My listener, a tobacconist in Leeds, stared at me as though rising damp had risen too far up my brainstem. In the British Isles, a mackintosh, a mac, or a mack, is a rainproof coat, invented by Scottish scientist Charles Macintosh by laminating two layers of cloth with rubber.

The Fameuse apple, a cultivar based on French stock, is still grown sporadically in its native Québec. Other once-popular Québec apples were the Pomme-de-neige 'snow apple,' Pomme gris(e) 'grey apple,' the Bourassa, and the St. Lawrence. Pomme-de-glace 'ice apple' was an early Acadian cultivar.

Two crab apples are native to Canada. The Pacific Crab Apple grows only in British Columbia. The hard, heavy wood of the crab apple makes it of little commercial importance. But pioneer grist mills in the Ontario countryside had gears and blades made of crab apple wood.

Canadian Paring Bee

Early settlers in the Canadas (Upper and Lower) liked to combine socializing with work. One such neighbourly gathering was the paring bee, also called apple frolic, paring frolic, and apple bee. It served the social function of preliminary courting ritual where young men and women from nearby farms could scout potential mates, while older married couples could gossip and exchange local news. Apples were pared, sliced, and hung to dry on long strings that might be suspended from rafters in the kitchen, attic, or cold cellar. A staple at Canadian pioneer tables throughout the winter months was stewed dried apples.

Canadian Apple Songs

"In the Shade of the Old Apple Tree." Canadian lyricist Harry Williams wrote the words to this Tin Pan Alley hit song of 1905. In his *Canadian Quotations*, editor John Robert Colombo reports that the lyrics were inspired by one actual apple tree that grew on Glen Edith Drive in Toronto. Williams was also lyricist of "It's a Long Way to Tipperary," adopted as the marching song of the British army in 1914. In the 1970s, George Hamilton IV wrote a country ballad, "When It's Apple-Blossom Time in Annapolis Valley."

Canadian Place Names

• Apple Hill, near the town of Casselman in southeastern Ontario

• Apple River, Nova Scotia

• Apple Tree Landing, former name of Canning, Nova Scotia, in the Annapolis Valley. Annapolis Valley apples enjoyed a long and bountiful export trade to Britain until the late 1920s.

ARBOR VITAE: THE CANADIAN ORIGIN OF THIS CEDAR'S NAME

A Canadian cedar tree or shrub named *Arbor vitae* means 'the tree of life' in Latin. Bestowed in 1558, according to one report by a King of France, the name commemorates the first, bleak, North American winter of 1535 for explorer Jacques Cartier and his men. Ill prepared for the rigours of the north, the white newcomers were only saved from death by scurvy when Aboriginal peoples showed them how to make cedar tea from the bark and foliage of eastern white cedar. The infusion was high in vitamin C, of which scurvy is a deficiency disease. Cartier sailed back to France with cedar seedlings that were grown in Paris in 1536 amid stories about the antiscorbutic wonders of this life-giving tree.

The arborvitae story made print in the works of Carolus Clusius, the humanist name of Charles de l'Écluse (1526–1609), a famous Flemish botanist, spreading the term to other European languages. For example, in German appeared the loan-translation *Lebensbaum* 'tree of life.' *Tulipa clusiana*, the Lady Tulip, a charming little species tulip suitable for Canadian bulb beds, is one of many plant names that honour this botanist.

Cedar as a Name

Cedar is one of those widespread and too inclusive common names in botany and horticulture. The trees called cedar in Canada, *Thuja* species, are of the arborvitae (informal) subfamily. No trees of the true cedar genus *Cedrus* are native to Canada. True *Cedrus* species include the Biblical cedar-of-Lebanon and the deodar.

ARCTIC CHAR & THE ORIGIN OF THE WORD *ARCTIC*

One of the most esteemed freshwater food fish of northern Canada and still shipped south to Canadian restaurants and fish markets, this char is *Salvelinus alpinus*. Brook trout and lake trout are also Canadian chars. There are two varieties of arctic char, one landlocked and the other pelagic but going into fresh water to spawn.

Why, incidentally, does English call far northern realms "arctic" regions? The idea was borrowed into late Middle English from classical Greek, where *arktos* is the word for 'bear.' The Greek adjective is *arktikos* 'pertaining to a bear.' But the Greeks used the terms to refer to one of the largest and brightest constellations in the northern skies, known to the Romans as *Ursa Major,* 'The Great(er) Bear,' and more familiarly known in English as The Big Dipper or The Plough. The Greeks thought of the distant, largely unknown lands lying under The Great Bear as dark, cold places perhaps devoid of human population. Hence our Arctic, land under the constellation of the Great Bear. And, of course, opposite (Greek *anti* or *ant-*) the North Pole is the land of the South Pole, hence the geographical name *Ant-arctica.*

In Greek myth, randy old Zeus, king of the gods and a major nymph-chaser, had a son out of divine wedlock by the nymph Calisto, who called her baby Arcas. Hera, queen of heaven and jealous wife of Zeus, was really ticked off, and seizing the opportunity to make a nasty pun (*Arcas-arktos*) caused Calisto's little bundle of joy to be turned into a large, revolting bear. But Zeus took pity on his now lumpish bastard son and set him up in the heavens to be forever with his papa in cloudland, and thus did The Great Bear come to adorn the northern night sky.

ARCTIC WILLOW TEA

There are dozens of species of ground-hugging dwarf willows in our north and they hybridize freely. Keeping low and clustered together is a protective strategy to keep out wind and freezing cold, and makes dwarf willows among the prostrate plant forms most common in subarctic and arctic regions. The bark of this scrawny, mat-forming shrub contains the antirheumatic chemical, salicin. Willow bark was imported into ancient Egypt to treat fevers and aches. More than 2,400 years ago Greek physicians prescribed extract of white willow for gout. Many of the First Peoples of North America, including the Inuit, chewed willow bark to alleviate toothache and, like the Montagnais of eastern Canada, also brewed a rich tea of arctic willow leaves and drank it to reduce headaches and for a warm pick-me-up.

Salix arctica takes its botanical name from Latin *salix* 'willow tree,' akin to the English word *sallow*, pale yellow, in reference to the leaves or bark of several European species. In Middle English, a sallow was one of the broadleaved willows. You'll find the chemical name for aspirin, acetylsalicylic acid, displays more willowy connections. Check out the history of aspirin on the web.

ATHABASCA

Athabasca was originally applied to the large, reed-ringed lake that straddles the northern Alberta–Saskatchewan border. 'Reed beds' in Cree are *athapaskaw*. The Athabasca boat was a speedy canoe useful to early fur traders in the area. That phrase was in print by 1824. There was also a clumsy wooden barge in use on the river of that name called an Athabaska scow. Once its cargo was unloaded, the crude planks making up the scow were dismantled and put to shore use. The Cree word also appears in the zoological name of Canada's largest land animal, the wood bison of Wood Buffalo National Park in northern Alberta and the Northwest Territories. Big male wood buffaloes can weigh 900 kilograms. The park is Canada's biggest, more than 44,000 square kilometres, and contains the largest herd of bison in the world. The scientific moniker of the noble beast is *Bison bison athabascae*, which is no sillier a name than Henry Wadsworth Longfellow. And the Canadian Navy still has a frigate named HMCS *Athabascan*.

BAFFLEGAB & GOBBLEDYGOOK OF CANADA CD

Selected CD Tracks Showing How Canadians Use English to Rant, to Lie, to Cheat, to Cover Up Truth, and to Peddle Bafflegab

Hey, dudes and dudettes, check out the hard copy below taken from some of the worst cases of gobbledygook ever uttered or written by a Canadian. For example, a current major phoney-baloney word is *bycatch*. Green Peace and The Suzuki Foundation have both expressed concern over this fishermen's cover-up word. The Pacific Seafood Processors Association told the *Vancouver Sun* (Dec. 7, 1988) about their "bycatch." It looks and sounds like a fisherman's honest and sturdy term. In fact, it is a cover-up word that refers to thousands of seabirds, seals, dolphins, whales, and sea lions that die strangled in ocean driftnets set to catch surface-swimming squid and other edible "sea-mass." Whenever you see the word used with approval, you know some kind of creepy lying is going on, because honest people don't use the word. Gobbledygook is often that simple.

What is gobbledygook?

Gobbledygook is language used to deceive, not to communicate. A medical services coordinator for a fire department in Canada reported that emergency personnel had found a victim "in a non-viable condition—he had no pulse and was not breathing." Well now, Mr. Coordinator. Can I call you Lem? That'd be what? Dang near ready fer a white nightie and little wings? Leastways, tuggin' at the Grim Reaper's hem, eh? I mean, you get a citizen up there in the higher realms of non-viability, you're saying: the buzzards are circling, right? I think what you're suggesting, Lem, is: this dude was rapidly approaching non-dudedom. Bone-yardwise, ready to be planted. Would I be close? Lem, seriously now and all kidding towards one side, could this guy be **dead**?

Gobbledygook is language spoken or written to evade responsibility, not to answer a question but to defuse it by coating the answer in a syrup of verbal glop. Acid rain in Canada becomes "atmospheric deposition of anthropogenetically derived acidic substances." Such language means to suffocate stark fact in a muffling blanket of mumbo-jumbo.

Gobbledygook can be an euphemism for the lowest motive. A Canadian funeral parlour is now a "Bereavement Resource Centre." As someone driving by their tasteful, glow-in-the-dark plastic sign wondered, "Gee, do they still take the dead?" A CBC-TV interviewer asks a surgeon about the source of a transplanted kidney. "From a cadaveric donor," says the pussyfooting sawbones. If he had not used euphemistic gobbledygook, think how influential this doctor (who had just benefited along with his patient from the process) could have been, by reminding people to sign the donor card on the back of their driver's licence and by stating that spare parts of the newly dead can keep some people alive. But no, he chose not to offend viewers and fudged the source with the rare adjective "cadaveric." Such misdirected gentility makes some want to jump up and yell, "You mean you cut it out of a stiff, eh, Doc?"

Gobbledygook is language wrapped in twaddling clothes and dying in a manger. It is twaddle because it often does not make sense. It's in a manger of the same straw that packs the heads and hearts of those who use it. And it is dying because it is language drained of vital reference. By obscuring common referents to which the listener or reader can attach everyday meaning, bafflegab hopes to slither off into the underbrush of unmeaning before one realizes that nothing concrete has been said. A bureaucrat from the British Columbia Ministry of Education comes to a school with bad news for its teachers, but never once uses the now context-sensitive word *teacher*. Instead, throughout his speech, this evader speaks of "on-site facilitators of pupil learning." Plenty of this spin-doctor-spiel is actually bad English and semi-literate, like the verbal garbage in the last sentence.

Origin of the Word Gobbledygook

No surprise is it to learn that this term sprang to the lips of a man who had to listen to politicians blabbing. During World War II, Congressman Maury Maverick of Texas made the word up one day in Washington, DC, after listening to more verbal bamboozlement than he could abide. In May 1944 Maverick told the *New York Times* magazine: "Perhaps I was thinking of the old bearded turkey gobbler back in Texas who was always gobbledygobbling and strutting with ludicrous pomposity. At the end of this gobble there was a sort of gook." The new word was so echoic and fitting that it passed immediately into popular speech. The congressman has an interesting last name. Could it be the origin of the word "maverick" to name anyone unorthodox and not part of a group? Yes, the congressman's grandfather was Samuel E. Maverick (1803–70) who was a Texas rancher and state politician who refused for certain practical reasons to ever brand his stock, vast herds of longhorn cattle. He then playfully claimed that all unbranded range stock might belong to him, following an agricultural precedent of pioneer America that unbranded animals on the open range, not rustled and unclaimed, belonged to whoever first branded them. Texas ranchers took to calling any unbranded cattle who wandered from a herd "mavericks." Then use of the term in Texas politics followed, and a maverick became any politician who would not follow his party's policy line.

Gobbledygook Track # 1

Now we'll continue to sample a few tracks from my CD of Canadian bafflegab.

In August 1987, the Health Sciences Centre in Winnipeg placed a Help Wanted ad for a "Co-ordinator, Occurence [*sic*] Screening, Quality Assurance Department." Uh-huh. Not too assuring a start. The word *occurrence* is misspelled, not once but four times more in the explanation that followed. Help is indeed wanted. But in the next paragraph are the real meat and potatoes of the advertisement. Should I wish to write 'meat and potatoes' in gobbledygook, I could say: the veridical carnal comestibles and solanaceous tuberosities.

The ad reads: "Occurence [*sic*] screening is an objective, criteria-based review of medical records conducted concurrently and retrospectively to identify and flag, confirm, analyze, trend, and report instances of suboptimal care attributable to health care disciplines. Under the general direction of the Director, Quality Assurance, the incumbent will co-ordinate the development, implementation and maintenance of multidisciplinary and integrated systems of occurence [*sic*] screening; will assess and review adverse patient occurence [*sic*] data; will assist with the identification of existing and/or new resources required to conduct occurence [*sic*] screening."

Now I am a mere medical layman in a state of mystification, but it appears all they want is a clerk to tote up procedural mistakes. But is that the job offered? I will never know, due to the ad's muzzy verbiage. By the way, would death be an adverse patient occurrence? I do want to say something positive. It is very assuring to be "under the general direction of the Director," as long as he's not directing their spelling.

This example and several others in this chapter are drawn from Rick Coe's excellent and unfortunately discontinued "Doublespeak Update" which appeared twice a year (1987–90) in the academic journal *English Quarterly*, published by the Canadian Council of Teachers of English when Mr. Coe was a professor of English at Simon Fraser University in Burnaby, British Columbia.

Gobbledygook Track # 2

Must gobbledygook always consist of many-syllabled senselessness? No, often it appears in language plain and bare. In 1996, Prime Minister Jean Chrétien's Liberal government brightened hopes of school-leavers with a "First Jobs" program. Canadian corporations were to help young people get into the workforce by hiring them for one year. "First Jobs" emerged from a brain-storming session with federal Treasury Board chairman Art Eggleton and the Boston Consulting Group, which then canvassed corporations for their ideas. Many of these same corporations continue in the process of massive layoffs designed to increase profit at the expense of Canadian workers. Durings the years 2002 to 2005 Ontario alone lost sixty thousand jobs in manufacturing. The young people in Chrétien's "First Jobs" scheme—really temporary help who can be let go after one year—were going to be paid near-minimum wages.

What "First Jobs" amounted to was the Liberal government, elected on a promise to create jobs, gave sanction and perhaps financial assistance to corporations to fire older, full-time employees working for higher salaries and to replace them with minimum-wage internships by temporary workers. "First Jobs" was a weasel term. A more accurate title would have been "Short, Meaningless Jobs Designed by the Liberals to Woo Corporate Canada."

Gobbledygook Track # 3

Song title: "School Days, School Days,
Dear Old Golden Fool Days."

Here is a list of sneaky phrases and wheedling euphemisms that Canadian public school and high school teachers once used to design computer macros to print out "personalized" report cards, and to reduce quarrels on parent interview days. This list or a variation once circulated widely among teachers in Ontario, British Columbia, and other provinces.

DON'T USE	USE
lazy	can do more when he tries
cheats	depends on others to do his work
below average	working at his own level
steals	borrows without permission
insolent	outspoken
lies	tends to stretch the truth
mean	has difficulty getting along with others
selfish	seldom shares with others
will fail	has a chance of passing if . . .

Remember this sickening list of lies was to be used by teachers charged with showing our children the proper use of English. To its credit, the Ontario Ministry of Education included this chart in its 1988 publication *Explorations in Language* and the author, Peter Evans, suggested another use for this list: give it to students for classroom use in learning about euphemism and dishonest language. Good for him! Parents shocked at this bafflegab might consider what they said the last time a teacher offered criticisms of their child.

Gobbledygook Track # 4
Song Title: "A Babble for the Teacher"

Another way to gloss over unpleasant facts in the parent–teacher interview is use by the teacher of the jargon of educational psychology, or the semi-literate tatters of such jargon that have become clichés. Suppose an impertinent mother comes to school and actually is bold enough to want to find out how her child, young Rupert, is really doing, no matter how upsetting a valid assessment may be. If the teacher were versed in educational doublespeak, and spoke in the same language he or she uses to write report cards, this little scene might ensue:

Mother: How's Rupert doing?
Teacher: The student in question is performing minimally for his peer group and is an emerging underachiever.

Mother: But Rupert's at the bottom of his class. He's a lazy klutz at home. Does he do anything well in school?

Teacher: The student exhibits prowess in manual plastic conception.

Mother: He knocks them dead in clay class? Makes bunnies from Plasticene?

Teacher: Well, I wouldn't put it quite that way. Rupert is also late in group integration and reacts negatively to aggression stimuli.

Mother: Yep, he's always been a loner and a crybaby.

Teacher: And he seems to have developed tardily in magno-muscle control facility.

Mother: Little Rupert falls on his head a lot. But then, so does his father.

There is no body part called a "magno-muscle" in anatomical literature. Utterly unknown to physiology is the concept of magno-muscle control facility. The teacher's English is that of the obfuscator and the liar, afraid to speak plainly because giving offence will upset the parent and take up too much of the teacher's already scarce time, hours that might be spent profitably reviewing more articles in educational journals. Then, too, the angry parent may be a member of or know someone on the school board. As all right-thinking persons know, when a student has the IQ of a beach pebble, it is ALWAYS the teacher's fault. It is NEVER the fault of the parent who married a spouse as stunned as a stump. Oh no, in modern educational theory, there are no such beings as stupid children, no, only bad teachers. By nature itself of course, all parents are perfect parents.

Gobbledygook Track # 5

Song Lyric:
"With constabulary duties to be done, to be done,
A policeman's lot is not a happy one."

In 1995, a knife-wielding intruder slipped past those guarding our prime minister's residence and penetrated the mansion as far as the Chrétiens' bedroom. Although the trespasser was caught before physical harm came to the prime minister and his wife, the RCMP sentinels were lax. This sloppy guarding called forth a paper blizzard of departmental studies. Here is part of one public RCMP document, *Security Breach — 24 Sussex Drive. Final Report, 1995-11-17*. One section of this report entitled "Shift Scheduling" begins with basic information: "The members attached to the Prime Minister's/Governor-General's Uniformed Security Detachment work on 12-hour shift rotations consisting of 2 days, 2 nights and 4 days off . . . A member rotates from post to post with commensurate breaks depending on resource numbers."

Then comes a review of whether or not a twelve-hour shift is too long for an individual RCMP guard. Here the reader asks himself how attentive anyone is after doing anything for twelve hours straight. The report continues: "Schedules impact morale and health, as well as operational efficiency. Often the greatest levels of efficiency improvement will result in unacceptable attenuation of 'quality of life' considerations. Hence a schedule that is acceptable to both the workers and the managers will likely consist of a negotiated trade-off and will often be less than maximally efficient. The demarkation of reasonable efficiency ranges that are also consistent with psychological, social and physical health is important. Quality of life [*sic*] considerations . . . translate into such issues as minimizing the number of consecutive duty tours in nights, maximizing the number of complete or partial weekends off during the year, and maximizing the predictability of working tours."

In plain English: Do cops get careless, tired, and sick after too many consecutive night shifts? Yes. Just like all the rest of us other human beings who have evolved as day-active mammals designed to sleep at night. But the report's author cannot bring himself to utter such clarity. It might sound like the RCMP was whining. Awwwww. Clear statements about too few guards getting dopey from too long, poorly designed shifts would not be stern, policelike and mature. But that is the excuse offered in this report for the bad police work.

In order not to make the RCMP sound like a bunch of complaining sucks then, the report puffs itself up with deceptive language: semi-sociological jargon mixed with a stuffy bluster of pseudo-psychological bureaucratese. A gobbet of gobbledygook like "unacceptable attenuation of 'quality of life' considerations" might read on the surface as brisk and concerned, until one pauses to ask what it means. In the context of the paragraph quoted above, it means: put guards on long shifts and they'll get clumsy, inattentive, maybe injured or shot by intruders. Scientific reports in correct English don't make formal mistakes like "unacceptable attenuation of 'quality of life' considerations." When a noun phrase is used as an adjective before another noun, one does not surround it with single quotation marks; one hyphenates the phrase so that it appears like this: quality-of-life considerations. The very act of putting 'quality of life' in single quotations is also a macho dismissal of the phrase, as if to say: I'm putting this in quotes because I'm a big, brave policeman and quality of life is only for weaklings. Yes, it's a tiny point. But little mistake after little mistake sticks in the alert reader's mind, until very early in perusal of the report, the reader sniffs the acrid reek of prose sweat, the stench of English sentences straining to be what they are not.

This prose wants to appear scientific. But it is only a cheap imitation of the general sound of scientific prose, the best of which communicates ideas, reports facts, clearly labels suppositions and hypotheses. This prose's little choo-choo ride towards respect runs off its rails in almost every paragraph. In the passage quoted, notice "demarkation" instead of the much more common Canadian and British and American spelling "demarcation." A quibble? Perhaps, but demarkation is already marked rare in many dictionaries.

Such copy also loves itself. There is a self-congratulatory smugness in the repetition of clichés borrowed from business reports and scientific abstracts, words like "commensurate," "impact" as a verb, "maximally efficient," "predictability." This is not English clear and simple and eager to tell you something. This is a ready-to-burst colostomy bag of words. It's full of crap, and the person who wrote it knows that. But the report had to be written. Orders descended from Ottawa politicians, from the Prime Minister's Office, from RCMP HQ as faces reddened and leaders became vulnerable to bad press about the break-in. Yes, after the break-in and after this report, some changes occurred in the way the RCMP guards our prime minister. But better prose, more clearly expressed, in an earlier report, might have prevented the frightening duration of the trespass.

An Ottawa civil servant once said that it had taken years to learn to write in a style such that his government department could not be held accountable for any error.

Gobbledygook Track # 6

Song Title:
"Release Me"

Here's another light sprinkle of federal flapdoodle, as found in *Budget Impact, National Defence* published in February 1994 by the authority of the Hon. David Collenette, Minister of National Defence. The paper concerned firing 8,100 military personnel and 8,400 civilian workers in the Defence Department by 1998. "The military reductions will be accomplished through attrition, restrictions on recruiting, occupational reassignment and encouraged release through the Force Reduction Program. The directed release of military personnel will only be used as a last resort." Isn't that noble? "Encouraged release" means if you quit when the Department of Defence asks you to, there will be a bonus of "additional leave entitlements and special annuity provisions." Sure, and what about an exit door prize, sergeant? How about pillows in a cheerful maple leaf pattern and pleasantly plump with shredded Somalia Inquiry documents? If you stick around and make the department fire you, or necessitate "directed release," well, the budget impact statement does not say, but it bodes ill for you. Maybe directed release involves being propelled off-base one midnight from the barrel of the regimental cannon, or a funsy going-away party where members of the disbanded Airborne Regiment perform colourful blood tests to see if you are Aryan? It's bad enough to fire people; but it is lower than pond scum to deny them any final dignity by trying to worm out of the firing by calling it directed release. Shame on the verbal charlatans who came up with this evasive claptrap. Perhaps all those with "release dates" can join in a plaintive chorus of "Release me, and let me go."

Gobbledygook Track # 7

Small print alert!

Be suspicious of small print. Use a magnifying glass always. Copy is not set in teeny type to save space, but to discourage people from reading the gobbledygooked message. Here is part of an application for a joint checking account once used by a Canadian chartered bank. By signing it, you agreed:

> that the Bank is hereby authorized to credit the said account with all monies paid to the Bank (i) at the branch of account or (ii) at any branch other than the branch of account for the credit of any one or more of us, the proceeds of any orders or promises for the payment of money, of bonds, debentures, coupons or other securities, signed to be drawn by or payable to or the property of, or received by the said Bank (i) at the branch of account or (ii) at any branch other than the branch of account for the credit of us or any one or more of us, and to endorse any of

such instruments on behalf of us of any one or more of them.

Whew! Any reader of that would wave the olive branch and sue for semantic peace. That is the worst English I've ever seen in small print. Would you entrust financial responsibility to an organization that approved such incomprehensible bank-speak? I would not. It could be rewritten in clear English using lists, clarifying punctuation, and nixing the not-legally-necessary repetitions. This is old-fashioned, pompous legalese, imitating the clotted English of Victorian contracts, and even as such it is an amateur's botched attempt at contractual precision.

Legitimate Uses of Jargon

The making of new words is a sign that a language is vital. But never be under the illusion that because a new label has been plastered on something, because it has been dubbed with a scrap of pseudo-scientific jargon, we will somehow know it more deeply.

On the other hand, all sciences need a private vocabulary. Some jargon is necessary. In one sense, all professional terminology is jargon, including that of medicine, law, education, business, sports, theology, etc., because the unique word-hoards of these fields contain terms not familiar to the general population. Linguists estimate that one-half of the vocabulary of all major world languages consists of scientific and technical terms. In Modern English, with more items of vocabulary than any other language that has existed, technical vocabulary makes up closer to 80 percent of all words. Jargon, of course, is not gobbledygook. The legitimate use of private vocabularies in science is meant to make complex statements precise and clearer than ordinary language would permit. Gobbledygook wants information made imprecise and unclear, in order to befuddle the reader sneakily.

BAKEAPPLE

Here's a one-hundred-percent Canuck word. In Canada the bakeapple is a Maritime fruit, also called baked-apple berry. It thrives in soggy bogs on Cape Breton Island and in other parts of Nova Scotia, Prince Edward Island, and Newfoundland. Farther north in Labrador and the southern Arctic, bakeapples grow on the sparse skin of moss and lichen that covers swampy areas, often in company with partridgeberries. Caribou and ptarmigan compete with humans for these sweet berries rich in fibre and vitamin C. Some Inuit people collect bakeapples in the fall and preserve them for winter use by freezing. Newfoundlanders sometimes call the plant *bog-apple*. Prince Edward Islanders occasionally use the term *yellowberry*. Bakeapple pie is still a popular pastry in our Maritimes. In Gordon Pinsent's 1974 Newfoundland novel, *John & the Missus*, a couple enjoy tea-buns and bakeapple jam.

Word Lore of Bakeapple

The Inuit word for this berry is *appik*. Late in the eighteenth century, says one cogent etymology, white traders borrowed the Inuit word, heard the *pp* as *b*, and combined it with the English word *apple*, to produce *abik-apple*, eventually further modified to bakeapple. Early German immigrants to Labrador called it *Apik-Beere* 'appik-berry.' Folksier origins say the raspberrylike fruit is amber and of wrinkled appearance, supposedly like a baked apple, but this was stretching metaphor a bit, as it resembles closely all the fruits of the *Rubus* genus. *Baie* is a French word for berry. One folk etymology of our Maritimes says that early French settlers first saw this berry new to them, and they inquired, in the improbable French of the folk story, "*Baie, qu'appelle*?" Berry, what's it called? English settlers who came afterward heard this as bakeapple, claims the tale. *Mais je pense que non*.

Rubus chamaemorus

Bakeapple is elsewhere called cloudberry and widely used in Scandinavian countries to make a sweet liqueur. Swedes ferment the berries to make a cloudberry vinegar. Lapps in Finland bury the autumn-collected berries in the snow for midwinter fruit. In Scotland it's cloudberry, and is the official badge of the clan McFarlane. One Slavic term for cloudberry is *molka*, a compressing of *malinka*, diminutive of the common Slavic word for raspberry *malina*. But standard Russian for cloudberry is *moroshka*, 'frostling' or little berry of the *moroz* 'frost.' The name for Santa Claus in Russian is *Ded Moroz* 'Father Frost.' Even the Vikings ate the juicy, amber berries of this creeping shrub that belongs to the huge Rose family of plants and to the raspberry genus *Rubus*.

The botanical name of bakeapple is *Rubus chamaemorus*. It grows all over the northern temperate zone of the world and in some adjacent arctic climates. *Rubus* is a randy genus where species interbreed at the drop of a pollen grain, so that there are dozens of species worldwide. *Rubus* is one of the Latin words for red, and is an old botanical name for any bramble bush. The Latin root pops up in the English word *ruby* and in learned adjectives like *rubefacient* 'causing redness.' The single flower of each bakeapple is white. The specific part of its scientific name, *chamaemorus*, means 'ground mulberry,' describing its low habit of growth. *Chamai* in classical Greek means 'on the ground' and *morus* is a Latin word for mulberry.

Canadian Bakeapple Place Names

Bakeapple Barren is an official toponym in Cape Breton Highlands National Park. Bakeapple Bay is an inlet of the larger Kolotulik Bay on the coast of Labrador, named to remind those sailing past in late summer that plentiful supplies of ripe berries awaited in bogs near shore. The Inuit word *appik* also appears in place names: Akpiksai Bay, Akpittok

Island, and Akbik, all indicating areas where bakeapples are plentiful.

BAKED WIND PILLS

The food words peculiar to Alberta reflect, first of all, cowboy humour and chuckwagon grub. Baked wind pills is cowboy slang for beans, heated up in many a black pot over a rangeland campfire. "Beans, beans, the musical fruit. The more you eat, the more you toot." While French and Métis fur trappers tending line in what became central and northern Alberta might have longed for their staple *fèves au lard* (pork and beans), what in fact they and the earliest buffalo hunters often ate, when the supply of salt pork dwindled, was rubbaboo (see entry in this book) and beans, in which chunks of pemmican (see entry) were diced and tossed into the bean pot.

BALSAM & BALM: WORD LORE GALORE

Canada's Balsam fir has major local names; my fave is "snotty var." Balsam Fir, *Abies balsamea* (Latin 'balsamlike') grows from Newfoundland through to northern Alberta under a variety of common names. The bark on young Balsam Fir abounds with raised resin blisters, hence Blister Fir. From the imposing shape of a mature tree with its distinctive upper spire comes an early pioneer name, Church Steeple. But the most colourful slang name for the Balsam

Fir was used in Newfoundland where an old fir tree with resin-clotted bark was a "snotty var," so-called because it was sticky. Var is dialect variant of fir.

British Columbia's coast has related species like Pacific Silver Fir, *Abies amabilis* (Latin 'lovely,' referring to the attractive foliage, hence the tree's use as an ornamental).

Also in British Columbia, parts of Alberta, and the Yukon is Alpine Fir, *Abies lasiocarpa* (Botanical Latin 'with woolly fruit').

Word Lore of Fir

Fir tree was *fyri* in Old Scandinavian, *furh* in Old English; is *fyr* in Danish and *Föhre* in modern German. The root abides in a common Old English collective word for woods or forest, *fyrhthe*, which produced two words encountered infrequently, unless one reads Scottish dialect poetry and woodsy English verse. In such rarified bowers of poesy a firth is a small wood, and a frith is scrub land or a hedge of underbrush.

Balm of Gilead Fir

Balm of Gilead Fir is an old and incorrect name for Balsam Fir. Gilead was a Biblical name for the Trans-Jordan and the site of manufacture of one of the ancient Near East's most famous products. Resins from a number of local trees and shrubs (none of them *Abies balsamea*) were there made into soothing salves, skin softeners, perfumes, incense and early cosmetics. This Balm of Gilead was expensive. In Genesis 37:25–26, Joseph's jealous brothers sell our hero to a caravan of unsavoury merchants who "came from Gilead with their camels bearing spicery and balm and myrrh, going to carry it down to Egypt."

But the most familiar citation occurs elsewhere in the Old Testament, in Jeremiah 8:22, where Holy Writ's greatest kvetch is complaining about how evil foreign doctors are. All medicine is balderdash, implies Jeremiah, and the only healing is with God. Jeremiah employs that hoariest of devices, the rhetorical question, when he asks, "Is there no balm in Gilead?" The answer is an obvious yes. The word in the Hebrew text is *sori* and referred to a resin obtained from a small evergreen tree of the cashew family, *Pistacia lentiscus*. Yes, a sister tree, *Pistacia vera*, gives seeds sold as pistachio nuts. English translators of the Bible chose different words to render *sori*. Wyclif used "gumme." Is there no gum in Gilead? has a certain alliterative appeal. But I much prefer Coverdale's "triacle." Is there no treacle in Gilead?

Word Lore of Balsam & Balm

This evocative word that now names a Canadian tree has travelled far, beginning perhaps in ancient Egypt in a word like *m'aam* 'embalming spice,' one of the spices used to mummify corpses. Note that the root still resides in our English verb embalm. Egyptian *m'aam* or one of its related forms like *m(b)'aam* was then borrowed by or is cognate with

Hebrew *basham* and Arabic *balasan* 'balsam.' The apostrophe in *m'aam* represents a glottal stop, a common sound in Egyptian, and still in Semitic languages where it is a letter of the Hebrew and Arabic alphabets. This quick opening and closing of the glottis is often heard by persons whose languages do not possess it as a plosive, that is, as a *b* or *p* sound, thus the appearance of the *b* in dialect forms and in borrowings. Speaking of which, the Greeks borrowed the Arabic as *balsamon*, from which the Romans made *balsamum*. The Latin form evolved into Old French *basme*, giving Middle English *baume* and modern French *baume* and modern English *balm* and *balmy*. A balmy wind was originally a healthy wind. To preserve a dead body "in balm" and other spices and by additional means was, in Old French, *embasmer*, later *embaumer*, which entered English as embalm. "Not all the water in the rough, rude sea / Can wash the balm from an anointed king," crowed Shakespeare's *Richard II*, illustrating the Elizabethan use of balm to mean any fragrant oil or perfume.

Balsam too meant any resinous ointment that preserved, healed, or soothed. In the bizarre alchemical notions of Paracelsus, balsam was a universal preservative essence found in all organisms. In spite of his dabbling in alchemy and sundry other strands of pseudo-scientific claptrap, Paracelsus did contribute to European knowledge of the medical properties of certain minerals. And we must digress to pass on the wonderfully Teutonic amplitude of his real name. He was born in 1493 and christened Theophrastus Bombastus von Hohenheim. *Ja wohl!* The word is still used in modern Italian in its curative or soothing sense: *La tua presenza è un balsamo per me* 'your being here is a comfort to me.'

Briefly the word was a verb. In J.L. Motley's *The Rise of the Dutch Republic* (1855), we read of one unfortunate who "fell down dead. We have had him balsamed and sent home." With a stern note to his relatives, no doubt, criticizing the bad form displayed by dying abroad.

Uses

Canada Balsam is a purified resin extracted from *Abies balsamea* and still used as a glue to mount slides in microscopy. Turpentine and varnishes are made from Balsam Fir resin, by evaporation and fractional distillation. What remains afterward is a hard yellow rosin. Abietic acid (*abies* Latin, fir tree) is one of the components of resin. With its fresh balsamic aroma and needles that persist in place long after the tree is cut, Balsam Fir has been a popular Canadian Christmas tree for more than a century, with almost a million sold every year at Yuletide. Yuppie cooks now trumpet the tasty virtues of balsamic vinegar, the term being a simple translation from Italian *aceto balsamico* 'remedial vinegar,' one of the wine vinegars made by aging the must of white grapes and then flavouring it with various spices and herbs, remedial because it found early use in Italian folk medicine.

Sieur de Dièreville, a French surgeon and plant gatherer, visited Port Royal in 1699 to spend a year studying Acadian people and plants. In his *Relation of the Voyage to Port Royal* published in France in 1708, he reported watching Aboriginal peoples resetting broken bones and then applying large pads of peat moss soaked with Balsam Fir resin (these together would have antiseptic and antibiotic properties). Birchbark was put over these pitched moss pads, and then splints were tied in place with "bandages of thinner bark strips." Other early travellers in the Canadas told of bush beds made by spreading several blankets over a nest of Balsam Fir branches, "and a very soft and aromatic couch they make." Native peoples also collected Balsam Fir gum and made teas of it to treat coughs, asthma, and, less successfully, tuberculosis. The needles were sprinkled on live coals inside sweat baths and the fumes inhaled to ease cold symptoms.

Early in their food-gathering rambles, humans must have noticed Balsam Fir resin stickily coating tree wounds, buds, and cones, protecting them from infection and from voracious birds and squirrels. Fir sap is a potent natural fungicide. When the trees suffer a fungus infestation, the quantity of resin produced by an individual tree increases measurably. Fir resin protects these hardy northern conifers from cold winters too. It acts like antifreeze for the roots, branches, and needles. Fir needles, coated with wax, can stay on the tree through their winter dormancy, and begin photosynthesis as spring thaw arrives, thus taking maximum advantage of the shorter northern growing season. The disadvantage is a forest floor strewn with resin-rich, dry needles, making vast stands of fir trees very susceptible to forest fires.

Surnames

English had a medieval tradesman called a balmer, one who made and sold spices and ointments. Balmer and Balme became surnames. But the English last name Balsam is deceptive, deriving from an ancestor who lived at Balsham in Cambridgeshire, whose name begins as *Baells-ham*, farm or village of an Anglo-Saxon with the common personal name *Baell*.

German has surnames like Forch, Forcher, Forchert, Forchner, and Forcht from an ancestor who lived in a *Föhrenwald*, a fir wood.

French has a wonderfully exotic matronymic (named after the mother) surname in Balmigère where the family took its name because the founding mother was an embalmer! In the Provençal language of southern France, to embalm is *balmeja* < *basalmum* Latin, balm + *gerere* to produce, to carry. The French word for a female embalmer is *embaumeuse*.

British novelist and Edwardian esthete Ronald Firbank had a surname that meant an ancestor lived beside a wooded slope (*gefyrhthe* Old English, wooded). A whole little subclass of British last names descend from *fyrhthe*, at first meaning a group of fir trees, then any forest or woods in general. Among such surnames are Firth, Frith, Frid, Freeth, Vreede, Freak, Freke, and Firk.

Everywhere over its natural range, the fir tree has supplied surnames: Estonian Kuuzik 'fir wood,' Finnish Kuusinen 'fir tree, spruce,' Latvian Egle 'fir tree' and Eglitis 'little fir tree.'

Canadian Place Names

Toronto has its very own Balmy Beach Canoe Club. Balmy Beach near Owen Sound, Ontario, has high summer breezes. So does Balm Beach, Ontario, on Nottawasaga Bay. Balsam Lake near Kirkfield, Ontario, was once fringed with firs. So is Balsam Grove north of Edmonton in Alberta. The map of Canada is furry with Fir Island, Fir Mountain, Fir River, and further pinaceous toponyms.

BALSAMROOT

This yellow-flowered perennial, a member of the daisy family, grows on sunny hillsides and flatlands from the foothills of Alberta into the southern interior of British Columbia. First Peoples, including the Interior Salish of British Columbia, dug the sweet taproots early in the spring and roasted them on hot rocks or in steaming pits. The roasted roots were eaten as a cooked vegetable, and also ground up and brewed in hot water as a drink sweetened with honey or berry juice. Early settlers sometimes used balsamroot as a coffee substitute. Balsamroot was translated into Greek-based botanical Latin to get the plant's scientific name of *Balsamorhiza sagittata*. *Sagitta* is the Latin word for arrow, and the species name *sagittata* refers to this composite's arrow-shaped leaves. South of the border the plant is called Oregon sunflower, and many Aboriginal peoples of the Pacific Northwest also gathered the little seeds in midsummer in buckskin bags, which were then pounded until the seeds were reduced to a meal. This nutty-flavoured starch was added to native stews and soups and also blended with berries as a dessert.

BANGBELLY

Bangbelly is a pudding or pancake of Newfoundland, baked, or more usually fried over an outdoor fire by fishermen or hunters. It's made with flour, baking soda, molasses, and pork fat. Fishermen used to substitute seal fat. Sometimes it was cut in strips and floated on top of thick pea soup. But a variety of recipes abound, including one that begins with blueberries, sugar, and hot water boiled into a bubbling mass, at which point balls of dough are dropped in until cooked. A belly-bang was coarse Elizabethan slang for a fart. Perhaps this noble provender takes its name from a mere reversal of the elements in belly-bang? Or, is it so heavy that it bangs the belly when eaten? But the origin may also lie in bang or bain, a hard-bread cake made by frying a batter of flour and water in tallow, from Québécois French *beigne* 'fritter.'

Supporting a transatlantic source is this next reference. In the best and best-selling book of Newfoundland recipes, Ivan Jesperson's *Fat-Back & Molasses*, Joan Andrews of George's Brook contributes a tasty recipe for Blackberry Bangbelly that originated in Dorset and was brought over by early English immigrants to Cape Freels, Newfoundland.

BEAR FOOT

This is an Aboriginal food-gathering device made of wood and shaped like the claws of a bear. It is used to harvest blueberries. This little hand-sized rake can be used to gather other wild berries as well.

BEAR'S BUTTER

Also called bear's grease, this is the rendered white fat of a bear, used as food mixed with wild fruit like saskatoonberries. Bear's butter is employed to fry food, to make medicine and to act as a cosmetic base. In a northern emergency, bear's butter can be smeared all over a human body to insulate it from arctic cold. As a commodity, bear's butter came to the official attention of Hudson's Bay Company factors, appearing in the minutes of an HBC council meeting in 1824: ". . . that the Gentlemen in Charge of districts be directed to use every exertion to collect Bears' Grease as it is likely to become a valuable article of trade."

BEDLUNCH

This neat Canadianism, a term exclusive to Prince Edward Island, denotes a snack taken before retiring for the night. Whether or not such nocturnal nibbles induce restful sleep is a question best left to biologists. One clue however may be found in the folk rhyme: "The later that you eat, the more unrest you meet."

BELLYBUSTERS

Sourdough biscuits and unleavened bannock made over an Albertan chuckwagon fire were both called bellybusters, testifying to their hardness and their indigestibility.

BIRCHBARK MOOSE CALLS?

Canoe Birch or *Betula papyrifera* is widespread across much of Canada and provided a smooth, waterproof shell for one of the yarest vessels ever invented by humankind. The canoe was light, easy to repair, lasting, and resilient, and was the first transport over the inland waters of North America. Voyageurs first traded for canoes and opened up what would become Canada through trading for furs. Native peoples of the eastern woodlands traditionally made the boats in early summer when birchbark stripped easily. After long swatches of birchbark had been sized and cut, white pine, spruce, or tamarack roots were dug up and boiled taut to make the tough thread used to stitch seams. Those seams were waterproofed and sealed with pine resin or spruce pitch applied with a hot stick. Canoe frames and thwarts were made from cedar soaked in water so it could be bent to the required shape.

Birch Moose Calls

The birchbark horn was a swatch of papery bark sewn into a cone shape. The Ojibwa and other Algonkian peoples blew through the cone making the papery layers resonate and imitating the anxious foghorn basso of a female moose in heat.

Rogan

rogan < *houragon* Canadian French < *onagan* Ojibwa, bowl, container

Birchbark rogans were used by First Peoples all across northern America. They were essentially waterproof bowls, buckets, and containers used to keep food for long periods of time, sometimes being buried or cached until needed. Birchbark strips were sewn tight with spruce-root thread and the seams sealed with spruce resin. Rogans also held maple syrup, up to five gallons in one case.

"BIRDCAGES" OF VICTORIA, BRITISH COLUMBIA

In 1860, the Colony of Vancouver Island opened the second session of its assembly amid a cluster of new public buildings erected the year before on the south side of Victoria harbour. The edifices featured fancy brickwork and pagodalike roofs whose shape reminded residents of a then-popular cage for pet birds. For the next thirty years, the nickname of the government buildings was The Birdcages. The soubriquet lasted until 1893 when construction began on a new government complex that in its turn was nicknamed The Marble Palace.

BLÉ D'INDE (INDIAN CORN)

This North American French term for corn first appeared in print in 1603. A variant was *blé indien*. Both mean 'Indian corn.' The French in North America called it *blé d'Inde* because some Aboriginal peoples encountered by early Europeans told them that the cultivation of corn occurred first in the islands *des Indes Occidentales* 'of the West Indies.' In fact, the Taino, the Caribs, and other island peoples brought knowledge of corn growing with them from the mainland. The earliest corn remnants found by paleobotanists at Tehuacán in Mexico have been carbon-dated as being 7,500 years old. Corn's cultivation had spread southward and northward long before Europeans arrived in the

"New" World. Explorer Jacques Cartier found it being grown plentifully along the St. Lawrence in 1535.

Although *blé* means 'wheat' in modern French, earlier it referred to corn in the sense of seeds of any cereal crop. Corn still has this meaning in British English. The word *blé* appears in French manuscripts as early as 1080, with subforms like *blet*, derived from the language of the ancient Franks where *blad* meant 'something harvested from the earth.' The ultimate Indo-European root of *blé* is **bhle-* 'flower, leaf, plant part.' The asterisk preceding an IE root citation labels the form as hypothetical, a root based on comparative research and conjecture as opposed to printed proof. Since the earliest speakers of Indo-European were pre-alphabetic, no inscriptions survive.

In standard French, corn is *maïs*, as it is maize in Great Britain, both derived from Spanish *maíz*. Spanish conquerors first encountered corn on the island of Hispaniola being grown by the Taino people. The Taino lived on several other Caribbean island groups such as the Greater Antilles and the Bahamas. They and their Arawakan language are now extinct. Corn in Taino was *mahiz*.

BLUE-BLOOD ALLEY IN VANCOUVER

In the final fifteen years of the last century, Vancouver's Richards Street and Georgia Street were lined with the mansions of plutocrats who had grown rich in the Vancouver boom. In 1893 a US financial crisis spread north. Capital for new investments dried up. So many loggers were out of work that the next year, 1894, Canada's first Labour Party was launched on the coast. Mortgages on the palatial residences along Richards and Georgia were foreclosed, and the formerly ritzy section of the town slumped into a five-year recession, earning a new nickname, Blue-Blood Alley.

BLUFF ON THE CANADIAN PRAIRIES

Bluff came to North America as a nautical adjective that meant 'broad-faced.' British navigators first applied the descriptive in such phrases as "bluff-headed ship, bluff cliffs, a bluff headland" and then in North America bluff was used as a noun to mean the cliff or headland itself. Nautical metaphors were in common use among early explorers of our plains. Consider a frequent synonym for prairie 'the sea of grass' and 'prairie schooner' for a pioneer wagon used by homesteaders.

Entirely Canadian in origin is the Albertan and Prairie use of the word *bluff* to designate a stand of trees, a little grove of trees alone on the generally treeless prairie. In our West, a bluff can be the high, wooded bank of a river, giving place names like Oak Bluff in Manitoba and Poplar Bluff in Saskatchewan. Canuck too is the infrequent adjectival form found in phrases like 'a rolling, bluffy prairie.' This Canadian sense of bluff has been heard in some northern American states like North Dakota, Montana, and Wisconsin. And *le bluff* has entered the Canadian French spoken in some of our Prairie provinces.

BOIL-UP & A PIPE

In Canada's Far North, a boil-up is a stop on the trail to brew some tea and take a brief rest. It's used as a verb too: "We'll boil up at the next ridge." Boiling places and boil-up places that are used frequently are sometimes marked as such on company or individual maps. Similar terms in the Canadian north are mug-up and smoke-up. Drink-up is saved for the return to town.

Another early (1806) term for a rest-break was a 'pipe.' In the days of the fur trade and later, from voyageurs' French *une pipe*, English picked up 'pipe' as a measure of distance. A pipe to explorers like Simon Fraser was the distance rowed or traversed between rest breaks. During such breaks but not usually en route, men would smoke a pipeful of tobacco.

BOSS RIBS OF PRAIRIE BUFFALO

This was the anatomically incorrect slang for meat attached to bones from a buffalo's hump. This fine-grained flesh, supported by the spinous processes jutting up from the cervical vertebrae, was esteemed as one of the most delicate and tasty parts of the buffalo, along with the tongue and the backfat. Being a popular boiled food, the boss had several slangy synonyms in pioneer English and French, including *the bunch*, *grosse bosse*, *the hunch*, and *the wig*. The boss was nicknamed the wig by British hunters because the buffalo's thick mane of neck hair flowed down over its hump, suggesting a bewigged head. Most exquisite in taste was the front part of the bison's hump, called *la petite bosse* by French hunters. It weighed about three pounds and was attached to the main boss above the neck.

BOUCANIÈRE (ACADIAN SMOKEHOUSE) & PIRATES!

Some Acadians still smoke herring (*hareng boucané*) in little shacks with fires made of spruce sawdust. Salted herring (*hareng salé*) is hung above the smokey fire for two or three weeks. Smoked herring is eaten hot, cold, and even sometimes flaked and put into soups and stews.

Those nasty old pirates, the buccaneers, took their name from the same root that gives *boucané* 'smoked.' At the end of the sixteenth century and throughout the following century, *boucaniers* were, first, rough French hunters on the Caribbean island of Santo Domingo who hunted the large herds of wild cattle sprung from escaped domestic stock brought earlier by Spanish explorers. These lawless ruffians dried and smoked their beef on a wooden grid called a *boucan*. The word could also refer to the little cabin in which the smoking was done. The French freebooters and criminals who infested the island and preyed on Spanish ships had borrowed the word and the technique from local Tupi people, in whose language *moka'm* or *bokaem* meant 'wooden grill on which meat or fish was smoked.' Soon *boucanier* came to refer to any Caribbean pirate. And *boucanier* entered English quickly, respelled for British ears as the word *buccaneer*. By 1719, novelist Daniel Defoe had his most famous character, Robinson Crusoe, declare that he had "been an old Planter at Maryland, and a *Buccaneer* into the bargain." Even earlier, in 1700, Defoe referred in print to "Buccaneering Danes."

In Québec French *boucane* is a slang word for bootleg hootch or homemade whisky, presumably because one needs smokey fires to make homebrew. One Québec phrase for 'smoked' sunglasses is *lunettes boucanées*.

BOUILLON D'HABITANT (FARMER'S STEW)

In ancient France, bouillon was the broth or stock rendered from boiling (*bouiller* 'to boil') vegetables or meat, and many a humble kitchen kept a stock pot ready to simmer in a permanent place on the stove. In classic French cuisine *bouillon* is the liquid part of a *pot-au-feu*. But among the first French settlers and explorers of what became Canada, a bouillon came to refer to a hearty stew of whatever vegetables and meat or fish were readily to hand. So pervasive was its use that the word passed into Canadian English. Various recipes and local adaptations of *bouillon d'habitant* 'farmer's stew' were carried across the country right to the Pacific and into our North by French traders, trappers, and much later by *bûcherons* 'lumberjacks.' One writer about the rolling lands of our Dominion was Stewart E. White who sings the delights of this stew in *The Forest* published in 1903: "[trout] mingled in . . . the famous North Country bouillon, whose other ingredients are partridges, and tomatoes, and potatoes, and onions, and salt pork, and flour in combination delicious beyond belief."

From the same verb *bouiller* 'to boil' comes another common food noun, *bouilli*, which in France, as still in Québec today, is a boiled dinner.

A Note on the Word Habitant

A few words are of interest here concerning the people who brought the old recipes to Québec and who through the centuries have grown so much of its food. At different times in the history of Québec, this familiar word has had different meanings. *Habitant* began as a legal term in the "new" feudalism of New France. A habitant was a free proprietor who held land in tenure within the seigneurial system. This system, in legal force from 1627 until 1854, was a way to distribute and occupy land in a new colony. Seigneuries were large tracts of land granted to the richest colonists of New France, often sons of French nobles. In return for their provision of teaching and medical services, convents and other religious bodies could also be seigneuries. These large tracts of land were also granted to high military officers and certain civil administrators. In turn, the seigneur divided his land grant into parcels, and leased these smaller farms by contract to tenants, called *censitaires* or *habitants*. The habitant was obliged to inhabit his plot, to put the land into fertile production as soon as possible, to grow enough food to sustain his family and to be productive enough to have some crops or money left over to pay his tenant's rent to the seigneur. This fee was the famous *cens et rente*, the *cens* being a small feudal tithe, the rent being money or its equivalent in produce. The habitant also had to pay a grain tax called *les banalités*.

The seigneur was given other rights pertaining to his land. A seigneur could set up a court of law, a mill, a commune, and sell licences to hunt, to fish, and to cut wood on his land. The habitant was under legal obligation to grind grain at the mill of his seigneur. As well, the seigneur could demand a certain number of days of free work from each tenant. This required labour was *une corvée*. As the *corvée* was technically illegal, it generated resentment, and was eventually suppressed. By the 1850s *corvée* gained a new meaning and denoted the volunteer work that local people performed to help build a barn, a new silo, or a local church.

As the nineteenth century dawned, almost

80 percent of Québeckers lived as habitants, and another system of land distribution, the township system, still familiar to us, began to grow alongside the seigneurial holdings. Tenured land favoured the wealthy seigneurs, and prevented economic and industrial progress, so, as the century reached midpoint, a bitter struggle to end the seigneuries ensued. Finally, in 1854, they were abolished and habitants could claim farmlands as their own.

By the end of the eighteenth century, a growing number of people had held no land even in tenure. They worked as farmhands for landed peasants, and they, too, came to be called *habitants* in North American French. Eventually in Québécois, *habitant* meant simply any 'farmer.' In modern Québec French, it also carries a subsidiary meaning reeking of classist put-down. For example, *un habitant* can mean 'a person with boorish manners.' *Faites pas l'habitant icette* could be translated: 'Don't try that country hick act around here.' In the nineteenth and early-twentieth century, *habitant* in English referred to anyone from rural Québec, not always in a pejorative sense.

BOURASSA & BORAGE & BURRO

There's a connection between Bourassa and borage and burro and burrito that is fascinating and that shows us something about the complex history of surnames brought from Europe to become well-known in Canadian history. We'll begin with the herb, borage. Its common names are bee bread and burrage (British dialect). Its genus name is *Borago,* Botanical Latin from *borrago* Medieval Latin, possibly from *abu 'araq* an Arabic phrase meaning 'father of sweat,' of moisture, of liquid, so named because early Arabic medicine used borage as a sudorific or diaphoretic, an agent that causes sweating. The English version descends this way: *borage* < *bourrache* Old French < *borrago* Medieval Latin.

But there is a second, more plausible origin. The mature plant is covered with stiff, prickly hairs. Consequently only the young leaves that taste pleasantly of cucumber are used to flavour drinks and salads. These rough, woolly hairs may account for a second, possible origin of the Medieval Latin word, namely in the Old French *bure*, *bourre*, and *bourre de laine* 'homespun cloth of brown wool.' It was the prickly material from which poor monks' robes were made, the same monks who would have collected borage in the wild and grown it in their herb gardens.

A long prominent Québec family takes its name from this cloth. One who made and sold *bourre de laine* had the French occupational surname of *bourrassier*. Bourassa is a regional variant, and the surname of Henri Bourassa (1868–1952), founder in 1910 of *Le Devoir*, one of Canada's most influential newspapers. Henri Bourassa was an important Québec politician who advanced French-Canadian nationalism. He was the grandson of Papineau. Robert Bourassa was Premier of Québec (1970–76 and 1985–94) and helped draft the Meech Lake Accord and supported the Free Trade Agreement.

Bourre or *bure* came into Old French from the popular street Latin of the Romans who conquered ancient Gaul. There *burra* meant 'rough wool' or 'a shaggy garment.' *Burrus* was an old Latin adjective for brownish-red, the colour of such clothing. Incidentally, it was also the colour of a small donkey used as pack animal, and Roman soldiers posted to the Iberian peninsula called the animal *burrus*, thus planting the verbal seed for one of the earliest words in the Spanish language, *burro*. In Mexico, a tortilla wrapped around a filling of spiced beef and other yummies looked to eaters like a little donkey loaded down with a colourful pack, and so the diminutive form *burrito* meaning 'little donkey' came to be applied to the food as well. *Burrus* was borrowed from or was akin to the Greek colour adjective *pyrros* 'fiery red' whose root is *pyr*, which is cognate with English 'fire.' Compare these English words: pyre, Pyrex, and pyromaniac.

Family: Boraginaceae, the borage family, a small group of European and Asian herbs grown for red dye from their roots and for their blue flowers, which are still used to garnish salads. Borage leaves are used to flavour punches and cocktails like Pimm's Cup.

Borago officinalis is the annual herb with

drooping blue, white, or pink flowers, often therefore planted up on a slope, so the starry florets are more easily seen. Borage is a prolific self-seeder and will appear year after year in the same patch. *Officinalis* is an interesting Medieval Latin adjective seen as the specific name of many older botanical plants that were sold in shops because they had medicinal and cosmetic uses. *Officina* is the Medieval Latin word for a workshop or shop, from which English gets, of course, the word *office*. *Officina* is a contraction of *opificina* from *opifex* 'craftsman, mechanic,' which in turn is made up of *opus*, Latin, work + *-fex, -ficis* Latin noun and adjectival suffix 'doing,' or 'making.' Compare *facere* Latin 'to do.' *Officinalis* as a specific in a plant name indicates the plant was widely used in medieval times (and often centuries before) for some human purpose. Borage was often added as a flavouring to tankards of wine and cider. The ancients believed borage essence drove away melancholy and gladdened the heart. Medieval students had the notion that a few young leaves of borage in their dinner wine would cheer them on to further study.

BREWIS

A traditional Sunday morning breakfast in Newfoundland is fish and brewis. Before the collapse of the cod fishery, the "fish" in this dish often used to be salt cod. Brewis is hard bread or hard tack, also known as ship's biscuit or sea-biscuit, soaked in water and cooked with salt cod, and often served with scrunchins, which are cubes of fat-back pork fried golden brown and tossed over the brewis as a garnish or mixed right in with the cod and bread. Hard tack is a dry biscuit or bread made of flour and water with no salt, often baked in large ovals. Hard tack keeps for months. It must be soaked or dipped in hot liquids to be eaten easily.

Origin of the Term Hard Tack

A majority of dictionaries mark the origin of the phrase *hard tack* as "unknown." I disagree. Hard Tack is a shortening of the nautical term *tackle*, originally the fishing equipment and gear on board a boat. Fishermen's or sailors' humour might easily have invented a joking reference to this biscuit, claiming it was harder than the wooden and metal tackle on the boat. English borrowed tackle from an early Dutch form like *takel*, itself related through a common Indo-European root to a Greek word of arrangement like *taxis*, so that tackle with its diminutive suffix was bits and pieces of equipment that had to be prepared and arranged on the boat before one set forth to fish.

Hard tack was cheap food first, then in England came to be applied to anything of low value or inferior quality. American English first applied the word *tacky* as a noun to name small, scruffy wild horses that roamed the Carolina colonies. Sometimes these tackies were captured and sold.

By the 1830s, some poor whites or southern crackers were being put down with tags like "piney-woods Tackies." Around the turn of the century, an American fad for costume parties where one came dressed as a hick or hillbilly produced the first common adjectival use in the phrase "tacky parties." Cartoonist Al Capp said that memories of these parties were partially responsible for the creation of his long-running cartoon strip, "Lil' Abner." Later in twentieth-century American English, tacky gained wide popular use as a pejorative adjective meaning cheap, seedy, in poor taste, or vulgar.

Origin of Brewis

Now we return to what many islanders consider the best use of hard tack ever invented. Brewis has several spelling variants and pronunciations but is usually said as "broos." In the lyrics of four different Newfoundland songs, brewis is rhymed with *spruce* in one ditty, with *news* in another, with *lose* in a third, with *youse* in the fourth. Local folk etymology claims the word derives from breaking, that is bruising, the hard biscuit, before soaking it—a practice reflected in one complimentary catch phrase of Newfoundland: "as fine a b'y as ever broke a cake o' bread." The folk etymology is colourful but incorrect. Brewis existed as a word in Middle English, a period of development in our language usually dated from 1150 to 1450. The earliest printed reference in English occurs around 1300 in *The Lay of Havelok the Dane* as "make the broys in the led" which means "make the brewis in the lid," that is, remove the convex lid of a pot or cauldron, turn it upside down and use the hollow to make a sauce. In this case, it means to ladle broth from the pot into the lid, then put the lid, still upside down, back on top of the pot, and make sops by putting hunks of hard bread into the liquid.

Brewis or browis (or one of a dozen variant spellings) entered Middle English and Scots from a Norman French form of Old French *brouetz*, a soup made with meat broth, itself a diminutive of Old French *bro* or *breu*. It caught on in English by popular association with an Old English cognate, *briw*, plural *briwas*, a word for soup. All of these words, including the English verb *brew*, hark back to the Indo-European mother tongue, where *bhereu* is a verbal root whose meanings include stirring, warming, and boiling. Distantly related words in English, fifth cousins of brewis, are braise, bread, breath, breeze, broil, broth, and imbrue. Latin cognates include the roots of English words like effervescent, ferment, fervent, and fry. The Bourbons who once ruled Naples, Spain, and France took their surname from a town in central France originally named after Borvo, a Celtic god of warmth.

Making Brewis

Skin and debone the dried salt cod and cut into pieces. Soak overnight in cold water. Change the water in the morning and boil the cod about twenty minutes until tender. Some Newfoundland cooks soak the hard tack overnight too, then boil it in its soak water the next morning and mix it with the cod. Scrunchins can be sprinkled on top. Some add potato hunks and wild herbs. Others make brewis with bacon or ham. Coastal cooks from Maine to Massachusetts make fish and brewis too, and sixteenth-century Scottish recipe books mention the dish.

The Brewis Bag

Some Newfoundland kitchens stock a special implement called a brewis bag, a netlike pouch in which to soak the pieces of hard tack and boil them, after which the pieces are dumped in a colander to drain. Thus, one who does not retain imparted information, who is scatter-brained or forgetful, may be chastised in Newfoundland with the outport snub: "He have a head like a brewis bag."

BROLLYWOOD, BRITISH COLUMBIA

American film crews love Vancouver for the excellent local movie-making facilities, good crews, and the Canadian film-union rates, cheap compared to Hollywood. Some US movie types call British Columbia and Vancouver "Mexico North." Of course, these wanderers from the Californian deserts do sometimes bitch about rain and changeable weather in the Lower Mainland of British Columbia. A comic place name thereto appertaining was coined in 1994 by Jim Sutherland, editor of *Vancouver* magazine: Brollywood. Come up and film; just bring your umbrella, or, as some Brits say, your brolly. In 2003 former movie action star Arnold Schwarzenegger was elected governor of California and Arnie vowed to end cheap runaway movie shoots in Canada. He spoke of punitive tax measures and bringing movies back to sunny California. His strictures have indeed had some destructive effect on American films being lensed in Canada.

BRYAN ADAMS

Born in 1959, the Canadian superstar rock singer and composer from Kingston, Ontario, is probably best known for his most played and popular song, "Everything I Do, I Do It for You." The music video of his 1998 hit "A Day Like Today" is considered one of the best rock videos ever made in Canada. In 1999, adding another quiver to his bow, Adams published a very popular book of his own startling and evocative photographs of women, famous and not, titled *Made in Canada*.

The majority of English surnames are based on the first name of the founding male ancestor of the family. Yes, it was oinky and chauvinistic of those frowsy Anglo-Saxons to deprecate female names, but, shall we revise history? No, herstory won't work as one peruses the history and rise of surnames.

Medieval English Form

As we might expect, Adams was in Medieval English a genitive form, Adames 'of Adam.' This could be appended in a parish registry to a first name like John, so that John Adames would mean John, son of a man named Adam. But note that it could also commonly refer to anyone of the household of a man named Adam. If that Adam had servants, his underlings' newborn children could be baptized with their master's name. So Adams can also mean 'servant of Adam.' If a family wished to make clear that the child being baptized was a legitimate heir of the founding ancestor, the relationship was stated plainly by putting "Adam's son" after the first name, so that John, Adam's son would become in time John Adamson.

Macadamian Nuts

In Scotland, MacAdam was the form, and one of that name, a surveyor, John Loudon McAdam (1756–1836) helped pave the way for better roads by suggesting many layers of broken stone as a roadbed. He also gave us a verb *to macadamize*. Another illustrious bearer of the name was John Macadam, an Australian chemist—the Australian tree whose fruit we eat as macadamia nuts is named after him.

Spelling did not become standardized in England until the spread of dictionaries and general literacy. So variant forms of the surname appear as Addams, Adems, and Adhams.

Diminutives of Adam

Sometimes the founding ancestor's pet name, often a diminutive form, was the origin of the surname. Pet names for Adam in medieval English included Addy, Ade, Adcock, Adekin, and Adnett. These pet names produced a profusion of Adam-based surnames that include Adcocks, Addey, Addis, Haddy, Addison, Addyman, Ades, Adey, Adkins, Atkins, Adnitt, and so forth. There is an Irish-Gaelic diminutive form, too, that appears in the name of the eighth-century Irish St. Adamnan, 'Little Adam.'

Saints Alive!

The majority of first names in all countries of Christendom were taken from the names of Christian saints, often by legal enforcement. For example, in 1563 the Council of Trent decreed that children baptized in the Roman Catholic Church must be given names that appear in the Catholic calendar of saints' names. This stricture was made to combat the then-growing Protestant habit of using Old Testament names. What the anti-Semitic Council of Trent was actually in a racist tizzy about, of course, was the fact that most Old Testament names were Hebrew, and Rome did not want the entire population of Europe tagged with Jewish names. Well, this may be a *goyishe welt*, but that ploy didn't work. A very large percentage of all first and last names in every language of Europe can be traced back to Hebrew originals in the Old and New Testament. Thus failed one bit of papal anti-Semitism.

Adam *as a Hebrew Word*

And so it behooves any bearer of the name Adam or Adams to know just what the name of the first man means in Hebrew. One striking feature of the Adam and Eve creation myth in Genesis is the pottery metaphor: a god formed humans from clay. This is a worldwide element in creation stories. Compare the Hebrew and Christian version in Genesis 2:6, 7 as translated in the King James version of 1611: "There went up a mist from the earth, and watered the whole face of the ground. And the Lord God formed man of the dust of the ground . . ." So, even today, in brickyards of the Middle East, does the brickmaker sprinkle water on the clay before he kneads it into shape. The Bible's name for the first man reflects this too. Adam means 'human being, person.' With only a slightly different voicing, adom means 'red.' Both may be related to Hebrew *adamah* 'clay' or 'red earth of Israel.' In Old Testament Hebrew it is usually *ha adam* and the definite article makes some scholars suspect that the name, like some others in Hebrew, was very early borrowed from neighbouring Assyrians. If so, it might stem from Assyrian *adamu* 'to make or produce.' Thus Adam would mean 'the made one, the created one.'

The Words **Human & Adam** *Related in Meaning*

The ultimately Latin word *human* also reflects this pottery myth in creation stories. The prime meaning of Latin *humanus* is 'clayey' or made of *humus* 'earth, soil, clay.' The Roman word for human being or man, *homo*, as in our species *Homo sapiens*, also stems from the same root. In Old Latin it was *hemo* 'the earthen one' or 'the person of clay.' The idea must have occurred early in human history, when primitive humans first dug up an interred body to discover bones and dust. *Dust thou art; to dust shalt thou return.*

BUFFALO BERRY

This prairie shrub, *Shepherdia canadensis*, offers a profusion of red, currantlike berries that are acidic and very, very sour, until nipped by fall frosts, at which time they sweeten up and make a delicious addition to buffalo stew (hence their common name). Buffalo steaks and tongues, salted and smoked to preserve them, made a very dry meat and needed a juicy garnish, even if it was acidic. Buffalo berries often served as this garnish. White settlers learned from the Cree and other First Peoples of our plains how to dry them as winter preserves. In 1851, explorer Sir John Richardson published an account of his search for the lost Franklin expedition under one of the long-winded titles popular with Victorian travellers. In *Arctic Searching Expedition: A Journal of a Boat-Voyage Through Rupert's Land and the Arctic Sea . . . With an appendix of the Physical Geography of North America*, Richardson mentions that buffalo berries make an excellent quick beer, fermenting in just twenty-four hours into a beverage "most agreeable in hot weather."

BUNGEE OF MANITOBA

Like Chinook Jargon on our Pacific coast, Bungee was a trading language or lingua franca used in the Red River area before Manitoba became a province of Canada in 1870. Bungee was made up of words from English, Cree, and from the local Ojibwa dialect of the Saulteaux people, with words from Orkney Gaelic, Scottish-English, and French tossed in as needed. The word *Bungee* comes from the Ojibwa *penki* 'small, little' and there are several explanations. One claims it arose simply because Bungay, Bungee, Bungie, and Bungy were slang terms for the Saulteaux who did use the lingo in dealings with local whites. Another reason might be that Bungee was *penki* 'small' talk because the grammar was simplified and the vocabulary was minimal. Like all trading languages and pidgins in the world, the number of words was small. A limited vocabulary is one of the reasons Bungee worked as a trading language. Few words meant it was quick to learn.

Bungee arose in Métis families where the mother was often Cree or Saulteaux and the father was Scottish or English. In "The Red River Dialect" from *The Beaver*, the magazine of the Hudson's Bay Company, S.O. Scott and D.A. Mulligan give examples of Bungee:

1. By me I *kaykatch* killed two ducks with one *sot* ('shot'). (Cree *kaikach* 'nearly.')

2. He fell off the rock *chimmuck* in lake. (Cree *chimmuk* 'head over heels.')
3. *Keeyam* = never mind, don't bother. (Cree)
4. *Neechimos* = sweetheart, honey. (Ojibwa *neeshee* 'friend.')
5. Slock the candle = snuff out the candle. (*Slock* is a Scottish dialect verb.)

Bungee has vanished from our Prairie soundscape, but trace phrases and stray words are heard now and then.

Is there any relationship between the name of this Canadian trading language and jumping off a high bridge to boing-boing-boing at the bouncing end of a bungee cord? Apparently not. No one has yet found a verbal connection. Bungee cord is strong, elasticized rope that is used in making a bungee jump. Most dictionaries mark this word *bungee* as "origin unknown." Bungee first appeared in English around 1930 in the form *bungie* or *bungy* (both with a soft *g* sound), meaning what English kids call a rubber and American children an eraser.

BUTTE

Frenchman Butte, Butte St. Pierre, Belbutte, and Central Butte are all in Saskatchewan. But this word for a hill with a flat top is in general use in all three of our Prairie Provinces. Although the geological formations are particularly common in southern Alberta at places like Picture Butte, buttes abound elsewhere, for example, on the outskirts of Paradise Hill in northern Saskatchewan near the Alberta border, one of which is Frenchman Butte. In the Nahani country of northern British Columbia and the Northwest Territories, a butte is a low, rounded mountain. Pronounced to rhyme with cute, butte often is the northern equivalent of the Spanish-American topographical noun *mesa* 'tableland of a flat-topped hill or mountain.' Butte came into Canadian English from early trappers' French. As early as 1375 CE *butte* in French meant a hillock or a knoll. Butte acquired its specialized North American meaning from *coureurs-de-bois* in the Canadian West.

BUTTER TART

Butter tart is a phrase and a confection that is 100-percent Canadian.

There is even a proper Canuck way to ingest this northern nectar of the oven. One holds the butter tart in one hand at lip height. One does not bring the flaky-doughed cuplet with its inner pool of sugared gold to the mouth. No. One stoops slightly inward toward the butter tart, not only to take an encompassing chomp but also to do obeisance to the gooey rills of embuttered ambrosia soon to trickle in sweet streamlets down the eater's gullet and, if he be too esurient a consumer, down his munching chipmunky chin.

In other words, when a real Canadian consumes

a butter tart, British Edwardian reserve is abandoned utterly. One must mess the lips and cheeks with the warm brown liquidity which is the centre of the true butter tart. Out in the boondocks it is permissible to jaw the tart so hard that a minor explosion of sugary elixir spritzes up one's nose or splatters an eyelid. But, be warned, peckish avidity of such revolting gusto will insure that you are banned forever from Rideau Hall and its dainty precincts.

"It's a nice little tart without much pedigree but I know you'll be amused by its lack of pretension," is how Toronto Moose artist Charles Pachter remembers one particular butter tart. Canadians are serious about butter-tartery and have been for more than one hundred years. One of the earliest recipes for this staple of Canadian cooking dates back to 1915. Renowned food writer Marion Kane states that the recipe is one of the few genuine Canadian recipes.

The butter tart has entered and lodged in our national mental kitchen. When I was senior producer for CBC Radio's *This Country in the Morning* in the early 1970s we ran several contests in which host Peter Gzowski sought to discover the definitive butter tart recipe. Scrumptious is the word that defined our judging of the tarty candidates.

There are many variations on the butter tart and debates have raged over what makes a proper butter tart. The seemingly innocuous question of adding raisins to the butter, sugar, and egg mixture gets some Canucks hot enough to melt their permafrost.

Sheldon Posen, Curator of Canadian Folklife at the Canadian Museum of Civilization, is doing research on Canadian sweet foods. The award-winning and exquisite museum is on the Québec banks of the Ottawa River, directly opposite Parliament Hill. Mr. Posen sent me this interesting email on the butter tart.

Bill:

No one else has a "butter tart." There are several relatives (or some would say, ancestors) usually cited, such as treacle tart (England), pecan pie (Southern US), black bottom pie (Mennonite), sugar pie (French Canada). But all of these use sweet syrupy bases (molasses, corn syrup, maple syrup) or rely for their identity on additions (pecans). Granted, most have butter in them, but that is not their defining feature. The classic Canadian butter tart uses creamed butter and sugar as its base. There may be little butter (1 T. in some recipes), but butter and sugar there always are. Though no one I've ever read has actually come out and said it (perhaps it's too obvious), this creamed butter-with-sugar base is the butter tart's defining feature—so unique in the sweet pie/tart world, in fact, that the medium diverts attention away from the sweetener. It's called, ahem, a BUTTER tart, not a sugar tart. An early case of the medium is the message?

Sheldon Posen

Clearly, our butter tart is a confection to be reckoned with, not perhaps as architecturally compelling as a Gâteau St. Honoré but nevertheless nicely Canuck, a dessert dulcifluent in its mellifluousness, if I may end this entry on a verbally saccharine note.

CABOT: FAMOUS NAME IN CANADIAN HISTORY

He was John Cabot, born Giovanni Caboto in 1450 and died in 1499. In this entry alone, I propose to mix biographical with etymological facts. Put it down to Cabot fever! The sea fog of history, with a damp guffaw at human fact-mongering, has shrouded the birth and death of explorer John Cabot. But he was probably born at Genoa in 1450 as Giovanni Caboto. The Genoese navigator later received financial backing for his voyages of discovery from British merchants at Bristol, became a naturalized British subject, and Englished his Italian name. He probably perished at sea off the coast of Newfoundland in 1499.

But his name festoons Canadian mappery. Cabot Head, Ontario, a place name bestowed by John Graves Simcoe to honour the explorer, bears Cabot Head lighthouse built in 1896 to warn ships entering and leaving Lake Huron. Cabot Head is a promontory of Ontario's Bruce Peninsula thrusting forth into the waters of Georgian Bay. Cabot Strait separates southwest Newfoundland from Cape

Breton Island. Cabot Lake in Labrador is drained by the Kogaluk River. Just west of Winnipeg is the little hamlet of Cabot. The capital of Newfoundland, St. John's, was so named to celebrate the traditional discovery of its harbour by John Cabot on the feast of St. John the Baptist, June 24, 1497.

The explorer is obliquely responsible for the early racist term "redskins." The racist notion that all North American native peoples had red skin began in published reports concerning explorer John Cabot's encounters in 1497 with the Beothuk tribes on the island that was later called Newfoundland. The Beothuks, victims of systematic genocide by whites and other native peoples, were extinct by the late-eighteenth century. Beothuks ornamented their skin with red ochre for ceremonial and spiritual purposes, hence appearing red-skinned to Cabot and his men.

Not named after early explorer John Cabot is *caboteur*, a French and then an English term for a boat or its captain. A caboteur is a wooden coastal vessel that plies the coast, does not often venture into open sea, but sails from port to port as a cargo vessel. Their individual chronologies prevent derivation of the boat term from the surname. *Caboteur* appears in a French written record as early as 1277. The surname Caboto first appears one hundred years later.

The precise origin of the surname Caboto is disputed, but it certainly begins with Latin *caput, capitis* 'head,' and probably arises from the name of a kind of boat. The following derivative forms are related, but even in classical Latin *caput* had expanded meanings like 'headland of a peninsula.' *Cabo* (from Latin *caput*) is a Spanish word for something jutting out, like a headland, a point, or a cape of land thrusting into the sea. There was a form *cabotz* in Old Provençal (also from Latin *caput*) that meant 'big-headed fish' or 'tadpole,' always a possibility as a sailor's jesting term for any small boat. *Caboto* also may be an early Northern Italian dialect version of the surname Caputo 'Big-head.' Early Northern French has *cabot, chabot* 'a small vessel that slowly sails along a coast from headland to headland, from port to port.' Modern English, French, and Italian now have cabotage, *cabotage*, and *cabotaggio* for 'sailing along a coast in a trading vessel' and 'coastal trade,' to which senses a twentieth-century meaning has been added. Cabotage is allowing a country to regulate airplane traffic in its own skies and over its own territory.

Latin *caput* is the source of our English word *cape* as in Cape Breton Island and our little head covering, a cap, a word that entered English from French through the language of Provençal. Up it pops in Spanish place names like Cabo de Buena Esperanza, the Cape of Good Hope. As a cape with a hood for the head, it gives French *capote* and thus the surname of American novelist Truman Capote. Mafia movies and American newspapers ring with an Italian derivative, *capo di tutti capi* 'boss of all the bosses.'

Sometimes in etymology what appears a simple borrowing of one word disguises a complex route indeed. Latin *caput* is the origin of the German slang adjective for broken, *kaputt*. We use this in English too but spell it with one t, *kaput*. But *caput's* path into German was long and twisting. We must go back to a French card game of the seventeenth century called *piquet*, a game for two players. In piquet, when a player was busted and had no tricks left, he or she was said in French *être capot*, to be capotted. Piquet and card games like it were popular throughout Europe. Capot entered German as *kaputt* and Italian as *cappotto*. In Italian hunting jargon, *fare cappotto* is to return empty-handed. Could the explorer's last name Caboto be a dialectical variant of *cappotto*? Yes, a jesting name recalling an incident of loss that befell an ancestor long ago.

Canada could have been called Cabotia! Now there's a thought to shrivel your maple leaf. Frighteningly, Canada was not the only name our forebears considered when in 1865 they began thinking about a name for the dominion they wanted to make from the provinces of Upper and Lower Canada, Nova Scotia, and New Brunswick. Let us rejoice that they chose Canada, and not Ursalia (land of bears), Borealia (northern place), Cabotia (after explorer John Cabot), Tuponia (acronym for The United Provinces of North America), or the hideous tongue-twister Albionora. Get it? Albion (England) of the Nor—th.

Our cartographical Cabotiana concludes by remembering that this Italian sailor's discoveries led to the opening of the North Atlantic fishery and to establishing England's now mercifully defunct claim to North America.

CADILLAC: AUTOMOBILE TAKES FUR TRADER'S NAME

He was Antoine Laumet de Lamothe Cadillac (1658–1730). In Québec by 1691 he was a commandant and fur trader. A few years later he founded a fur-trading fort at Detroit, hence the name of General Motors' luxury car. Charges of empire building sent him down to Louisiana as governor from 1710 to 1717. Further charges of sharp dealing sent him with great wealth home to France in 1718.

Cadillac is the name of a place near Bordeaux and of a little town in the Dordogne that springs from the name of a Gallo-Roman territory of ancient Gaul, *Catiliacum*, itself composed from a Latin cognomen mentioned by Cicero and Pliny *Catilius* and the Latin locative suffix *-acum*. *Catus*, an adjective in street Latin, meant 'smart, intelligent' and the noun *catus* was a tomcat. The diminutive of that noun *catulus* meant the young of any animal, especially puppy or kitten, and was the nickname of an ancestor of the greatest lyric poet of ancient Rome, Catullus.

CALGARY REDEYE

This simple brew is beer and tomato juice. Redeye was an earlier Canadian slang phrase for any cheap, homemade, often bootleg whisky, as were these terms, some imported to the frozen north by our American cousins: blaze-belly, bug juice, coffin varnish, embalming fluid, moose milk, pink-eye, prairie dew, rotgut, and snake poison.

CALLAGHAN: A LITERARY SURNAME OF CANADA

Barry Callaghan (1937–)

Barry is a poet, founder of a literary press (Exile Editions) and a literary magazine *Exile*, short story writer, novelist, television producer, host, critic, translator, and professor of English at York University in Toronto since 1966. His published works include *The Hogg Poems and Drawings* (1978), *The Black Queen Stories* (1982), *The Way the Angel Spreads Her Wings* (1989), *When Things Get Worse* (1993), and *A Kiss Is Still a Kiss* (1995). One of Callaghan's most engaging works is *Barrelhouse Kings: A Memoir* (1998), about growing up in Toronto as Morley Callaghan's son. The memoir bubbles with Barry's frolic and passion, the self-portrait of a man of big talent who takes the space life has given him and occupies it to the fullest. *Barrelhouse Kings* is a masterpiece waiting to be discovered by any reader who likes Canadian autobiography served rare and sizzling. Most recently McArthur & Company has published several volumes of Barry Callaghan's collected prose, some of the craftiest, most splendid expository English written in this country.

Morley Callaghan (1903–90)
How can men and women find spiritual anchorage during the time storm of human life? How do we juggle love and faith with greed and selfishness? How ought a person to live faced with the certainty of eventual death? These questions, central to the fiction of Canada's most intelligent novelist to date, were not ones most Canadians cared to ask themselves in the twentieth century, and that is one reason Morley Callaghan was not as appreciated in Canada as he was in the rest of the English-reading world. His moral genius is however a compelling reason to revisit the work, for the quiz of life did rivet Morley Callaghan, a Roman Catholic from Irish Toronto and a deft wielder of clean prose in novels like *Strange Fugitive* (1928), *They Shall Inherit the Earth* (1935), *More Joy in Heaven* (1937), *The Loved and the Lost* (1951), *The Many Coloured Coat* (1960), *A Passion in Rome* (1961), *A Fine and Private Place* (1975), and *A Time for Judas* (1983). Some of his best short fiction is collected in the 1959 *Morley Callaghan's Stories*.

A strong memoir of Parisian literary life appeared as *That Summer in Paris* (1963), containing Callaghan's famous account of his 1929 boxing matches with Ernest Hemingway and F. Scott Fitzgerald. Callaghan describes superbly that heady summer, a high point of his career when he was selling short stories to Ezra Pound's *Exile* magazine, to *The New Yorker*, *Harper's Bazaar*, and *Atlantic Monthly*.

For more than forty years beginning in the 1940s Morley Callaghan was also a provocative presence on CBC Radio broadcasts as panelist and radio essayist. When I was senior producer in the early 1970s at *This Country in the Morning*, it was my pleasure to book Morley Callaghan for conversations with Peter Gzowski. The novelist was a most charming talker—bright as brass with an Irish sparkle and the gab gift of a Jesuit wizard. Callaghan was also a sly debater who easily led interviewers like Gzowski down whatever garden path Morley had decided he would meander. Especially enjoyable were spring mornings when Morley would walk over to the CBC Radio studios on Jarvis Street from his house across the ravine on Dale Avenue, settle into a chair in Studio E, and just chat about things and people he had seen on his jaunt and what those sights might mean.

The History of the Callaghan Surname

Every true Irish surname in its full form, O'Callaghan, for example, is a patronymic, that is, it expresses descent from a father or famous ancestor by means of various prefixes added to the founder's name. The earliest hereditary surnames in Ireland used the prefix O or its earlier form *Ua* meaning literally 'grandson.' For example, the first true surname in Irish history was recorded in 916 in County Galway at the death of a great lord named *Tigherneach Ua Cléirigh*. Nowadays he'd be an O'Clery. Although some think of the Gaelic *Mac* as a Scottish prefix, in Irish, too, *mac* has the literal meaning of son.

O'Callaghan, in Irish *O'Ceallacháin*, means 'grandson or descendant of a man named Ceallachán.' Now the common diminutive suffix in Irish often appears as *-an*. *Ceallach* is an ancient Irish single personal name meaning 'bright-head,' or 'shining pate.' What precisely did it betoken to ancient speakers of Irish? Clever, famous, or bald: take your pick. The diminutive suffix could signify actual physical shortness, but more usually diminutives in personal and surnames imply affection. They are little tails of verbal endearment pinned to the names of loved ones or added to the name of a fondly regarded clan chief. Older etymologies suggested Callaghan means 'strife' or 'frequenter of churches.' These are false.

Ceallachán 'Little Clever One' was a historical personage. He was a king in what is now County Cork in the Irish province of Munster. He died in 954, and we know that the first Callaghan to pass on the hereditary surname was Murchadh Ua Ceallacháin who lived in the eleventh century. Ancestral Callaghan territory comprised land bisected by the River Blackwater near present-day Mallow, land the O'Callaghans ruled for four hundred years from castles at Clonmeen and Dromaneen—homes and fields that by the seventeenth century spread over more than 20,000 acres. In 1996, O'Callaghan was the forty-seventh most populous family in Ireland.

CAMAS OF BRITISH COLUMBIA

Salish First People taught early white visitors to our Pacific coast, including explorer David Thompson, to eat and to make root bread from the sweet, starchy bulbs of this plant, which are found two to six inches below ground in their preferred habitat of wet meadows. Other common names: Camas, camass, commas, kamass, or quamash. There are more spellings for this once staple food bulb of Western Canada than you can shake a digging stick at. Camas was the name in Chinook Jargon, which in turn borrowed it from the Nootka language where *camas* means 'sweet,' in reference to the edible bulbs. The original Nootka name for the place that became Victoria on Vancouver Island was *Camosun*, 'place where we gather camas,' hence the name of Victoria's own vibrant Camosun College.

Once Pacific coast peoples used to harvest the bulbs of this blue-flowered member of the lily family and bake them immediately in ground ovens. They could be eaten hot or could be dried and stored for winter rations. Another name for the plant was bear grass, because black bears would grub for the tasty bulbs in the summer. Humans, however, harvested them in the plump-bulbed autumn.

There is one fly in the paradisal ointment here and that is death camas, a nasty little plant that sometimes grows with camas and has bulbs similar in appearance, but it never has a blue flower. Death camas blooms a sickly white. *Zygadenus venenosus* is highly toxic to humans and other animals. Care had always to be taken at harvest. Indeed native peoples usually weeded out death camas when it flowered from among the food camas. In 1878 there was a camas war when the US Army fought the Nez Percé people, after white settlers had let their pigs loose in the camas prairies that Nez Percé had used for centuries as natural gardens.

Several species including *Camassia cusickii* and the Canadian *Camassia quamash* make good garden subjects, planted like tulips in the fall and left undisturbed until overcrowding occurs. In its natural setting in British Columbia, camas likes mountain meadows that are wet in the spring and that dry up well by midsummer.

Camas were noticed by the nineteenth-century Canadian painter Paul Kane on his sketching tours of 1845–48. Kane published his field notes in 1859 as *Wanderings of an Artist* and wrote this of camas:

"They are found in immense quantities in the vicinity of Fort Vancouver, and in the spring of the year present a most curious and beautiful appearance, the whole surface presenting an uninterrupted sheet of bright ultra-marine blue, from the innumerable blossoms of these plants."

CANADA BLOODROOT OR PUCCOON

Also called *sang dragon* or Dragon's Blood or tetterwort, this plant is a member of the genus *Sanguinaria,* the name derived from Latin *sanguis*, blood. Its name in Algonkian languages is poughkone, often Englished as puccoon. All its names refer to the red dye that could be extracted by making a powder of the dried root of this member of the poppy family native to eastern North America. White pioneers learned from First Peoples to make a red dye for clothing and woven baskets. Puccoon also produced ceremonial face paint.

The larger family to which bloodroot belong is *Papaveraceae*, the poppy family, a large group of annual, biennial, and perennial herbs. *Papaver* is the Latin word for *poppy flower.* The word was borrowed into Old English as *popig* and by Middle English was *popi*. Both *opion*, the Greek word for poppy juice, and *opos*, Greek, vegetable juice, as well as *papaver*, seem related to a Mediterranean root with a reflex in ancient Egyptian hieroglyphics as *peqer* 'poppy seed.'

The species that Canadians know best is *Sanguinaria canadensis*, which blooms late in April or early in May, with a single, short-lived, waxy, white flower, and does best in the rich soil of shaded woods. By midsummer the plant has completely died down. There is a bloodroot with a double flower that can make an attractive addition to the shade garden, if care is taken with soil preparation.

By the very earliest English visitors to North America bloodroot was called tetterwort. *Tetter* is an Old English word for any of various skin diseases like ringworm, impetigo, and eczema. Extract of *Sanguinaria* was used in the eighteenth and nineteenth centuries to treat warts and nasal polyps. A British doctor, J.W. Fell, read about the native peoples along the shores of Lake Superior who treated skin cancers with red sap of bloodroot and he tested it to his satisfaction in the 1850s.

In Russia, bloodroot is a folk remedy for skin diseases too. The Rappahannock people of eastern North America made tea from bloodroot as a specific against rheumatism. And other eastern tribes applied the crimson roots of Sanguinaria directly to decayed teeth as a remedy for toothache. Members of the poppy family contain many physiologically active substances that man may learn to extract and use. For example, biochemists have isolated an alkaloid called sanguinarine from bloodroot, but any therapeutic efficacy is so far much in dispute.

CANADIAN PRISON SLANG: BENNY, BILLY & DUNKER

David Boyd of the Ontario Ministry of Health and Long-Term Care writes, "Late in my life I worked at a penitentiary. The inmates wore a benny, a wool coat with four buttons. Sometimes they carried a shank (knife) hidden in the sleeve. Food was brought up to the cell blocks in heated carts. The soup was in one billy, the spuds in another, the beans in another. The meat course was usually in a hot-tray at one end of the cart.

"Sometimes they made coffee using a dunker to boil the water. The dunker was an electric plug attached to a cord, the two wires at the end of the cord were soldered to two metal washers which were fastened together with a nut and bolt, insulated from touching with fibre washers. When plugged in (immersed first in a large jar of water) the current flowing between the washers would bring the water to a boil. This often blew a fuse, so the guards were supposed to search for dunkers and confiscate them."

CANADIAN WILD GINGER: A PIONEER TOOTHPASTE

Canadian wild ginger, *Asarum canadense*, clings to the damp humus of shady forest hummocks. Its dense, kidney-shaped leaves usually hide the brownish-purple flower that grows at ground level. Why would a flower pop out half buried in soil? Simple. Wild ginger is a plant that is pollinated by crawling insects, not flying insects. Flying insects respond to high flowers at the top of their respective plants. Creepy-crawlies like the nectar near them on the ground. Wild ginger spreads also by a creeping rhizome.

First Peoples taught early white settlers to peel the root for use as a spicy flavouring. To pep up pioneer baked goods, wild ginger root was boiled with sugar as a bread and pastry spice. Many Algonquin tribes of eastern Canada made a wild ginger tea to relieve jumpy heartbeat, although today cardiac arrhythmias are best treated by a doctor. Other native North Americans steeped the roots and poured the liquid into the ear to treat minor earaches. A pioneer toothpaste of powdered black alder and black oak bark was made palatable by adding an equal portion of ground-up wild ginger root. On the West Coast, a Pacific species, *Asarum caudatum* (Botanical Latin 'with a tail,' referring to the lobes of the calyx that are formed like a long tail) provided a spring tonic tea when Skagits people and their neighbours to the north boiled the leaves of wild ginger.

Modern science has extracted from wild ginger, aristolochic acid, which has some anti-microbial effect, and from the root, a broad-spectrum bactericide of limited use in some prescription cough medicines. A final caution about wild ginger root is that some of the essential oils have caused cancerous tumours in laboratory tests.

The Genus name of wild ginger *Asarum* comes from Botanical Latin, which borrowed it from *asaron*, a word in ancient Greek for a wild ginger. It belongs to the large plant family called *Aristolochiaceae*, the birthwort family, named after its type genus *Aristolochia*, a plant like Dutchman's Pipe, believed by the ancients to assist labour in childbirth < *aristos* Greek, best + *locheia* Greek, childbirth. See . . . even long, jaw-breaker words can be broken down into their usually quite simply component word parts. Once you know the parts that make up long, long words they never again seem frightening and complex. And, you have learned a tip or two that will make these long words easier to spell!

CANOLA

Canola could have been listed under any of the Prairie Provinces where more than two million hectares of this crop are grown annually, because it supplies seed, meal, and oil of high commercial value. In 1994–95 canola surpassed wheat as the largest cash crop in Canada. It used to be called turnip rape, from *rapum*, the Latin word for 'turnip.' But, let's face it, turnip rape suggests sexual shenanigans and so hurt sales of the product. Even rapeseed as a term was tainted by the fact that it is spelled and pronounced exactly like sexual rape (which is from an entirely different Latin word *rapire* 'to seize and carry off'). This happened in spite of the fact that rapeseed has been a valuable source of nutritious vegetable oil for more than four thousand years in Asia.

Canadian farmers first grew the yellow flowers of this crop during World War II when rapeseed oil proved to be an effective lubricant for ship engines. After the war, Canadian scientists led by R.K. Downey hybridized rape to produce an oil high in monounsaturated fats and low in cholesterol. The euphemism canola was formed by compounding *Can* (Canadian) + *ola* (Latin, *oleum* 'oil'). Canola oil is used extensively in food processing, in margarines, salad dressings, soap manufacture, synthetic rubber, and as a fuel and lubricant.

CAPE BRETON PORK PIES

These little date tarts contain no pork, but perhaps the pastry shells were made long ago with pork fat instead of butter. The filling is chopped dates simmered in brown sugar and water until "just gooey." Yum! Sometimes a sinful mantle of butter icing tops the tart.

CARIBOU

In Québec, the Algonkian word for the North American reindeer had a later playful extension of meaning when it came to refer to a drink composed of red wine and often homemade whisky, or wine mixed with pure grain alcohol. But among some French settlers who ventured westward, *le caribou* referred to another local potable, namely dandelion wine mixed with gin.

By 1665, the name of the animal entered early Canadian French from one of the languages in the widespread Algonkian family, perhaps from Mi'kmaq *xalipu* 'pawer, scratcher.' In one of its most characteristic movements, the caribou uses its front hooves to scrape snow away to get to the grass and moss beneath the snowdrifts. This large reindeer was probably one of the first animals encountered and named during the waves of migration that brought North America's First Peoples across the Bering Strait twenty thousand to forty thousand years ago. In Quinnipiac, one of the extinct Algonkian languages, once spoken in what is now Connecticut, the word was heard by a European listener to the language as *maccaribe*, showing its putative Proto-Algonquin compound origin in a form like **mekalixpowa*, made up of **mekal-* 'to scrape' + *-ixpo-* 'snow' + *-wa* 'animal agent.'

One of the nineteenth-century folk etymologies is amusing. Some French speakers re-spelled caribou as *carreboeuf* and suggested it might have derived from *carré boeuf* 'square ox.' It did not. However, one alternative spelling, cariboo, did give its name to the famous region of British Columbia that enjoyed the Gold Rush in 1860, and to several derivative phrases like Cariboo fever and Caribooite, a bit of historical slang applied to placer miners who hit the Cariboo Trail during the gold rush.

CATSKINNER

Drivers of giant caterpillar tractors used in northern construction projects particularly for clearing trail invented this Canadian term in the early 1930s. It was formed by analogy from mule-skinner, a phrase of brutal origin that meant in its first instance a mule-driver who used the whip so frequently that it might flay the poor beast of burden. Catskinner is also used in abbreviated form in the north, as 'skinner.'

CHARLOTTETOWN

The central block of downtown Charlottetown, bounded by Grafton Street, University Avenue, Kent and Queen Streets has been called the Dizzie Block for many years. Is it because it was once the only block of buildings in town worth circumambulating, and hence the walker-around-Charlottetown became dizzy after repeated circlings? Or is it because the block is so small that walking around it even once very fast would make one dizzy?

Charlottetown now has many pleasant venues and vistas, and is still the friendliest capital in Canada, whether one is strolling, zipping about in one's Bimmer, or being borne high in a gold-lamé litter by six slaves. Actually, if I were you, I wouldn't try that last form of transport in Charlottetown, especially if you "come from away."

CHEECHAKO

Prospectors heading north to the Klondike Gold Rush of 1898 brought this Pacific coast word for 'greenhorn' or 'newcomer' with them and it is still is wide use throughout Canada's Far North. Cheechako is Chinook Jargon, *chee* 'new' + *chako* 'come.' Another definition of a cheechako was a prospector who had never seen the ice go out in the spring. Such tenderfoots were different than old Gold-Rush hands who called themselves sourdoughs, even if they had only been in the Yukon gold fields for a few months, even if they had not yet staked one claim. Sourdough was dough fermenting with yeast; a portion of this leavened dough was saved to start the next batch of bread. Both terms were widely introduced into Canadian and American English by the popularity of Robert W. Service's books of frontier poetry, especially by *Songs of a Sourdough* (1907) and *Ballads of a Cheechako* (1909).

CHIARD

Chiard means 'ground meat' in Québec, and also has the more general slang sense of 'grub.' *Chiard* also names a tasty fried hash: hamburger or leftover meat chopped up and fried with potatoes and onions, seasoned with the most popular herb in *la belle province*, savory. Diced salt pork was once a favourite ingredient of *chiard* or *chiards blancs* (white hash because of the potatoes). Once fried, this "grub" would keep for a day or two, and could be packed as a meal for a fisherman, hunter, or trapper going out on a short trip. In fact, it has variant names like *chiard de goélette* 'fishing-boat hash' and *chiard du pêcheur* 'fisherman's hash.'

Extended figurative meanings occur as well, where *un chiard* is 'a mess,' 'a large crowd of people,' and 'a small fight, a scrap.' "*Quel beau chiard!*" "What a major-league screw-up!"

CIPAILLE OR SEA PIE?

Here is a word for a layered meat pie familiar to all who love Québec cookery. Not so well known is the delightful linguistic dispute attached to this term. Both the French and the English languages claim its origin. According to most recent etymological probings, Québec's *cipaille* is just the English phrase *sea pie* wearing French spelling. Borrowed from British nautical slang—where it named leftovers of meat and vegetables layered in a big pot since at least 1751—sea pie now is a deep-dish meat pie made by layering assorted uncooked, cubed meats inside a pastry-lined Dutch oven. Herbs, onions, potatoes are added, then bouillon, and perhaps wine. Nineteenth-century British sailors spoke of two- or three-decker sea pies.

But one alternative source is warmly embraced by French etymologists who state that *cipaille* derives ultimately from Latin *caepa* 'onion' because both the dish and the bulb have many layers. To arrive at the French form *cipaille*, one might posit an intermediary diminutive or affectionate form like **cepallus* 'little onion.' **Cepallus* is a hypothetical construct. That's what some linguists call an informed guess, and that's what the asterisk means. However, *caepulla* 'onion bed' is an attested form in a farming handbook written in postclassical Latin in a manuscript dated around AD 350. Latin *caepulla* is the source of the modern Italian word for onion, *cipolla*. In fact, the Italian could be the transmission form into French, through one of the southern French dialects, in a chain that might look like this: *cipollo > cipallo > cipaillo > cipaille.*

Which origin is correct? Well, the British sea pie is the earliest in print, by 1751. But that is no proof that French borrowed it from English. We must await printed or written evidence that *cipaille* appears earlier than sea pie. Then perhaps we can begin to sift such evidence.

On every list of traditional Québec foods, *cipaille* was and is a particular favourite at *Réveillon*, the Christmas feast after Midnight Mass on Christmas Eve. Throughout the province there are many regional variations of *cipaille*, and in some places the food is called *tourtière* (see the entry in this book), although that term usually describes a shallow-dished, thinner-crusted, unlayered meat pie. The Aboriginal Montagnais people of Québec adapted wheat flour, which arrived with white settlers, to create their own distinctive version of *cipaille* where the meat is a selection of wild game. In their earliest recipe, the dish was cooked in an earthenware pot and the dough pastry was put only on top of the pot contents near the end of the cooking. A big sea pie is still the favoured provender of a high feast among the Montagnais and may simmer for six hours, with each vast pot feeding twenty-five feasters.

Traditional meats in a *cipaille* included venison, pheasant, hare, or duck. After imported spices had been made regularly available in the province, the sweet pungency of cloves became de rigueur in the *cipaille* of some districts of Qu'bec. Nowadays, the ubiquity of these wizened little flowerheads of the tropical clove tree have made cooks blasé about their inclusion. Often, today, spicing of *cipaille* consists of salt and pepper and the trite mélange of cloves, nutmeg, cinnamon, and allspice.

CISELETTE (PORK & MOLASSES DESSERT SAUCE)

Literally the word means 'little chisel,' but I have no idea why it was applied by Acadians to this old-timey sauce made by frying diced pork or salt pork in its own fat. After the pork dice has browned, it is removed, and molasses is added to the remnant pork fat in the pan. The molasses is heated gently to boiling and then the fried pork dice goes back in. *Ciselette* is offered with *crêpes*, fresh bread, or toast. It was widely popular throughout Acadia, and different communities had different pet names for this molasses sauce. It was called *bagosse*, an old French dialect word that could mean 'deceptive blather, homemade liquor, or shoddy merchandise.' Other terms for this sauce were *bourgaille*, *bourdomme* (from *bourdonner* 'to hum like a bumblebee or cicada,' based on the sound of the ingredients as they fry in the pan), *mousseline* (*sauce mousseline* is usually based on whipped cream, with the original implication that it was like fine muslin cloth), and *tamarin aux grillades* (this is possibly an Acadian kitchen joke that means basically 'monkey cutlets,' the tamarin being a South American monkey related to marmosets). *Tamarin* in French also refers to the tropical fruit of the tamarind tree, whose acidic pulp is used for preserves. Tamarind juice is still made into a laxative drink. Take your pick, but, somewhere in this phrase, there's a little jest.

COLCANNON NIGHT IN NEWFOUNDLAND

The famines of the 1730s and 1740s in Ireland brought waves of Irish immigrants to Newfoundland, and with them, dishes like colcannon, crubeen, and pratie oatens. Colcannon was first boiled cabbage and mashed potatoes topped with butter. This is clear from the original term in Irish Gaelic *cál ceannfionn*, literally 'cabbage fair-headed.' But it's a lively little Irish joking reference and was really like calling the dish in English "blonde cabbage"—blonde because of the potatoes. As different cooks personalized the ancient recipe, colcannon came to be a boiled hash of as many as seven or eight vegetables, sometimes with bits of meat tossed in. Chopped chives, parsley, and a piquant hail of fresh-ground pepper can spice up the basic blandness of the recipe. Like its British sister dish, bubble and squeak, colcannon can also be fried into a kind of cake. In Ireland and parts of England it was traditional to serve colcannon on All Hallows' Eve.

Colcannon Night

Colcannon Night and Snap-Apple Night are still frequent synonyms for Halloween in many Newfoundland communities. To snap at apples is similar to bobbing for apples. Very ancient custom held this late October evening to be ghost-thick, ghoul-swarmed, ripe for magic, and fit for prophesy. For a millennium or two, All Hallows' Eve has been an evening when properly performed rites might help one discover a lover or find out what marital fate awaited the young. Thus four objects were traditionally hidden in the large dish of colcannon served on Halloween: a ring, a coin, an old maid's thimble, and a bachelor's button. So, when spooks leave a broomy spoor across the night sky, one eats this cabbage-and-potato hash with care. Whoever finds the ring will marry soon. To the coin-holder, riches will accrue, while celibacy awaits both the thimble-getter and button-discoverer. Happily for eaters, one Newfoundland variation reduces the surprises in colcannon to several large buttons. If a girl finds a button, she will marry. If a young man finds a button, he will remain forever a bachelor.

The Folk Etymology

The spurious origin of colcannon says the word consists of cole, an old name of cabbage still seen in coleslaw, plus the military weapon, cannon. This compound "arose when Irish peasants turned cannon balls into kitchen implements by using them to pound vegetables into a paste." So runs a quotation from *Cupboard Love: A Dictionary of Culinary Curiosities* by Winnipegger Mark Morton. He does not bother to label this supposititious flapdoodle as just that: a wild guess by folk unacquainted with Irish Gaelic and even perhaps, most modern dictionaries. I have shared a flagon of the nut-brown ale with Mark Morton in the eatery attached to Winnipeg's best bookstore, McNally Robinson, and I can report that he proclaims himself no etymologist. Like all protestations of modesty by academics, however, this claim must be taken with a dose of salt.

The True Etymology

Irish Gaelic *cál* reflects an ancient Indo-European word for cabbage, literally vegetable on a stalk (IE **kaul* 'stalk'). Related forms are: Old English *cal* (giving colewort 'cabbage plant,' an older name for one loose-leaved variety), Old Scandinavian *kal* (giving English kale and modern Norwegian *kaal*),

German *Kohl* (giving *Kohlrabi*), Latin *caulis* (think of cauliflower, a plant in the same botanical family as cabbage; think too of various words for cabbage, derivatives of caulis in the Romance languages, for example Spanish *col* and French *chou*), Greek *kaulos*, Medieval Dutch *kool* (in MD cabbage salad was *kool sla*, giving modern English *coleslaw*). Finally, showing the true spread of this cabbage word, a cognate appears in ancient Persian as *kelum*.

Perhaps the most appealing derivative is a French term of tender affection used by lovers and maybe by mothers speaking to small children, *mon petit chouchou*, a sweet intimacy one might translate as "my little cabbage-wabbage."

Irish Gaelic

Colcannon is an Anglo-Irish compression or slurring, a frequent habit in daily speech, of the Irish Gaelic name for this dish *cál ceannfionn*, literally 'cabbage fair-headed.' The adjective comes after the noun in Gaelic. *Ceann* means head; *fionn* means white or fair, when describing people it usually refers to a light complexion or to blonde hair. You will recognize the Gaelic word for white or fair in common Gaelic female names like Fiona, and in less common but no less beautiful girl's names like Finola, Fionnula, or Fenella, all from the Gaelic *Fionghuala* "with white shoulders."

The initial part of the compound adjective *ceannfionn* is the Gaelic word for head, *ceann*, which appears in Gaelic surnames like the Irish O

Cannan 'son of white head,' that is, son of a founding ancestor who was of fair complexion or blonde hair, and also in its Scottish cousin McCannan, with the same meaning.

COTEAUX OF CANADA

This continental French noun meaning 'small hill, slope of a low hill' came early to Québec, and is still there in place names like Coteau-du-Lac and Coteau-Landing. Voyageurs and trappers spread it across our west where coteau is still used today in Canadian English and Canadian French to describe high prairie. A coteau is a plateau or a series of low ridges. In 1843 in his Narrative of the Discoveries of the North Coast of America, Thomas Simpson described a "route . . . through a more open country, consisting of rising grounds, or coteaux with bare ridges, and sides clothed with dwarf poplar and brushwood." The word came into medieval French from Late Latin *costellum* 'little side, hillock, slope of a hill,' itself a diminutive of the Latin word *costa* 'rib, side, sea-coast.' That Late Latin diminutive *costellum* gave rise to the well-known Italian surname Costello, remembered by older folk as one half of the 1940s comedy team, Abbott & Costello. The locative surname suggests a founding ancestor who lived on the lower slopes of some elevated Italian landscape.

COULEE

French *coulée* gave us a word for the deep, dry bed of a stream or river, the bed having sloping sides unlike a canyon's steeper, perpendicular sides. Coulee has a southwestern American synonym in gulch or dry gulch. British trappers called them dry sloughs, but the French-Canadian voyageurs' term stuck. *Coulée* 'the running, flowing of a liquid' entered continental French from Latin *colare* 'to run liquid through a strainer.' Think of the name of a common kitchen implement perforated so that cooking liquids can be strained off vegetables, namely, a colander. Colander has the same Latin root as coulee. Alberta has a community called East Coulee, and an interesting doublet occurs in southern Alberta's Etzikom Coulee, where *etzikom* is the Siksika (Blackfoot) word for coulee.

COW CHIPS & BODEWASH

"Cowchips" as a term for dried buffalo dung used as a fuel began on our Canadian prairies as a loan translation from the Canadian French of early voyageurs and fur trappers. It appeared at first humorously as *bois de vache* 'cow wood' and also in the slightly more refined phrase *bois des prairies* 'prairie wood.' Buffalo chips were called bodewash too, which is a direct Englishing of *bois de vache* that shows up in the Manitoba folk saying "squished flatter 'n a bodewash chip." Anyone who could find the chips of buffalo dung strewn about the prairie used them since there was little wood available. The dried dung of cattle burns with a very heavy odour. On the other hand, buffalo chips are relatively odourless and in plentiful supply, a fuel just lying there in the early "buffalo days" of prairie settlement before the vast herds were slaughtered.

CUSHION CACTUS FRUIT OF ALBERTA

In southern Alberta this squidgy midget cactus hugs the slopes of dry coulee ridges. Only its tiny but nasty spines protrude from the fingerlike mounds of the central fleshy mass of the cactus. Desert botanists sometimes call these little segments of cushion cactus, *tubercules*. This Alberta cushion cactus has the botanical name of *Coryphantha vivipara*. The genus name is made up of two Greek roots, *koryphe* 'hilltop, summit' and *anthos* 'flower,' and is so called because it bears flowers on the "hilltop" of its cushion. Latin *viviparus* 'bearing live young' as a species name in botany denotes that the plant bears little miniature plants on its leaves or in its flowers. Cushion cactus has striking, glowing dark red flowers in June. The greenish-red fruit is harvested later, after first frost on the prairie, and has a delicate gooseberrylike flavour. Although the fruits do drop off the plant and ripen on the ground, care must be taken if picking them off the plant, since the fruit is often obscured by bristling spines.

DAMPER DOGS & FLACOONS OF NEWFOUNDLAND

Damper dogs are quick bread, wads of bread dough fried quickly on the lid (damper) of a hot woodstove, usually a treat for children, who were fed the damper dogs so they wouldn't gobble up all the fresh-baked bread. Although the phrase *damper dogs* is pure Newfoundlandese, damper appears in eighteenth-century British slang as any little, between-meal nibble that takes the edge off or dampens the appetite. By 1833 damper is Australian slang for an outback bannock, Australian bush-bread, unleavened bread of flour and water baked in hot ashes, if no stove were handy. Newfoundland synonyms include damper boys, damper cakes, damper devils, or joanies. The verb *to damp* meaning 'to dull, to check the force of' and its later extension to dampen appear to have been borrowed into Middle and Early Modern English from German *dämpfen* 'to dim, to wet down, to lessen.'

Flacoons

When the hunk of dough cut off to make a damper dog is flattened into a pancake shape, these little breads were sometimes called flacoons in Newfoundland. I suggest flacoon may stem from the fact that the dough was rolled flat by using a bottle, in Old French and Modern French *flacon* 'small bottle, flask,' which is the root of a more familiar English bottle word *flagon*. The process of verbal transformation in the borrowing was much like the process that gave one Anglo-Irish word for boy or youth, *gossoon*, from French *garçon*.

DIGBY CHICKEN

A bit of Nova Scotian self-mockery is present in the gently satiric phrase *Digby chicken*, which refers to a tiny herring that is smoked, salted, and stored for winter use. Some Nova Scotians also call fillets of the little fish, Digby chips, both named after the Nova Scotia fishing port that commemorates Admiral Robert Digby, commander of HMS *Atlanta*, one of the ships that conveyed the Loyalist founders of the town to the shores of Nova Scotia in 1783. Herring were gutted, scaled, cleaned and plunged into a barrel of brine for two days. Then a hardwood fire was started in the smokehouse. When it was roaring merrily, damp sawdust was tossed on to make dense smoke. Sometimes the sawdust was made from aromatic wood like spruce. The herring, placed on a grid made of greenwood saplings, was then put over the smouldering fumes to smoke for two or three hours.

"DOG PATCH" IN EDMONTON

Now known as Riverdale from its site in the valley of the North Saskatchewan River, Dog Patch is an older community of small, gentrified houses. Once, however, as heart of the downtown it received poor newcomers who may have reminded luckier residents of the mythical community of Dog Patch where cartoonist Al Capp's L'il Abner dwelt, a hamlet composed of hicks, rubes and rural innocents. Dog Patch's small homes were subject to flood damage in early days. Also in the river valley area is Rossdale, known as The Flats.

DOLLAR BILL: A CANUCK BUCK

Although they are not Canadian, we use words like coin, dollar, mint, money, and penny every day, and they have interesting sources. Take dollar, for example.

In AD 1516 there was a silver mine in northwestern Bohemia in the valley of St. Joachim (now Jáchymov in the Czech Republic) that produced sufficient ore that silver coins could be minted there. In sixteenth-century German, the coins were called *Joachimsthalern*. In the singular this was *Joachimsthaler*. German *Tal* or *Thal* 'valley' is akin to our English word *dale*. The Germans abbreviated the coin's name to *Taler*. Plattdeutsch and Dutch changed the *t* to *d* giving *daler*, and it was this form that English borrowed. By the eighteenth century it was spelled dollar. Meanwhile, as Spanish *dolar*, the name had been transferred to the Spanish *peso* or "piece of eight," so-called because it was worth eight *reales*. By the time of the American War of Independence this Spanish dollar was the most widely circulated coin in all the British colonies.

Thomas Jefferson wanted nothing to do with the British pound sterling. In 1782, he suggested in *Notes on a Money Unit for the United States* that the Spanish dollar was "the most familiar [coin] of all to the mind of all of the people. It is already adopted from south to north." And thus by the *Coinage Act of 1792*, the dollar became the basic unit of US currency, and was later adopted by Canada, Australia, New Zealand, and many other countries.

DOLLY VARDEN TROUT

The Dolly Varden trout is a fish of our Pacific and Western rivers and lakes, including some in central and northern Alberta. Not a trout, it's actually a char with gaudy orange speckles on a greenish skin. Dolly Varden is a character in Charles Dickens' novel *Barnaby Rudge*. The 1841 historical romance centres on the anti-Catholic riots in London in 1780. Dolly Varden is a buxom flirt, the daughter of a locksmith, who knows how, within her means, to dress flamboyantly enough to attract men and yet earn the approving comments of women. Dolly is a charming little coquette, and his prose makes it clear that Charles Dickens approved most heartily of her. So did his Victorian readers. During the book's first printing Dolly Varden bonnets became all the rage in London. Thus it was quite natural a century later for some literary angler to name a vividly speckled Canadian fish after Dolly.

DOUGH GODS

In the cookhouses and around the chuckwagons of cattle-ranching operations in south and central Alberta, *dough gods* was a slang phrase for the flour dumplings often tossed into a big, black soup kettle. The nickname arose presumably from the lordly bobbing of the dumplings on or near the surface of the boiling broth.

DOUGLAS FIR OF BRITISH COLUMBIA

French: *sapin de Douglas* < *sappinus* Late Gallic Latin, one of the European pine trees. The word seems to blend the Germanic and Scandinavian root **saf* 'sap of a plant or tree,' here the resin of the pine, **sappus* in its Gallic form, with *pinus*, Latin, pine tree. The ancient Indo-European root probably also shows reflexes in Latin words like *sapor* 'flavour' and *sapa* 'the must of wine.'

Douglas fir, the largest tree native to Canada, is said to reach 100 metres high. The giant coastal species of Douglas fir, *Pseudotsuga menziesii*, is one of the most valuable timber trees in the world. The common name commemorates David Douglas (1798–1834), a Scottish naturalist who was one of the first to identify this fir tree to science. As a collector of botanical specimens he travelled in Upper Canada in 1823 at Amherstburg.

By 1825 he reached Fort Vancouver and then collected along the Columbia, Saskatchewan, and

Hayes Rivers, travelling to meet Sir John Franklin's expedition on Hudson Bay in 1827. Two years later he returned to collect along the Okanagan and Fraser Rivers. Douglas introduced the greatest number of North American plants to international botany, and some fifty species bear his name. The specific honours Archibald Menzies (1754–1842), a Scottish naval surgeon and botanical collector who sailed with Captain George Vancouver aboard *Discovery* in 1790, bringing many specimens and seeds back to England for study and classification at Kew Gardens. Menzies may have described the tree a few years before Douglas did.

Douglas fir is one of the best structural timbers, formerly used in bridge building, and coated with creosote still widely used to make underwater pilings for piers, decks, and docks.

There is a smaller (to 140 feet) variety of Douglas fir that grows inland in British Columbia and a few places in Alberta. *Pseudotsuga menziesii* var. *glauca* is sometimes called Blue Douglas fir because its needles are grey- or bluish-green (Botanical Latin, *glaucus*).

DUCK POTATO & WAPATOO: CANADIAN TERMS FOR ARROWHEAD PLANT

Other common names for the arrowhead plant are *flèche d'eau* 'water arrow' and tule and wapatoo 'white food.' The seemingly lowly Canadian duck potato belongs to the genus *Sagittaria* (*sagitta* Latin, 'arrow'), a plant family found chiefly in freshwater streams and swamps in temperate and tropical regions of the northern hemisphere. Leaves shaped like an arrowhead give this plant its name. The Latin word for arrow also hits the target in Sagittarius, the sign of the zodiac that means 'the archer' in Latin, referring originally to the constellation.

The two common species in Canada are the more southerly *Sagittaria latifolia* with its lata folia or broad leaves, and the more northerly *Sagittaria cuneata* with cuneate or wedge-shaped leaves. Arrowhead tubers grow in the muddy guck of shallow streams and marshes across Canada, where wild geese, ducks, beavers, and muskrats chomp them with gusto. Observing the animals feasting on tubers, native peoples found wapatoo could provide good food even in the winter. Adult Aboriginal people used digging sticks to harvest arrowhead tubers, but children jumped into the streams and found tubers by squishing them between toes in the warm muck and yanking them loose. Wapatoo was then boiled or roasted in hot ashes. Wapatoo is Chinook Jargon, borrowed from an Algonkian language where *wap* or *wab* is the root for 'white.' Wapatoo means 'white food.'

DULSE

Dulse is an edible seaweed, a red alga, also called salt-leaf. Although it is described as tough and flavourless by those who dislike it, dried crisps of purply dulse are chewed by themselves and added to soups and stews as salty thickeners. Along the coasts of our Canadian Maritimes, dulse grows in the intertidal zone at the low-water mark, attached to rocks or other seaweeds by a holdfast shaped like a disc. Many Canadians say the best dulse in the world is harvested along the rocky shoreline near Dark Harbour, on the west side of Grand Manan Island, New Brunswick. But some Nova Scotians who go out collecting would argue vigorously about that contention.

Word Lore of Dulse

Dulse was borrowed directly into English at a rather late date, circa 1698, from Scots Gaelic *duileasg* < *duil* Gaelic, leaf + *iasc* Gaelic, fish, hence in origin it is a playful, Celtic nickname, leaf-fish, because it came from the sea like fish and was an edible leaf. In Welsh, it's *delysg* or *dylusg*, in modern Irish (Erse) *duileasc*. Sometimes in Scotland, it is spelled *dilse*.

Dulse is *Palmaria palmata*, which grows on both shores of the North Atlantic Ocean. Longfellow wrote that "the tide is low, and the purple dulse is lovely." The genus name Palmaria, is botanical Latin from *palmaris* Latin 'the width of a hand,' also influenced by *palmatus* Latin, 'with lobes that resemble a human hand with the fingers stretched out.' Dulse has dark red, palmately divided fronds. It belongs to the family *Rhodophyta*, the red algae family, whose name is made up of two Greek word elements, *rhodo-* 'rose-coloured, red' + *phyton* Greek 'plant.'

The Rhodophytes
The Canadian coast has about 175 Arctic, 350 Atlantic, and 500 Pacific species of seaweed, many of them algal. Algae are divided into greens, browns, and reds. Most seaweeds are red and brown algae. Rhodophytes are a division of the algae, which store floridean starch, a compound that makes them sweet, mucilaginous, and sticky. Many commercial products of a gluelike consistency are made from red seaweeds, for example agar-agar, algin, and carragheen. They are hydrocolloids used to thicken, stabilize, or emulsify products like ice cream and toothpaste.

DUMB CAKE

In some other parts of Canada, a bake-over was and is a pleasant, social get-together at which women made pies and baked goods, perhaps for sale at a church bazaar, together at one house. Newfoundland has preserved an old Irish spin on such an occasion: the making of a dumb cake. Unmarried young women and still hopeful spinsters gathered to bake and eat one cake. During the making, baking, and consumption of the cake, no talking was permitted. In the relative silence of the proceedings, said the old superstition, fate would grant a maiden a prophetic vision of the man who would marry her. Until they consumed the last crumb of the dumb cake, be they virgins or old maids, not a whisper could escape their lips.

"DUTCHMESS" IN NOVA SCOTIA

Dutchmess is the pride of local cooking in Lunenburg, Nova Scotia. Dutch is *Deutsch*, the German adjective meaning 'German.' And mess is not a mess meaning an untidy jumble. It's mess meaning a serving of food. Lunenburg Dutchmess, sometimes called *Hauskuchen*, is salted cod and potatoes dressed with bacon bits or salt pork scraps and onions. By the way, all meanings of the English word *mess* stem from Old French *mes* 'a portion of food put in front of the eater' from the verb *mettre* 'put' or 'place.' Latin had *missus* to mean one of several courses during a meal.

EAU CLAIRE IN CALGARY

This part of Calgary, with many high rises and condos, lies between the Bow River and the big buildings of commerce. Its name derives from a turn-of-the-century Eau Claire Lumber Company, which milled logs at the site. *Eau claire* in French means 'clear water.'

EDMONCHUK, ALBERTA?

Edmonchuk began as a politically incorrect reminder of the great contribution that Canadians of

Ukrainian origin have made to the city and to the province of Alberta. Edmonchuk can be used as a racist sneer, true; but I have heard it playfully tossed back into a smug, waspy face by a Ukrainian-Canadian with a big laugh. Sometimes the knife wielded in a verbal chop can nick the speaker too! The city, once centre of the Western fur trade, was named Fort Edmonton by a clerk in the local Hudson's Bay Company post, who named it in memory of his birthplace, Edmonton (Edmond's town), now part of London, England.

EEL PIE

Canadian eels can be speared through a hole in the spring ice or caught in late fall when they are fat and sluggish and just beginning to burrow into bottom muck. They can be fried or broiled, or even chopped up into an eel pie and put into a dish lined with stuffing. Add lemon juice, mild onions, seasonings; top with puff pastry. Make béchamel sauce and add it to the pie after it has baked for an hour and a bit.

Eel is a lovely, slithery slip of a word, Germanic in origin. Compare German *Aal*. And yet its legitimate adjective *eely* never became widely used in English. The eely connivings of Ottawa lobbyists would seem a most apt use. More obscure still is a splendid English word that names a place where these snakelike fishes abound and are caught, an eelery.

EH? DID CANUCKS INVENT EH?

One interjection, one sound, one word seems to identify Canadians wherever in the world we travel. Imagine this statement by a gentleman of the Canadian persuasion fresh from a psychiatrist's office: "So I go to this shrink, eh, and he goes like I don't have no confidence, eh? I go, 'No way, man.' He goes I should take assertiveness training. Weird, eh? Like I'm always supposed to be seeking approval, eh, from, you know, other people? I felt like he could kiss my Royal Canadian, eh? But, sayin' it woulda been too pushy. Dyuh think?"

How We Hosers Use Eh

Eh comes in two basic flavours, two broad categories of usage: final interrogative eh? with a rising intonation, and narrative eh with a sustained or flat intonation and found in the midst of spoken Canadian English sentences. Pop culture icons like Bob and Doug Mackenzie, those two hosers on SCTV, played in the 1970s to the 1980s by Rick Moranis and Dave Thomas, popularized and used eh? repeatedly as a marker of Canadian speech. The two actors were simply reproducing what they heard in everyday Canadian life. But the popularity of SCTV in the United States also helped some Americans and more Canadians become aware that eh was a characteristic of Canuck talk.

An Essay or Eh-say

Long before the hosers, of course, academics were

writing their eh-says too. Professor Harold B. Allen in "Canadian-American Speech Differences Along the Middle Border" (*Journal of the Canadian Linguistic Association*, 5 [1959]: 20) wrote "Eh? . . . is so exclusively a Canadian feature that immigration officials use it as an identifying clue."

It is natural that we Canadians share a proprietary need to claim certain speech habits as our own. Differentiating ourselves from Americans is important to our notoriously fragile sense of self. But we cannot go too far and claim eh is exclusively Canadian. Chaucer used it, eh? That's Geoffrey Chaucer, English poet, author of *The Canterbury Tales,* written between AD 1387 and 1400. Chaucer used Middle English ey? and variants in some of the same ways Canadians still do.

Eh is Six Hundred Years Old!

The interjection is well over six hundred years old. I know it hurts but, no, three rink rats did not meet in a secret cellar under a hockey arena in Sudbury one night back in the forties after a game and too many brews to coin the evocative particle. Yeah, but only Canadians use it. Oh, right! Check out these famous Canadian usages:

> "And who is to look after the horses, eh?" (Emily Brontë, *Wuthering Heights*, 1847)
>
> "So you think he might be hard on me, eh?" (Charles Dickens, *Bleak House*, 1852)

"I suppose you're a smart fellow, eh?"
(Henry James, *The American*, 1867)

"Breakfast out here, eh?"
(George Bernard Shaw, *Arms and the Man*, 1894)

"Breathe; fresh air. Good, eh?"
(Joseph Conrad, *Typhoon*, 1903)

"So this is Brooklyn, eh?"
(Arthur Miller, *Death of a Salesman*, 1949)

"Oh, she's coming, eh, Ma?"
(Paddy Chayefsky, *Marty*, 1954)

"Not like some people we know, eh?"
(J.D. Salinger, *Zooey*, 1957)

"Let this cup pass from you, eh?" "Right."
(Harper Lee, *To Kill a Mockingbird*, 1960)

"Eh, Nat, ain't that so?"
(John Fowler, *The French Lieutenant's Woman*, 1969)

Of course Morley Callaghan, Robertson Davies, Margaret Laurence, Stephen Leacock, W.O. Mitchell, Farley Mowat, Mordecai Richler, and dozens of other Canadian writers use eh as well. Its usage is widespread. Australian and South African novels contain the interjection. The examples from British and American authors quoted above, which demonstrate many of eh's categories of usage, were collected by a great Canadian lexicographer, the late Walter S. Avis; and they appear in his definitive article "So eh? is Canadian, eh?" (*Canadian Journal of Linguistics*, 17, no. 2 [1972]: 89–104). It is well worth perusal. Professor Avis' view is the scholarly and the commonsensical one and I quote it: "Eh?. . . did not originate in Canada and is not peculiar to the English spoken in Canada. . . . On the other hand, there can be no doubt that eh? has a remarkably high incidence in the conversation of many Canadians these days . . . in Canada eh? has been pressed into service in contexts where it would be unfamiliar elsewhere. Finally, it would appear that eh? has gained such recognition among Canadians that it is used consciously and frequently by newspapermen and others in informal articles and reports." Earlier in the same study, Avis writes "eh? is a feature Canadians share with Britishers but one which some Americans consider unusual." Americans say huh? more often than eh?

Precise Definition of Eh

So what is eh? In the always magisterial (and often correct) words of the *Oxford English Dictionary*, eh is "an exclamation of instinctive origin . . . an interjectional interrogative particle often inviting assent to the sentiment expressed." Wordy, eh? An interjection is a marginal lexical item like oops, ouch, wow, tut-tut, tsk-tsk, ugh, and yuck. It is a part of speech thrown into a sentence for emotive effect. Compare the Latin origin of interjection in *interiectio* literally 'something thrown in between.'

Manifold Uses of Eh

Eh has many functions in Canadian speech. By itself it often asks the listener to repeat something not heard: "Eh? Yes, my hearing aid works. Isn't it wonderful about those Dead Sea squirrels? They found more of them. People were putting them in desserts. What did you say?" Canadians use it very frequently as a spoken question mark, inviting the agreement of the person they are speaking to. "She was like Mother Teresa, eh?" It is a question tag much like the French terminal *n'est-ce pas?* or the German *nicht wahr?* Of course, eh? along with *eh bien* and *hein?* has been an interrogative tag in Parisian and Québécois French for many centuries.

Eh in Canadian Fiction

In English, subtle shades of expressive connotation occur in the manifold uses of eh. Avis distinguishes eight main categories of usage. Here are three examples chosen by Professor Avis from the short stories in Margaret Laurence's *A Bird in the House* (1970):

> 1. There is the eh? that seeks agreement after an elliptical statement of something observed by the speaker. "Taking life easy, eh?"
> 2. There is the eh? that reinforces an exclamation.
> "Gee! What a night, eh?"
> "What an admission, eh?"

3. There is the eh? that reinforces an imperative. "Yeh, I know,"Aunt Edna sounded annoyed. "But let me say it, eh?"

All those uses caught by Margaret Laurence's ear for Canadian speech also display a quality in the way Canadians overuse eh that Professor Avis neglected to mention. The many ways we toss eh into sentences show us constantly attempting to involve the persons being spoken to, to draw a response from them, to seek their agreement. It is a residual, uniquely Canadian, pioneer bashfulness, a polite hesitational spacer in daily discourse. What do you think, eh? Sure, I can keep right on spieling like a snake-oil barker selling Kickapoo Joy Juice, eh, but I'm also very concerned that you are listening, that you are not offended, and that you are in general agreement with the drift of my conversation. It's a way of being nice, eh?

The Yokels' Eh

One must not fail to include the ehs repeated *ad nauseam* in the slovenly speech of the unlettered oaf and the shambling halfwit. That use is not nice. Professor Avis put it well and more temperately: "Its frequency of occurrence is high generally—among some individuals so high as to pose a threat to communication."

Moreover, some of the British immigrants who first brought eh to Canada had been taught "over 'ome" that using eh was rude—and, sir, a damned impertinence! We know this from several, centuries-old expressions of reproach that became common in Britain. In fact, in print as early as Jonathan Swift's *A complete Collection of polite and ingenious Conversation* (1740) is a catch-phrase said by their superiors to vulgar persons who used eh or hay. Upon having her ears affronted with such a low interjection, the pearl-encrusted dowager would shake her wattles, look with scorn through her tortoise-shell lorgnette at the varlet who had dared to utter the particle, and dismiss him with: "Hay is for horses." If the particle spoken was eh, a variant Cockney response was: "'Ay is for 'orses." All forms of eh and hay continued to be branded vulgar well into the 1930s in England. Thus, as Eric Partridge reports in his *Dictionary of Slang and Unconventional English* (1984), we have a British RAF retort: "Eh? to me! Why, you'll be saying *bloody* to the CO next!" Later British army slang had "Eh? to me, you offensive little twit; next you'll be saying 'hell!' to the Queen. GET OVER HERE!"

So, say eh for aye, if you like. Just don't flog it to death. It's still a fine marker of Canadian speech, as good as a maple leaf pin on your backpack, to ID you as a Canuck in a world where being Canadian is not nearly so dangerous as being some other nationalities.

FIGGY DUFF

Newfoundland balladeer John Burke (1894–1929)

sang of the island "where the figgy duffs are seen, that would sink a brigantine." This is a Newfoundland boiled pudding with raisins. In some British dialects, fig was a synonym for raisin as early as the sixteenth century.

A common recipe involves moistening stale bread crumbs, squeezing the water out, then adding raisins, brown sugar, molasses, butter, flour, spices like ginger, cinnamon, and allspice, and a teaspoon of soda dissolved in hot water. Mix this well, put into a dampened pudding bag made of cloth, and steam for two hours. Or stick the bag in the oven with a Newfoundland meal like a Jigg's dinner for one hour, and cook a main course and a dessert at the same time. Serve with coady sauce. Variations abound in the recipe and in the spelling of this treat: figged duff, figgedy duff, figgity duff, figgy pudding, figgity pudden. In British culinary history, figgy duff is related to a very old recipe, suet pudding, in which a bit of hard fat was tossed into the mix for flavour.

Even centuries after immigrants brought the word and the food to Newfoundland, it was still heard in England; for example, in 1846 a Cornish writer extols "a thoomping figgy pudden." In Cornwall and Devonshire, fishermen took to sea with figgie-dowdie, a West Country raisin pudding. In the popular Christmas carol "We Wish You a Merry Christmas," you are also wished "a figgey pudding." But this is the medieval European *figee*, a dish of true figs (fruits of the common Mediterranean cultivated tree *Ficus carica*). Figgey pudding consisted of dried figs stewed in wine.

Fig = Raisin?

How did fig come to mean raisin as well as true fig? Well, it was a little gefuffel that happened when raisin entered English right after the Norman Conquest in 1066. Raisin had two meanings in French, and in early English, too. Raisin stemmed from Latin *racemus* 'a cluster of grapes, a raceme of grapes.' Raisins of the sun were grapes partially dried on platforms under Old Sol. In the English language, as the word *grape* came to mean the unprocessed fruit itself, raisin came to mean the dried fruit. Interestingly, grape also came from a French word *grappe* that first meant 'a cluster of grapes,' itself from another noun *grape* which was the hook that vineyard workers sometimes used to harvest grape clusters. It is related to English words like grapnel and grappling hook, both referring to an anchor with sharp claws.

Now the true fig, when first introduced to England, was a relatively expensive imported luxury. Figs appeared on the tables of the rich in London, at court, and on groaning country boards at the feasts of wealthy nobles. But most of the Anglo-Saxon peasantry would never see, let alone eat, a fig. They heard the word though, perhaps from fellow Anglo-Saxons who were servants at the tables of the high and mighty. Well, underlings could have figs too, but they would be the less expensive and more available raisins.

On Your Duff

Duff is just a northern British pronunciation of dough, on the analogy of other similarly spoken spellings like enough and tough. “Get off your duff” displays a metaphor in which the human buttocks are compared to plump rolls of dough. On The Rock, a humungous duff, a pudding fit for Paul Bunyan, was sometimes called a stogger, because you could stog your gob (stuff your mouth) with it, and because the cook had to stog a large pudding bag to make it. Often a Newfoundland cook set aside a particular day or days of the week on which to make this pudding. Such happy apppointments were “duff days.” Another name in Newfoundland for this big boiled pudding is lad-in-a-bag.

FIREWATER

As early as 1743, both French and English translated an expression in Algonkian languages that denoted the cheap brandy or diluted whisky that white traders often bartered for furs with Aboriginal peoples. In the Cree tongue it was *iskotawapo* < Cree *iskota* fire + *wapo* water. In Ojibwa, firewater was *ishkodo-waaboo*. English traders also used the indigenous term in barter speech where *scuttaywabo* was frequently heard. The phrase suggests two things. High-proof alcoholic beverages like strong rum or whisky would ignite if tossed into a fire or if a lighted taper was brought close to a cup of booze. It was firewater also because of the taste, feel, and effect of alcohol on someone drinking such potent spirits for the first time. But it was chiefly firewater to Aboriginal peoples because more sophisticated traders like the Blackfoot people soon realized, when trading with whites for whisky, that they had to test each batch of rotgut whisky by fire, because white traders diluted the alcohol to make it as weak as they could and still barter furs for it.

The term began in Canada. For example, James Isham wintering at Haye's River for the Hudson's Bay Company in 1747 lists, among his observations on local words, "brandy: scut ta wop pou." Although some of the most evil whisky traders were Americans along the border, both the British and Americans in the nineteenth century blamed the introduction of alcohol to native peoples on whites who came to the Canadas. Here's a taste of blame from James Fenimore Cooper's famous frontier novel of 1826, *The Last of the Mohicans*: "His Canada fathers . . . taught him to drink the fire-water, and he became a rascal." Forty years later the term had spread to standard British English, as here in 1861 in another popular novel, *Tom Brown at Oxford* by Thomas Hughes: "His father . . . had a horror . . . of the fire-water which is generally sold to undergraduates."

FIREWEED TEA OF THE YUKON

Some Aboriginal peoples of the North like the sugary pith of fireweed obtained by splitting a young stalk and scooping it out. Elk and deer browse in fireweed fields, and bees produce a dark, sweet-smelling honey which makes it worth putting beehives near fireweed. Beekeepers also plant fireweed close to northern apiaries because the honey produced is of superior taste. French-Canadian voyageurs called fireweed *l'herbe fret* and cooked it as greens. In Russia, fireweed leaves are brewed for *kapporie* or kapor tea. Other names for this wild plant, which is invasive on cleared or logged-off land, are mooseweed or willow herb. Its most common name signifies that fireweed is among the first plants to bloom on land after a burn-over. Campers in our North may brew up a refreshing backwoods tea by pouring hot water over the tender young leaves of fireweed. The tea is light green and sweetish. Just make sure you have correctly identified fireweed before teatime, so that there will be an after-teatime.

August 17 is Discovery Day in Yukon Territory, recalling the big strike of 1896 that began the Klondike Gold Rush. A sprig of fireweed often decorates posters and advertising concerning Discovery Day because the pink-blossomed fireweed, *Epilobium angustifolium*, is the official flower of the Yukon. When the pod dehisces after midsummer, it sends out delicate aerial flotillas of silky-winged seeds across thousands of northern acres. The specific adjective *angustifolium* means 'with narrow leaves.'

There is also a broad-leaved species, *Epilobium latifolium*, called mountain fireweed or river beauty, whose deep pink flowers are truly startling spread across a damp arctic-alpine meadow or scattered beside a northern streamside.

The young shoots and flower buds of fireweed and mountain fireweed have been eaten raw or cooked as emergency foods. *Coureurs de bois* and colonists learned from Aboriginal herbalists to make a poultice for skin sores from the ground-up root of fireweed.

FIRST MERIDIAN OF MANITOBA

Two thousand years ago Greek map-makers thought of drawing imaginary lines on the earth to help locate places for travellers and sailors. This grid of lines is now made up of meridians of longitude and parallels of latitude. A meridian of longitude is half of an imaginary circle around the earth drawn from north to south, passing through both poles. On our Canadian prairies, early surveyors who were laying out townships and parcels of land for settlement selected a meridian line a few miles west of Winnipeg from which to begin and called it the First Meridian. Townships in Manitoba were numbered to a second initial meridian east just east of Lake of the Woods, and to a second initial meridian west just west of the Saskatchewan–Manitoba border. The term, highly suitable for our Prairie surveys, is a little confusing since geographers also call a line of longitude that passes through Greenwich, England, the prime (or zero) meridian. This was selected in 1884 as the meridian from which to start measuring how far east or west a location was.

FLIPPER PIE OF NEWFOUNDLAND

The classic piece on seal-flipper pie appears in *Newfoundland*, a 1969 book by feisty Newfoundland writer, Harold Horwood: "Canadians (and other foreigners) often make the mistake of supposing that this famous Newfoundland delicacy consists of the animals' paws. Not at all. The paws are called pads and are usually discarded. The flipper is the front shoulder, corresponding to a shoulder of lamb or a shoulder of pork, except that it is much tastier than either. It is heavy with rich, lean meat, the colour of red mahogany, so tender that you can cut it with a fork, and of a hearty, gamy flavour like that of wild duck." Horwood is quoted thus in the second edition of the *Dictionary of Newfoundland English*.

Flipper dinners and flipper suppers, often put on by service clubs as fund-raisers, are a feature of April on the island. Sealing ships returning from the spring harvest on the ice floes of Labrador or the Gulf come back to harbour with barrels of flippers, so awaited in St. John's that they sell out quickly.

One folk saying speaks of those who are peckish as "hungry as dogs at a flipper barrel."

Flipper pie is an ancient recipe with roots in Scandinavian countries and the Outer Hebrides off Scotland. But the earliest fishermen who crossed the Atlantic for Grand Banks cod and who eventually tested the coast of Labrador saw Inuit people eating *utjak* 'seal flippers,' raw and cooked.

One simple recipe comes from cooks at Happy Valley and Goose Bay in Labrador. A difference of opinion exists about parboiling the flippers first. Some say this produces a horrible, oily smell that gets back into the meat, doubling its "sealiness." Most cooks soak the flippers in cold water and baking soda for thirty minutes and then trim off the fat. Next dredge the flippers with flour and brown with pork fat, onions, and bacon in a frying pan. Then cover and bake two or three hours until tender. Finally, cover with a biscuit pastry and bake for twenty or thirty minutes more. Serve with lemon wedges. A gravy is sometimes added before the pastry is applied.

FOULE

The French word for 'crowd' was used by French-Canadian trappers to refer to the great autumn migration of caribou from the Arctic Ocean south for food and shelter in the pinelands. And *la foule* is still used in northern Canadian English to describe this massing of caribou.

FREDERICTON

The Green is a spacious scroll of lawn stretching along the Saint John River where for more than a hundred years residents of Fredericton have ambled, taken the air, and lolled on the grass to sunbathe. In days of yore, band concerts and riverboat excursions began here as well. Spritzing happily in front of City Hall, and a common meeting spot, is Freddie the Fountain, more recently dubbed Little Nude Dude.

Fickle Finger of Fate
This is one nickname for a well-known former landmark of the city, a four-metre-long hand pointing straight up to heaven, which once adorned the steeple-tip of Wilmot United Church. It had to be taken down for safety reasons, but is on display inside the church. Members of the early British garrison in Fredericton called it Thumbs Up and many residents made appointments to meet one another in the shadow of The Finger.

FRICOT (ACADIAN STEW)

Fricot is *the* Acadian food dish, so common that "Come and Get it!" can be translated into *Acadien* as "*Au fricot!*" It's a thick, hearty soup of potatoes with meat or fish or seafood, always eaten with a spoon. Acadian clam chowder is *fricot aux coques*. Acadien fricots often have dumplings, too, called *grand-pères* 'grandfathers' or *poutines*.

Fricot à la poule 'chicken stew' is part of every Acadian cook's repertoire. Note the constant Acadian use of *poule* 'hen' when chicken as a food is meant. One seldom sees the standard French *poulet* 'young chicken' in old Acadian recipes for the practical reason that one did not kill a laying hen. Eggs were too important to have their production cut short by slaughtering the hen at too young an age. Since older hens were used in most chicken dishes, such recipes often called for long simmering.

At Christmas and New Year's, rabbit stew was an Acadian favourite. For *fricot au lapin des bois*, rabbits were often snared so that they would retain more blood, making them tastier than if the rabbit was shot and then bled copiously. If no meat at all was available for a stew, an Acadian mother might prepare, with a wink, *fricot à la belette* 'weasel stew.' This meatless, onion-and-potato dish was tricky and sly like a weasel, and really only pretended to be a stew. Another jokey name for this recipe among Acadians on Prince Edward Island is *fricot à la bezette* 'stupid cook's stew,' implying that the inclusion of the meat or fish was forgotten.

In standard French, Acadian stew would be *un ragoût acadien*. But the word *fricot* was in continental French by 1767 meaning a feast. By 1800, it was in use in France to denote a meat stew and then prepared food in general (*faire le fricot* = *faire la cuisine*).

FROLIC IN NEW BRUNSWICK HAS JUMPY ORIGIN

Pioneer neighbours rallied around to help put up a barn, make quilts, dry apples. What might be a quilting bee in Upper Canada was a quilting frolic in New Brunswick's early days. A stick-to-your-ribs meal, dancing, and several cups of good cheer might follow all the communal hard work. British immigrants brought the term to New Brunswick. Frolic came into English from Dutch *vroolijk* 'happy, joyous.' Compare its cognate synonym in German *fröhlich*, as in the German for Merry Christmas, *Fröhliche Weihnachten!* The Indo-European root **fro* means 'hop.' It has descendants like German *Freude* 'joy' and even English frog whose root meaning is 'the hopper.' Classical Sanskrit, ancient tongue of India and sacred language of Hinduism, has the related *pravate* 'it hops.' So a frolic is semantically close to a high school hop of the 1950s.

FUNGY

Fungy or fungee (pronounced FUN-jee) as a noun is of Nova Scotian origin. It's a deep-dish blueberry pie, perhaps first named in Yarmouth County. *The Dictionary of Canadianisms on Historical Principles* states that the word is of unknown origin. Not really. It is an extension of the sixteenth-century adjective *fungy* 'full of air holes, spongy like a fungus.' In Newfoundland, fungy bread was poorly baked with too much yeast or other riser and consequently had big holes. The watery component of blueberries is driven off the fruit when it bakes, and bubbles of steamy vapour often make little holes in deep-dish blueberry pastries, so that some early cook probably referred to this concoction as a fungy sort of pie. And the name, like blueberry stain to dental enamel, stuck. See the entry below for grunt.

GEODUCK OR GOOEYDUCK

Gooeyduck is the wonderfully slurpy slang word for a tasty clam of Canada's West Coast, one that inhabits the saltwater tidelands of our Pacific waters. It was not named because the glistening innards reminded someone of a duck pressed into a goo. One may dine on that in Paris. Another spelling is geoduck. The word is from the Nisqually language, from which it was taken into Chinook Jargon, the old trading language of southern British Columbia. The gooeyduck is the largest burrowing bivalve in the world, and that habit caused the West Coast Nisqually people to call it *gwe-duk* or dig-deep. Its very deep burrows make it a tricky clam to harvest.

The geoduck (pronounced GOOee-duck) can attain a mature weight of more than seven kilograms and have a neck as big as a fire hydrant. The length of this neck or siphon accounts of the Chinese name which translates as "elephant trunk clam." To zoologists it is *Panopea abrupta*. It's one of the longest-lived animals on earth. Scientists analyze the growth rings on gooeyduck shells. Some are more than 100 years old. One caught specimen was 146 years old. Geoducks eat and breathe using their long siphons to stick up above the sand line of a beach. One tube of the siphon extracts algae and oxygen from sucked-in sea water, while the other tube spits out water so processed.

There is already a black market trade in these clams which are illegally shipped to Hong Kong and Japan where a single gooeyduck sells for more than sixty Canadian dollars. Japanese prize them especially in geoduck sashimi, an example of a traditional Japanese dish (bite-size slices of raw geoduck) now made with this Canadian clam.

GIN POLE

To preserve meat for a shorter time in our pioneer West, fresh beef or buffalo was cut up and stuffed into gunny sacks or clean flour bags that were tied to a pulley and hoisted to the top of a pole reaching 9 to 15 metres high. This gin pole held the meat above "the fly line" where blowflies could not deposit their eggs in the meat, and so the beef was prevented from turning maggotty. The cooling prairie breeze at such higher heights may also have helped preserve it temporarily. The name derives from a hoisting gin, a device usually consisting of three poles united at the top and used to raise heavy weights with an attached windlass, pulleys, and ropes. Gin here is a contraction of engine or its Old French form, *engin*.

GORBIES OF MUSKOKA

A localism in the central Ontario tourist area of Muskoka is gorby, used by some inhabitants of the area, mostly younger people, to describe loud tourists of the yahoo persuasion. "Oh-oh. Another busload of gorbies!" This does not imply that visitors, upon whom much of the Muskoka economy depends, are treated badly by locals. Muskokans are polite to a fault, in the view of this frequent visitor. But it is pleasant to know they have a little phrase to dismiss the vulgar litterbugs and motorboating cretins who happen through the district now and then.

The origin of gorby is, I believe, in the 1950s camping slang term GORP, an acronym that stood for Good Old Raisins and Peanuts, a trail mix suitable for canoe nibbling, easily packed, and not subject to immediate spoilage. However, when people who were practically born paddling a canoe across a small lake to a store see a tourist and canoeing neophyte set off on the same trip with thousands of dollars' worth of yuppie camping equipment and three pounds of GORP to sustain them in their fifteen-minute canoe trip across the lake, then it seems natural that gorpy, later gorby, might arise as a mild put-down.

GOW OF BRITISH COLUMBIA

Gow is a legal Canadian export worth more than one million dollars a year but you may not know the word. Gow is a rough Englishing of a Japanese word that signifies little eggs. Gow is a delicacy in the cuisine of Japan. It is herring roe (fish eggs) spawned on a small piece of seaweed. Some British Columbia fisheries actually plant severed fronds of algal seaweed within schools of spawning herring, and harvest the result for immediate air freighting across the Pacific. The delicacy was known to some coastal First Peoples of British Columbia whose ancestors may have brought the discovery with them eons ago when they first crossed the Bering Strait to enter North America.

GRID ROADS

You know you're in Saskatchewan when you hear this term describing the best system of municipal roads in Canada. Incidentally, Saskatchewan has the longest road system in Canada: more than 200,000 kilometres! The grid roads were laid out 1 mile apart east to west and 2 miles apart north to south, with a correction line, a little hop every 24 miles in the north to south line to compensate for the difference between the line as surveyed and the true meridian of longitude.

GRUNT

Grunt or slump or fudge is a steamed pudding or dumpling made with blueberries or huckleberries. But one can also enjoy in a Nova Scotia kitchen rhubarb grunt, raspberry grunt, and even apple grunt. In *Folklore of Lunenburg County*, Nova Scotia, the great Canadian folklorist Helen Creighton gives one definitive recipe: "Put berries in a pot, cover well with water and cook. Cool and add sugar. Drop baking powder dough in it." Maritimers enjoy many variations, including one made from the little red cranberrylike fruits of foxberry or cowberry, *Vaccinium vitis-idaea*. Grunt is the toadish plorp! sound made as baking drives pockets of heated water vapour out of the gelatinous mass of the cooking berries. Grunt can be a main course as well as a dessert.

HALIFAX

Known in the argot of the Royal Canadian Navy as Slackers, Halifax was so dubbed because of slack time during shore-leave granted when ships are in port. The area around Brunswick and Gottingen Streets is called Dutchtown, because of early German immigrants. In the mid-eighteenth century it was the German Mission. Dutch is an illiterate clerk's misspelling of Deutsch. One neighbourhood nickname that remains in use is Dutch Village, on the outskirts of Halifax. Haligonians colourfully nickname local buildings as well. The site of the old Churchfield barracks on Brunswick Street near the corner of Cogswell is the Twelve Apostles. They are twelve attached barracks for married soldiers built on the old army cantonment model. Still standing, they are now privately owned. Summit Place next to Sackville Landing is a squat, green-glass edifice waggishly known as The Green Toad. It was the Kodak Building until leaders of the G-7 Summit held meetings there one weekend. And there is the notorious Liquordome where five loud pick-up bars are all connected together so the bleary searcher after sex can wander from one pie-eyed emporium of plonk to another, getting only his whistle wet. Still controversial is the obliteration of Africville, once home to a small community of African Nova Scotians. Africville was expropriated and the residents removed by force to create SeaView Park and the McKay Bridge and its overpasses and underpasses. My thanks for these notes go to Lou Collins, the honorary civic historian of Halifax.

HALLELUJAH POINT IN VANCOUVER

This spot near the collection of totem poles in Vancouver's Stanley Park was named after Salvation Army revival meetings held in this pleasant setting for many years. Stanley Park, named after an early Governor-General of British Columbia, Lord Stanley, actually began long before British Columbia entered Confederation, when bigwigs in the Royal

British Navy, fretful about the possibility of any future dust-ups with pesky Yankees from the south who had been complaining about the manifest destiny of Oregon and Washington territory to be part of the United States (it was manifest, was it not?) looked at the thousand acres of land on Burrard Inlet and reserved it for military use. In 1886, the first meeting of Vancouver City Council passed a resolution to open the land as a public park.

OFRA HARNOY: THE MEANINGS OF A CELLIST'S NAMES

Born in Israel in 1965, Canada's internationally renowned cellist began her mastery of the instrument under her father Jacob's tutelage at the age of six just before the family immigrated to Canada in 1972. From the Royal Conservatory of Music in Toronto she has gone on to perform to great acclaim as soloist with most of the major orchestras and in solo recitals all over the world. Ms. Harnoy has recorded more than forty solo albums, and received many prizes including two of Canadian music's Juno Awards and other honours like the Order of Canada in 1995.

Harnoy originates as a Russian-Jewish surname. The Russian noun denoting the colour black may be transliterated as *chornoi*. Although the name in some instances was adopted freely by Jewish families during their dispersion through northern Europe, in many more cases the name is the result of anti-

Semitic local laws that forced Jewish people to assume permanent family names in the language of the national authorities who ruled over them. In some Russian *shtetlach* (Yiddish 'little towns') this was accomplished by ordering Jewish residents to congregate in the town square while some functionary divided them—men, women, and children—into four groups differentiated by the hair colour or stature of the father: darkhaired, lighthaired, tall, and short. Then various Russian words for these attributes suffixed with Slavic patronymics became the legal surnames of these Jewish families. A darkhaired or dark-complexioned ancestor may lie behind such Slavic-Jewish surnames as Harnoy, Charnoy, Chorny, Charnin, Charnis, Chernoff, and Chernovsky. Fair-skinned ancestors might have been given surnames containing the Slavic root for white *byelo-*, names such as Belsky, Byelov, and Byelin. When such divisions for forced naming happened in Germany, the resulting Jewish last names were Schwartz 'dark' or 'black,' Weiss 'white' or 'lighthaired' or 'with pale skin,' Gross 'tall,' and Klein 'short.' This happened in other European countries as well. Consider some Hungarian Jews whose surname is Fekete, the Hungarian word for black or darkhaired. One proviso must be repeated: some families did get to choose their goyish surnames. But many did not.

Ms. Harnoy's given name is the beautiful Hebrew Ofra, the feminine of *ofer*, the Hebrew word for fawn. Both male and female words for young deer are still popular today in Israel as first names. Curiously, Ofra appears in the Old Testament as a man's name (First Chronicles 4:14). This has led some scholars of Hebrew etymology to suggest that Ofra may derive instead from a different Semitic root and may mean 'she who turns her back.' I suggest that these meanings are simply the same radical in different reflexes, that is, that the root meaning of *ofer*, the Hebrew word for fawn, is 'creature that turns or shows its back.' What is more memorable about young fawns than their beautifully flecked backs, evolved by nature as camouflage?

HAW EATERS OF MANITOULIN ISLAND

Haw eaters are Canadians born and raised on Manitoulin Island. Their local word for themselves comes in three forms: run together as haweater, with a hyphen as haw-eater, and primly discrete as haw eater. They like hawberries, the dark red fruit of a species of hawthorn common in northern Ontario. Haws can be lovingly ovened in pies, tarts, and strudels. Visitors to Manitoulin buy tasty haw jams too.

The word was brought to Canada by early immigrants from England and Scotland. One of the oldest berry names in English, haw pops up plump and ruddy in a glossary dated around AD 1000. Hawberry and hawthorn share an initial element which is cognate with Old High German *hag* 'enclosure.' The first meaning of haw in English was fence. Hawthorn bushes were early used to fence yards, hence hawthorn is fence-thorn. Our later word "hedge" is related to haw, and still hemming and hawing in some rural English dialects is churchhaw for churchyard.

By the fourteenth century, 'enclosed yard' and 'pen for domestic animals' were common meanings for the word. Geoffrey Chaucer (AD 1340–1400), the first great poet in English, used it that way in "The Pardoner's Tale" from his *Canterbury Tales* written in Middle English: "Ther was a polcat in his hawe, That . . . hise capons hadde islawe." There was a polecat in his yard that his castrated roosters had slain [by pecking it to death]. A polecat is a smelly European weasel. Charming vignette. Chaucer used the word in its fruity sense in "The Former Age": "They eten mast hawes and swyche pownage." They ate acorns and chestnuts (mast), hawthorn berries, and such pannage (pig food).

A Dutch cousin of *haw*, Middle Dutch *hage* 'ground enclosed by a fence, park' gives both of the two names of the capital city of the Netherlands: *'s Gravenhage* 'The Count's Haw, or Park.' Modern English "The Hague" stems directly from the other name of the city in Dutch *Den Haag* 'the hedge.' Both names refer to woods that were royal hunting grounds surrounding a medieval palace. Such pleasant ripples in the pond of words waft us back to Lake Huron and the largest freshwater island in the world, namely Manitoulin, and so to . . .

Debajehmujig, Teller of Tales

Manitoulin Island is home to one of the most imaginative storytelling groups in Canada. Is narrative magic aloft in island air, spun of mystic wisps only haw eaters may gather? Seems so. The Ojibwa word *debajehmujig* 'storyteller' is used to name an inventive Ojibwe theatre group based in "Wiky." Some of the actors and craftspeople belong to the local Obidgewong band. Wiky is Manitoulin's affectionate short form for the Wikwemikong Unceded Reserve at the eastern end of the island. Wikwemikong means 'bay of the beaver.' Note the adjective "unceded" in the reserve's name. Thereby hangs a tale. In 1836 the stoutly named Sir Francis Bond Head, Lieutenant-Governor of Upper Canada, put his signature to a treaty that ceded Manitoulin Island to the Ojibwe and Odawa peoples for their sole occupancy. But, surprise! surprise! in 1862 the white government cancelled the treaty and allowed white settlers to homestead almost anywhere on the island. The Aboriginal leaders of the Wikwemikong peninsula said no, and Wiky remained unceded.

In August 1994 the De-ba-jeh-mu-jig Theatre Group staged a performance piece called "The Manitoulin Incident," written by Alanis King-Odjig, local playwright and artistic director of the company. Acted smack-dab in the ruins of a Jesuit mission at Wiky where some of the white duplicity had actually taken place, the play was a night of marvels: giant thunderbirds on stilts, a woman impishly playing Sir Francis Bond Head, three languages: Ojibwa, English, French ricocheting off the Jesuitical bricks, puppets, drums athrob in the dusk, masked dancers. See this astounding company if you can. They usually perform in conjunction with the Wikwemikong pow wow held on the first weekend in August, and each production runs for a few weeks on Manitoulin before a fall and winter tour. Their hits have included a 1990 piece, *Toronto at Dreamer's Rock*, and one that wowed me, King-Odjig's 1993 *If Jesus Met Nanabush*. Nanabush is a shape-shifting half-mortal and trickster god of the Ojibwe. He smiles on this company, and so will you.

HÉBERT: FAMOUS SURNAME OF QUÉBEC

***Anne Hébert** (1916–2000)*

One of Québec's most influential novelists, also a poet and playwright, she was the author of *Kamouraska* (1970), filmed by Claude Jutra, and *Les Fous de Bassan* (1982), filmed by Yves Simoneau. Ms. Hébert was one of the great wordsmiths of Québec French. Her *mots justes* were French words that rang like precise bells on the ear and on the page. Her French had none of the flabby wobble of much of twentieth-century French fiction and expository prose. She was a superb editor of her own writings and was able, perhaps better than any other writer of her century, to flench off the blubbery excesses to which French is prone and so to produce a lean, fatless tendon of prose that flexed to permit thought and emotion to reside cleanly together in the same sentence, neither quality overwhelming the other.

On her mother's side of the family, Madame Hébert is related to two famous figures in Québec literary history: nineteenth-century historian François-Xavier Garneau and the influential twentieth-century poet Hector Saint-Denys Garneau, her cousin and her friend. When Saint-Denys Garneau died of a heart attack while canoeing alone on a lonely Québec river in 1943, it deeply affected Anne Hébert's life and her calling to literature. Her first novel was *Les Chambres de bois* in 1958. Her influential volumes of poetry include *Les Songes en équilibre* (1942), *Le Tombeau des rois* (1953), and *Mystère de la parole* (1960). A collection of poetry, *Le jour n'a d'égal que la nuit*, appeared in 1993. Her other novels include *Héloïse* (1980) about ghostly vampires haunting the Paris subway system. Hébert lived in Paris for more than thirty years because, she said, "Montréal is too American; Québec City is too small; and Paris is very, very beautiful." Three years before her death, doctors told her she had cancer and Ms. Hébert returned to Québec City to live out her life at home. Among her later works were *L'Enfant chargé de songes* (1992), *Aurélien, Clara, Mademoiselle et l'officier anglais* (1995), *Est-ce que je te dérange?* (1998), and her last book, *Un habit de lumière* (1999).

Hébert is a variant of Herbert, a French surname based on an ancestor's given name, Old German *Hariberht*, made up of *harja* 'host' and *berhta* 'bright.' After the Norman Conquest, Herbert spread widely throughout Great Britain as a male given name.

HEPATICA

No better introduction to this early little beauty exists than the entry by our pioneer writer Catharine Parr Traill. In *The Backwoods of Canada* published in 1836 she wrote, "The hepatica is the first flower of Canadian spring: it gladdens us with its tints of azure, pink, and white, early in April, soon after the snows have melted from the earth. The Canadians call it snow-flower, from its coming so soon after the snow disappears." Two species brighten eastern Canadian woodlands, *Hepatica acutifolia* (Botanical Latin, 'with sharply pointed leaves') and *Hepatica americana*. The earliest British settlers thought of it as Noble Liverwort. Indeed, it is named for the mottled, liverish colour and the shape of the leaves that come only after the pale purple flowers have faded. The genus *Hepatica* derives from the Latin word for liver, *hepar*. It is familiar to anyone who has studied human anatomy in medical words and phrases like hepatic function, hepatitis A and B and C.

The wild plant hepatica is a member of *Ranunculaceae*, the buttercup family, named after its typical species, the buttercup, *Ranunculus* < *rana* Latin, 'frog' + *-unculus* Latin, diminutive suffix, 'little, tiny.' *Ranunculus* is Latin for 'little frog,' so named because buttercups like damp places just as amphibians do.

HERE'S A HO!

When all glasses are charged with bubbly champagne or sudsy beer, this drinking toast can still be offered in Winnipeg and other places in Manitoba, and some among those tippling will remember the origin. "Ho!" was the word used to begin the attack in great community buffalo hunts of yore. In those early days, a buffalo's horn was commonly used for certain ceremonial toasts and that may have influenced the choice of "Ho!" Sodbusters and stubble-jumpers would toast that way to make sure no one mistook them for a bunch of high-falutin' cigarette dudes (old Prairie slang for a 'city slicker').

HERRING-CHOKER IN NEW BRUNSWICK

This old slang term for any Maritimer was applied usually to New Brunswickers, probably because the Bay of Fundy has a run of spring herrings (alewives, a good bait fish) that come in to spawn in April and May. In the fall a herring run of a different species more highly prized for eating arrives, as A. Murray Kinloch points out in "The English Language in

New Brunswick 1784–1984," his lively tour of the topic that appears in *A Literary and Linguistic History of New Brunswick* (1985).

HEWITT OF HOCKEY SHOOTS & SCORES!

Foster Hewitt (1902–85) carried one of the most famous names in modern Canadian history. He was *the fons et origo* of hockey broadcasting, Mr. Hewitt spoke one of the first play-by-play descriptions of a hockey game using an upright telephone as a radio microphone on March 22, 1923. Foster did the first game from Maple Leaf Gardens in 1931, raising an already high voice to an excited scream of "He shoots! He scores!" Mr. Hewitt borrowed from Italian the word *gondola* to name his broadcast booth high over the ice at Maple Leaf Gardens. In the 1950s Hewitt easily made the transition to televised hockey commentary. Through the CBC's broadcasting of *Hockey Night in Canada*, he is indelibly linked with Saturday at home in the minds of several generations of Canadians.

In 1969 my first job in Toronto at CBC Radio on Jarvis Street required me to disembark at the College Street subway and then walk along Maitland Street behind Maple Leaf Gardens and so enter the CBC Radio building from its back door. One brisk and snappy day early in November soon after I began my first CBC assignment, I was trotting along Maitland when out of the Gardens came a red-faced little figure bundled up in a very expensive winter coat. My jaw dropped. It was Foster Hewitt! Now I have never asked anyone for an autograph in my life. I don't faint when movie stars are discovered nibbling shrimp at the next table. But I did grow up listening and watching Foster Hewitt. I greeted him and told him how much a part of my childhood and of our family Saturday nights he had been and still was. He was in person a shy and modest man. But he took the time to chat amiably with a fan, asked me what in particular I was doing at the CBC, and spent some ten minutes with me telling with some relish a few CBC anecdotes not for general publication. I may have encouraged this, as I began our conversation by relating several tales-out-of-school myself. Afterward, as I walked on to work, I finally felt "big city" for the first time since moving to Toronto. I was a kid from the boonies and now I had truly arrived in the city. That night I phoned home and told my dad I'd met Foster Hewitt. "Try to keep your head now, Bill," Dad said.

Hewitt is a very old English surname that originated in the county of Kent. Last names arise from four basic sources: the first names of ancestors, the places ancestors lived, the nicknames of ancestors, and their occupations. Hewitt belongs to the class of English surnames that originated as the name of the place where the founding ancestor lived.

At Hewitts in Chelsfield and at Hewitts in Willesborough (Kent) lived a family named *de la*

Hewatte whose first appearance in printed records occurs in the year 1270. Nearby occur records for de la Hewett (1301) and atte Hewete (1338). Note that the variation in spelling was great until English orthography was standardized through the widespread use of dictionaries at the end of the seventeenth century. The Old English word *hiewett* 'place hewed' or 'cutting' referred to a farmstead or acreage where trees had been cut down, that is, a clearing.

Individuals had one name to begin with. As population density increased, with the rise of towns and villages, a method was needed to differentiate clearly between two or more persons both with the same single name. For example, a village might have two persons named John. In the parish register of births and deaths, one might be a John whose father's name was Robert. He would be entered as John, son of Robert, and eventually his patronymic surname would be John Robertson. Another John might dwell at a clearing in the woods, at a *hewitt* in Old English, a place prominent and known to all local folk. He might be first styled John at the hewitt; and soon his name was shortened to John Hewitt and became hereditary.

HIGH MUCKAMUCK

Now referring to a pompous official, high muckamuck once meant merely someone with plenty of food to eat. High muckamuck is a term

I remember my father using as a way to describe any arrogant SOB of an official. As he was a school principal, it sprang up often when he spoke of school boards. The term, first in Canadian, then borrowed into American English, was taken, with a touch of folk etymology, from Chinook Jargon, the west coast trading language of the last century. *Hyiu* meant 'much' and came into the catch-all trading language from the Nootka tongue of Vancouver Island where *ih* means big. *Muckamuck* was food in Coast Salish. In the days when food gathering took much time and skill, anyone who had lots of food was an important and successful person, hence a high muckamuck. Its mucky sound in English made it appropriate as a deflator of ballooning egos. Muck-a-muck was borrowed into West Coast English very early as a synonym for food. Even a verb, to muck-a-muck 'to eat heartily,' appears in pioneer journals and diaries.

HOODOO

Who grew that hoodoo that you knew came from voodoo? Every kid who ever traipsed the badlands of Alberta near Drumheller and saw hoodoos has played comic variations on silly hoodoo sentences. Hoodoos are odd-shaped pedestals of earth or pillars of rock that develop through erosion by wind and water, especially in areas where the sedimentary layers alternate between soft and hard material, for example in horizontal strata of shale and sandstone. You can see them in Alberta's Dinosaur Provincial Park, down in the border country near Alberta's Milk River, on the banks of the Columbia River north of Cranbrook and in the Okanagan Valley in British Columbia. I saw small hoodoos on a raft trip I once took down the Kootenay River. And there are plenty in Hoodoo Valley near Leanchoil on the edge of Yoho National Park in British Columbia. French-Canadian voyageurs called them *demoiselles* 'young ladies.'

Hoodoo is general across the west of North America, and is not of Canadian origin. *The Dictionary of Canadianisms* (1967) states that hoodoo is "of African origin, related to voodoo." No, it is not related as a word to voodoo. In the eighteenth and nineteenth centuries, black slaves of Hausa origin brought with them to their enslavement in the American south a distinct magic practice called "hoodoo." The word comes directly from the Hausa language where the verb *hu'du'ba* means 'to arouse resentment, produce retribution.' Note that the word *voodoo* comes from another African language called Ewe where *vodu* refers directly to a specific demon or tutelary deity. Voodoo passed into American English by way of Louisiana Creole *voudou*. Very early in America, hoodoo came to mean 'jinx' or 'cast a spell on' as a noun and a verb: "Something hoodooed me out in the swamp last night. I think it was my ex-husband."

American Aboriginal peoples of the Northwest picked up the word from English-speaking fur trappers and, like them, used hoodoo to refer to any malignant creature or evil supernatural force. That's how it came to be applied to the curious columns of earth or rock. Hoodoos were thought to be evil in the mythologies of many first peoples. For example, in Siksika (Blackfoot) mythology, the strange shapes were giants whom the Great Spirit had turned to stone because of their evil deeds. Deep in the night, the petrified giants could awaken and throw boulders down upon any humans passing nearby.

HOOTCH

Hootch and hootchinoo are one-hundred-percent Canadian booze words. Hootch, now a term for homebrew or a popular synonym for any liquor, was first popularized in the Yukon during the days of the Klondike Gold Rush, and has now spread across Canada.

Hootch is short for hootchinoo, a cheap, inferior whisky made during the Gold Rush. Hootchinoo is the mangled English form of a word in the Tlingit language, *khutsnuwu*, or Grizzly Bear Fort, the name of a people and their village on Admiralty Island, where hootch was first brewed from molasses, yeast, local berries, and other ingredients best left veiled from mortal knowledge.

Tlingit is a member of the Na-Dene family of northern languages. It is spoken by a people now inhabiting southern Alaska and some offshore islands. In 1981 approximately 1,500 people still spoke the language. *Tlingit* in the Tlingit language means 'the people.' As for the roots of the name *Na-Dene*: in Chipewyan and in Proto-Athapaskan, *dene* means 'person.' *Naa* in related languages like Haida and Tlingit has to do with roots meaning 'house,' 'living,' and 'tribe.' Thus, the semantic sense of Na-Dene is 'our people.'

HURT PIE

Hurt, with a welter of spellings like eart, heurt, hirt, hort, hurt, whort, and several diminutives like hurtle and whortle, is a very old English berry name. *Hurtes* appear in print by 1542, but its cousin hurtleberry appears earlier in 1450. The word has disappeared from Standard English, but is still common in many British dialects. In Newfoundland it refers to a number of species of the *Vaccinium* genus including blueberries, blackberries, bilberries, and huckleberries. In fact, Mark Twain's eponymous Huckleberry Finn takes his nickname from an American alteration of hurtleberry. Newfoundland has ground hurts, stone hurts, and black hurts. This abundant berry ended up early on in hurt pie and other dishes like hurt cake, hurty pudding, and in a delicious brew of fermented blueberries called hurt wine, still offered with Christmas cake to lucky mummers who come calling during the holidays.

INTERVALE OF OUR MARITIMES

This word, also seen as "interval," brought up to our Maritimes by immigrants from the New England states, is a synonym for bottomland, the rich alluvial soil in the flood plain of a watercourse. New Brunswick's many rivers rejoiced in deep intervales, sometimes called riverbottoms. Here's a pioneer quotation from around 1780: "The interval lands on the St. John are wonderful, not a stone, and black mold six feet deep."

IRISH MOSS PUDDING

Also called sea-moss pudding, this Canadian Maritime dessert is similar to a blancmange, but an edible seaweed is the jelling agent instead of gelatine. Whipped egg whites replace the more usual cornstarch. One old recipe was thought especially helpful for invalids or anyone with "a delicate digestion" and this was Irish moss jelly, in which a small handful of cleaned, dried Irish moss was boiled in two cups of water and then cooled. A cup of milk was stirred in and a little sugar added. Highly restorative, according to many an Island grandmother!

Irish moss, Canada's most valuable commercial seaweed, is one of the red algae, usually *Chondrus crispus*, but several other seaweeds are sometimes called Irish moss. It is called carrageen in Scotland and Ireland, and was named after a town near Waterford in Ireland, Carragheen. But the town may have owed its moniker to an Irish term for the moss, *cosáinín carraige*, literally in Erse 'little foot of the rock.' *Chondrus crispus* is related to another edible seaweed called dulse. See our entry on *dulse*.

Irish moss is exported from Prince Edward Island and processed to yield a hydrocolloid, carrageenin. All of us use products every day that contain carrageenin as an emulsifying and stabilizing agent. For example, it holds together the ingredients in many toothpastes, shampoos, cosmetics, pharmaceuticals, and prepared foods like chocolate milk, ice cream, and commercial salad dressings. Check the list of ingredients on any commercial food product that might qualify as "goopy." Carrageenin is also used to clarify liquids like beer, wine, coffee, and honey. In many frozen foods, carrageenin helps retard the formation of ice crystals in products that can be kept cold for long periods.

Irish Moss Industry on Prince Edward Island

Gathered as well along the coasts of Nova Scotia and New Brunswick, Irish moss has been an important commercial crop on Prince Edward Island for so long that some unique Island terms have grown up around its collection, notably the noun *mosser*, referring to one who harvests the seaweed. A mosser is also a high, stormy wind that wafts Irish moss toward the shore. Such winds help produce the underwater waves of turbulence that rip Irish moss fronds from their holdfasts on seabed rocks in the lower tidal and subtidal zones.

Water-plumped and tempest-rolled, rows of green strands festoon shores in the north of Prince Edward Island near Tignish, Miminegash, Cape Tryon, North Rustico, and Covehead. Moss that reaches a beach is forked into piles by *combers* using hand rakes. *Horse mossers* collect Irish moss near shore by rakes and wire-mesh scoops pulled through the water by a *moss horse*. Such horses are usually large and fearless, for they sometimes have to haul moss in water right up to their necks and work among several dozen other horses when twenty or thirty horse mossers all harvest one stretch of shore after an especially bountiful storm. A former term for profit from such a sea-gift was *moss money*. In olden days, children often had the job of cleaning freshly harvested moss of pebbles, shells, sea wrack, and other unwanted seaweeds. On Prince Edward Island one such impurity is called *monkey fur*, being the seaweed genus *Halopteris*, whose thick brown strands are matted through the Irish moss and make it hard to dry. Another tangly intruder has the Prince Edward Island nickname *shoe-string*. It's a green, eelgrasslike seaweed of the *Chondra* genus and must be plucked from a mosser's haul if the harvester wants top price from processors.

Popular Canadian balladeer Stompin' Tom Connors who wrote the rollicking "Bud The Spud" about Prince Edward Island's potato industry also celebrated seaweed in his "Song of The Irish Moss" where he wrote "You can hear them roar from the Tignish Shore / There's moss on Skinner's Pond . . ."

JIGG'S DINNER

This is a boiled dinner of salt beef and vegetable dish, although salt pork can be used, too. The salted meat is soaked overnight in cold water, then boiled for three-quarters of an hour, at which time the cook adds turnip, carrots, cabbage, and potatoes, boiling until the potatoes are done. This makes a hearty repast for a fisher who's been jigging, that is, using a weighted hook with a line and no bait to catch squid or cod by jigging the line, jerking it up sharply. A jigger line often has two or more hooks attached. Is this the origin of the name *Jigg's dinner*? The verb *to jig* is also used in Newfoundland to mean "to hook a husband." As a noun, a jig can mean a romantic date. Could a Jigg's dinner have been an honest way to convince a potential husband that the female cook preparing the meal knew how to feed a hungry man? In any case, it's a word woven into the tough fabric of island life. Even official Newfoundland place names refer to this method of fishing—spots like Jigging Cove, Jigging Head, and Jigging Point.

But here's an email that expands the search for Jiggs, probably with the correct answer:

My understanding of "Jigg's" comes not from cod catching, but from a newspaper comic I read as a kid, "Bringing up Father." *The main characters were a monster of a wife Maggie and her unfortunate husband Jiggs. Jiggs (I've since learned) was an Irishman who came into money but was always hankering after his old standby dinner of corned-beef-and-cabbage; Maggie, aspiring to higher-status dining, always tried to keep him from getting it. It wasn't until I moved to Newfoundland to take up graduate studies in the 1970s that I heard corned-beef-and-cabbage referred to as a "Jiggs dinner." It took me back to childhood evenings on the floor of the living room reading the comics in the* Toronto Star *with Maggie shouting, "Insect!" as Jiggs tried to sneak out for his beloved victuals. I believe they use "Jiggs dinner" in Boston as well.*

Sheldon Posen
Curator, Canadian Folklife
Ethnology & Cultural Studies
Canadian Museum of Civilization

JILL-POKE

In the jargon of New Brunswick lumbering this noun named a major nuisance for log drivers: a timber pole that had one end stuck in the mud of a riverbank and the other projecting dangerously out into the current. Jill-poke was also heard in early Maritime lumber camps as a label for anyone in camp who was a 'pain-in-the-ass.' "Get that drunken jill-poke's face out of the molasses!" It's a nifty, jabby chop and should be resuscitated for use in political invective. Why, two or three of our glorious, jill-pokey leaders come to mind almost immediately.

JOLLOP

A jollop on Prince Edward Island is any big mess of food made from kitchen leftovers. Spelled like dollop, jollop is seventeenth-century English farm slang where a jollop was the wattle of a turkey or rooster, the implication being that when you wolfed down such goopy leftovers, you really had to move your jowls, that is, your wattles. Jollop appears to be a compound of jowl + lap, analogous to dewlap.

JUNIPER TEA

From southern Alberta's foothills to British Columbia's interior mountain ranges grows Rocky Mountain Juniper, *Juniperus scopulorum*, Latin 'of the rocky cliffs.' In spite of its specific, this conifer grows best in rich, well-drained, moist loam but can be seen clinging to a lofty precipice now and then. But it is one of only two Canadian junipers that attain tree size. Always used in moderate amounts, the berries can be steeped in boiling water for fifteen minutes to produce a warm drink said to be good for mild stomach troubles and for coughs. Even the young, tender tips of juniper boughs, minus the berries, were used to make a pleasant and refreshing tea.

The ripe berries, really the cones, of several other juniper species are used as part of the flavouring of the French liqueur, Chartreuse, and, most famously, to flavour gin. Juniper berries begin green and take two to three years to ripen to a dark blue when they are harvested to add piney zest to pâtés and to game meats like venison and rabbit.

European immigrants found First Peoples burning juniper needles as incense and as an inhalant to cure coughing, as well as using the berries in herbal remedies. But note that raw, unprocessed berries and boughs of some juniper species can be toxic to livestock and are reported to have poisoned humans, although grouse, pheasants, and other birds bolt the berries with impunity. The teas made from juniper are for occasional, herbal use, and should not be taken daily.

KAHAHOOSA OR JACK-IN-THE-PULPIT

In Canada, Jack-in-the-pulpit has had many names: *gouet à trois feuilles*, Indian turnip, and *kahahoosa*. Jack belongs to the arum family of plants. The most common foliage pot plant in the world is an arum, good old leafy standby *Philodendron*. Jack-in-the-pulpit, *Arisaema triphyllum* (Botanical Latin < *treis* Greek, three + *phyllon* Greek, leaf) the familiar little arum of our moist woods, refers in its specific name to the three little leaflets of which each leaf seems to be comprised.

French-Canadian lumberjacks encountered the

plant in Québec woodlands and thought the spathe that bends over the jack or spadix like a little pointed flap looked like one of their implements, a hand-held log-hook or *gouet*, hence the French-Canadian name, *gouet à trois feuilles* 'hook with three leaves.' Iroquois peoples named it *kahahoosa* 'papoose cradle,' because it looked like the backrack Iroquois women used to carry their babies. Indian turnip was a pioneer name for the plant.

The corms of jack-in-the-pulpit can be eaten only when well cooked. Consumed raw, they burn the tongue, mouth, and throat, and are highly poisonous. Scottish settlers called it Devil's Ear. Medical records contain case histories of those who ate jack-in-the-pulpit raw and died from a hideously painful gastroenteritis. Colonists in early Virginia dubbed it American wake-robin, but the name has no practicality as a folk term because it was used to refer to at least six separate plants, all of different plant families, including the trillium.

KARTOSHNIK—DOUKHOBORS' POTATOES

This is a Doukhobor recipe from Saskatchewan based on a much older Russian version of potato cakes. Cooked potatoes are drained and mashed. Eggs and cream are whipped together with a pinch of salt and folded into the mashed potatoes. After a final brisk stirring, the mixture is spread on a greased pan and baked for half an hour. The potato cake is cut into squares and the *kartoshniki* are served immediately with butter. In its form, *kartoshnik* looks like a Russian alteration of the German word for potato, *Kartoffel*.

Remove the Slavic agent suffix (*-nik*) and what remains is *kartosh*, possibly one of the many German words introduced in Russian during the rule of Catherine the Great, who was a German-speaking Hapsburg. *Kartoffel*, the German word for potato, began as a mangled borrowing, *Tartoffel*, from a seventeenth-century Italian term for the tuber *tartuficolo*, itself a diminutive form derived from an unattested Medieval Latin compound like **territuberum* 'earth tuber.' Yes, linguistic use of the adjective *unattested* always means it is only an educated guess.

About seven thousand Doukhobors, members of a pacifist Christian sect, came to Canada to Saskatchewan in 1899, after they were attacked in their native Russia for refusing to serve in the Russian army. Their pacifist protest in Russia included the public burning of large piles of military rifles. Their peaceful farming in Saskatchewan was interrupted when the provincial government enforced certain laws, such as making Doukhobors swear allegiance to Canada and forcing them to enrol their children in public schools. Rather than succumb to these demands, some Doukhobors moved on in 1905, to the remote West Kootenays in British Columbia, where today perhaps thirty thousand still live. A radical anarchist sect of the

Doukhobors called themselves The Sons of Freedom. Canadians may remember their arson, bombings, and nude protest marches in British Columbia during the late 1940s and early 1950s. But most members of this religious group were and are peaceful.

The name *Doukhobor* began in Russia as an insult. In 1785, a Russian Orthodox archbishop, from the lofty summit of his archbishopric, denounced the sect by calling them Doukhobors. *Dukh* is Russian for 'spirit,' if capitalized for the Holy Spirit, if lowercased for any spirit or goblin. *Borets* means 'fighter' or 'wrestler.' Thus *Dukhoborets* can mean 'one who wrestles with the Holy Spirit,' and without the capital letter *D*, in Russian slang, it is 'spirit-wrestler,' the equivalent of 'holy roller' in English. A double-whammy insult, indeed. Nevertheless, after being called this in Russia, the members of the persecuted sect decided to adopt the name, nullifying the insult, because *Dukhoborets* can also mean 'fighter **for** the Holy Spirit.'

KIACK

Kiack is a rough-scaled, bony little fish called the alewive in English, and *ki'ak* in the Mi'kmaq language. It is often fished during the spring salmon run when it comes up maritime rivers. Its zoological name is the daunting *Pomolobus pseudoharengus* or apple-bellied false herring. The little fish does have a naturally big belly, and this gave the English common name too, an alewife being just what it looks like, a woman who kept an alehouse, sampled her brew copiously, and had a fat stomach. In Nova Scotia, kiack became an insult, too. Kiack was a term of derision in early Nova Scotia for anyone who ate alewives, implying that they were poor, rustic, and could not afford to indulge in civilized "town" food.

KINNIKINNICK

Atungawiat, bearberry, Yukon holly, kinnikinnick: all these terms refer to the bearberry. *Atungawiat* is the plant's name in one of the dialects of Inuktitut, the many-dialected language of the Inuit. Other English terms are Bear's Grape and Indian tobacco. And like many plants useful to humans, the bearberry has local names, too, such as Yukon holly. It's a member of the heath family of plants. Precisely, atungawiat is northern bearberry, the sweet dark fruit of *Arctostaphylos alpina*, a low shrub of the Barren Grounds; it is related to the more southerly kinnikinnick but much sweeter, a true tundra treat. The tiny flowers look like white bells with pink rims, and the dense mats of leathery, evergreen leaves hug the northern ground, in some places like a green carpet. The red fruit of the bearberry is much munched by bears, hence its common name and the botanical label of the more southerly species: *Arctostaphylos uva-ursi*. *Arctostaphylos* means 'bear berry' in botanical Greek. *Uva ursi* means 'grapes of the bear' in Latin.

In all the northern climes of the world, humans have made tea from the dried leaves of bearberry, usually by a simple steeping for five minutes in boiled water. The red berries are also added crushed to tealike infusions. Early white fur trappers and prospectors often soaked the leaves of bearberry in whisky before steeping them to make tea. As a natural herbal remedy, the tea has been used for kidney and bladder troubles. Russians call the tea kutai and in their country it's widely used for various stomach disorders. Because the red berries are persistent through the long winter, atungawiat is an important emergency ration for those lost and hungry in the Arctic barrens. Eaten raw, the berries are dry, floury, and tasteless, so they are mixed with other, sweeter wild foods, if possible.

Kinnikinnick is another common name for this plant. The word with the root (*kinn*) reduplicated means 'mix-mix' in Cree and Ojibwa, hence mixture, specifically a smoking mixture that might contain dried bearberry leaves, dried sumac leaves, red-osier dogwood bark, and tobacco. This very pungent Indian tobacco was smoked in a pipe.

Every native language seems to have a word to denote this widespread plant. Among the Chinook people, bearberry is *iss-salth*. The Cree call it *tchakoshe-pukk*; in the Chipewyan language it's *kleh*.

KITSILANO IN VANCOUVER

The Kitsilano area of Vancouver starts roughly near Kits Beach and runs along the south shore of English Bay out towards the campus of the University of British Columbia on Point Grey. Kits extends up to 16th Avenue. Kitsilano was home during the early 1970s to a rainbow of countercultural activities along 4th Avenue: a Greenpeace office, the Divine Light Mission, the Soft Rock Café, and happy hippies, students, and young British Columbians just starting in the workforce. John Gray's Kitsilano novel, *Dazzled*, records the flower-power giddiness of those days: 4th Avenue incense shops, love beads, psychedelic posters, a Doors LP wailing like a stoned banshee from every back porch. Between 1971 and 1976 more than fifteen hundred condominium apartments were built in Kitsilano, many of them handsome low-rise buildings in natural British Columbian wood. During the eighties and nineties, yuppies brought their Porsches, designer jeans, designer water (Perrier), and designer lives to Kitsilano to dwell in the most expensive small bungalows known to Canadian real estate. Persisting over the years, head shops, health food stores, used bookstores, and trinket emporia remained to peddle kitschy ephemera. This may be the origin of a snobbish and punning nickname for the Kitsilano area: Kitschilano. Vancouver's somewhat gentrified Ambleside Park, at the north side of the Lions' Gate Bridge, is similarly often called Amblesnide. And famous newspaper cartoonist Len Norris dubbed a pseudo-British part of West Vancouver with the playful nickname of Tiddlycove.

The name Kitsilano belonged first to a Squamish chief Khahtsahlanogh who settled in Stanley Park, east of Prospect Point, around 1860. In the Coast Salish of his Squamish band, his name means 'spirit man,' although other experts claim it is 'chief man of our band.' When around 1913 the Canadian Pacific Railway decided to make a new housing subdivision of some land nearby, the chief's name was Englished so it would rhyme with Capilano across the inlet. In 1913 the government of British Columbia bought eighty acres near the mouth of False Creek that had become known as the Kitsilano Indian Reserve. They intended to make a great new harbour at False Creek. As for the comic tag, remember that Kitschilano is a pun. As someone who lived two blocks from Kits Beach for one happy year (1976), I do not think it is in any way a valid comment on a wonderfully diverse neighbourhood. But the word *kitsch* is worth a comment.

Kitsch

Kitsch began as a simple German noun for shoddy goods, trash, junk, or flashy gewgaws. One German verb meaning 'to cheapen' is *verkitschen*. Kitsch is also used in Yiddish with the same meaning. The word *kitsch* had appeared in English early in the twentieth century, but it really entered the vocabulary of North American English after becoming a buzz word in art criticism. Its spread in academic discourse can be traced directly to American art critic Clement Greenberg's accurate prophecy in his famous essay "Avant-Garde and Kitsch" printed in the *Partisan Review* in 1939. Greenberg had sensitive antennae, finely tuned to pick up alterations in the artistic Zeitgeist, and he early recognized that, in the twentieth century, high art (for example, Mondrian's experiments in space and colour) and mass art (the labels on food, plastic toys, advertisements) were distinct but—the wily prediction—destined to influence each other profoundly.

Mass art is trashy but has vulgar elan. One thinks of Noel Coward's remark about "the potency of cheap music." The artist can make the art objects he creates partake of this kitschy street energy by borrowing it. The artist picks up a used egg carton, sprays it orange, and glues it to his latest construction, which also contains a plastic birdcage, a Dinky toy, a doorbell that does not ring, and a whalebone corset with most of the stays missing. Kitsch is sometimes defined by this separation of form from original function. The egg carton has its dull, daily usefulness as an object that holds and protects eggs and then is tossed into the paper-recycling bin. But now, glued to an artwork, the piece, as kitsch, gives off new visual and semantic vibrations as part of a campy construction. "It's good because it's awful," wrote Susan Sontag in

"Notes on 'Camp'" in her book *Against Interpretation*. We admit the garish or sentimental crappiness of the original object; at the same time we enjoy its very kitschiness.

In less formal criticism of popular art, kitsch is still used in its original German sense to mean 'low-brow junk of poor quality': for example, "That painting of a bullfighter on black velvet is pure kitsch."

KRALL AS IN "DIANA OF THE KEYBOARDS"

In 1999, Canadian jazz pianist and vocalist Diana Krall recorded one of the best-selling Canadian jazz CDs of all time. Under the CD title "When I Look In Your Eyes," Ms. Krall and her trio, with some silvery and soulful strings courtesy of Johnny Mandel, brought new life to old standards like "Let's Fall In Love," "Do It Again," and "I'll String Along With You." Ms. Krall won a Grammy for her jazz performance on that CD, and it was nominated for best album. In Canada she won a Juno for best jazz album, also replete with sweetly swung classics. Ms. Krall tours in Canada and abroad to continuing international huzzahs.

Krall is a Sorbian surname from Lusatia in the northwest of Germany. Lusatia is a small German province between the Oder and the Elbe Rivers. Sorbian is a Slavic language in which *kral* means 'king.' Compare the Czech word for king, *král*, and the Polish *król*. The reflex of this Slavic root appears in Russian as *korol*. The name first appears in print as *Crol* in 1369, then as *Kral* in AD 1374. Merely for the purposes of onomastic comparison, consider too a great Canadian football player from the first half of the twentieth century, the Toronto's Argonauts mighty triple-threat player, Joe Krol. He could run; he could pass; he could kick. His nickname? "The King."

Sorbian is a living language with some one hundred thousand speakers today and two very distinct dialects, although some linguists would say that Lower Sorbian and Upper Sorbian are separate languages because of the vocabularic and phrasal differences. The Sorbian surname Krall was early borrowed into German, usually as Krahl, and is widespread throughout Germany and Europe with that spelling.

Does the surname mean that a founding ancestor was a king? Almost never! But, of the perhaps one dozen different origins, all are connected with the regal meaning of the word. *Kral* or king begins in many a family record as the nickname of the founding ancestor. He might have been called, let's say, Ivan Kral (John the King) because he swaggered like a king or displayed some other regal bearing in his person. He might be Ivan of the kral, because he was a servant in a royal household. In medieval times, even someone who played a king in a pageant or play might be a kral or king. At certain holidays, especially the medieval Feast of Fools, a King of

Misrule was elected from among the townsfolk in many parts of northern Europe including places where Slavic-speaking peoples lived. This Ivan too might be called kral thereafter. A jousting tournament also had an official called a king. Ivan, kral of the joust, might proudly bear this nickname for the rest of his life and then see his descendants adopt it and turn it into an inheritable surname. Sorbian parents are also recorded in legal documents as having christened a male child with an additional or byname of Kral, in hopes that he might attain royal qualities later in life.

Finally, let us return to the north German plain and Lusatia, land of Sorbian speakers. They call themselves Serbja and, yes, that's the same word the Serbians of the former Yugoslavia use. Perhaps these two peoples, the Sorbians and Serbians, were once branches of one ancient Slavonic tribe, one branch settling in Lusatia, the other pushing southward to what would be Yugoslavia (literally 'south-Slav-land'). Another older name for Sorbian is Wendish. These Wends or Sorbs have left permanent marks on the map of Germany. Near Lusatia is the great German city of Leipzig, whose parks and fairgrounds have filled with trade fairs for seven or eight hundred years. Leipzig is just a German attempt at the city's original name, Lipsk, which is Slavic for 'place of the lipa,' that is, lime or linden tree. A few kilometres away is bombed old Dresden, also wearing a German version of its original Slavic name, *Drezdzane* 'boggy woods people' aptly named for the impassable marshlands encountered by early Slavic settlers. Russian *t* becomes *d* in some southern Slavic languages, so we can compare *drezdzane* with *tryasyenye* 'boggy' in Russian.

LABRADOR TEA

Labrador tea is *Ledum groenlandicum* (Ledum, Botanical Latin < *ledon* Greek, the name for a European evergreen shrub we generally call Rock Rose + *groenlandicum* Modern Botanical Latin, 'of Greenland'). This evergreen shrub of the heath family has been a staple hot drink or infusion of northern peoples since the first humans crossed from Asia to America some twelve thousand to forty thousand years ago, give or take a day. One *Ledum* species is circumpolar, so anthropologists posit that First Peoples may have brought knowledge of its refreshing and medicinal properties with them. The tea is made by lightly steeping cleaned, crushed, dried leaves. Arctic explorer Sir John Franklin in his 1823 *Narrative of a Journey* reported that the tea smelled like rhubarb. It acted as a mild digestive and perked up one's appetite. The Hudson's Bay Company for a time imported the leaves into England where they enjoyed popularity under the peppy name of Weesukapuka! Canadians spelled it in a variety of ways, usually referring to the plant as wishakapucka, their attempt at the Cree term, *wesukipukosu* 'bitter herbs.' The leaves might also be added to kinnikinnick as part of the standard native smoking mixture.

LAKE WINNIPEG GOLDEYE

This tasty, freshwater fish has the most renown of Manitoba's finny legions. Although native to Lake Winnipeg, *Hiodon alosoides* swims in other waters of our Northwest as well. Algonkian-speaking First Peoples called it *nacaish*, which early French trappers and voyageurs heard as *la quesche* or *lacaiche* or *lacaishe*, the latter two still being its names in Canadian French. Cree people like to ponask or ponash goldeye, that is, clean and split the fish, attach it to green twigs and roast it over an open fire. See the *ponask* entry. Smoked Winnipeg goldeye was once a steady menu item on CPR dining cars. Goldeye was also frequently part of official dinners where an all-Canadian menu was thought appropriate, for example, at hoity-toity Ottawa feasts where our politicians might be feeding traditional Canuck fare to American lobbyists.

LASSY MOGS

Lassy and lasses are common short forms for molasses in the province of Newfoundland Labrador. Mogs are small cakes made of flour, baking powder, butter, salt, etc. When sweetened with molasses instead of sugar, they are, of course, lassy mogs. Mog may derive from a British dialect verb that meant "to go slowly" because the little cakes rose slowly when baked. But Mog and Moggy were also dialect nicknames for Margaret in certain rural areas of the British Isles, so these cakes may simply be lassy Margarets. The origin I think most likely is that mogs may have been made at first by stamping out the dough with a cutter consisting of an empty mug turned upside down.

LOGGING JARGON OF BRITISH COLUMBIA

From the "sawdust nobility" of lumber barons to the humble "whistlepunk" who relayed signals from workers with axes to those running donkey engines used to pull cut timber, British Columbian loggers' lingo has a long provincial history, a stock of jargon that has words now obsolete, together with words fresh as the aroma of a Sitka spruce bough. The West Coast forest industry depends on Canada's tallest and broadest conifers, the chief commercial trees being Douglas fir, western cedar, balsam fir, hemlock, and Sitka spruce, whose coastal stands thrive in the mild, wet climate and make up 40 percent of Canada's commercial lumber potential. Charles B. Crate, one of the editors of the *Dictionary of Canadianisms* (1967), has done much pioneering study of British Columbian localisms, including those from logging.

Birling

Scotsmen brought the verb *to birl* to Canadian lumbering. In Scots dialect, to birl is to spin something, like a coin on a table, so that it makes a noise. Birl, especially with a thick burr of the *r*, originates as an imitation of the whirring sound made by a spinning object. It was a natural verb to apply in Canadian logging to the practice of spinning a floating log while remaining balanced atop the log. Logs are spun to propel them out of shallow water, off snags and sandbars where they have become stuck, and to make it easier to change their direction. Birlers were competitive. Competition at a local camp soon led to district log-rolling contests where the deftest act of birling could win big bucks.

Crummy

Crummy meaning 'lousy, of poor quality' derives from an extension in mid-nineteenth-century American English of the word *crumb* 'body louse.' In British Columbia logging areas, from the late 1930s, a crummy was an old boxcar or caboose in which loggers were transported from towns to the current cutting site at the logging camp. A bit later, beat-up buses and trucks used to haul forest labourers were crummies. Now in British Columbia crummy can mean a schoolbus, or any vehicle that carries workers to and from distant work sites. This usage has spread down into the state of Washington too.

Davis Raft

The Davis raft met special conditions of West Coast logging. Sometimes booms had to be towed by tugboat to sawmills across rough ocean. Even if the tow was short, rafts sturdier than those used in eastern lumbering were needed, and one was invented in 1913 by a Mr. Davis of Port Renfrew, British Columbia. The Davis raft consisted of layers of logs "choked" into bundles by withes and chains. In Old English a withe was a tie made of several slender willow shoots twisted together. The Davis raft was almost 500 feet long, 30 feet deep, 16 feet above sea level, and held an astounding 3,600,000 board feet of timber.

High-Line Logging

The size and height of British Columbian trees like the Douglas fir made necessary new logging techniques. Skyline or high-lead logging involves the use of a spar tree. A standing tree is topped and trimmed and given extra support from guy cables anchored to the ground. It is then rigged with a series of high cable-lines and pulley-blocks by which the logs cut afterward are hauled from the cutting area to the yard. In very large operations there are now mobile spar trees that are gigantic diesel-engined cranes that do all the complicated skylining.

Jaw-Bone

Unemployed loggers sometimes had to "live on the jaw" or "call my jaw." Jaw was short for jawbone, a word widespread in the Canadian West, a synonym for credit obtained at a store. Its first appearance in print is 1865 in the pages of the *Cariboo Sentinel*, the feisty newspaper of Barkerville, near the Willow River east of Quesnel,

British Columbia. Barkerville was the terminus of the Cariboo Gold Trail, which began in 1862 with William Barker's rich strike. The slang term arose because one had to use his jawbone in trying to talk a line of credit out of a merchant. Matthew Macfie from England visited the interior during the Fraser River Gold Rush and wrote this in *Vancouver Island and British Columbia* published in 1865: "Credit is 'jaw-bone'; and in one store on the road to Cariboo, the full-sized jaw-bone of a horse is polished and suspended on the wall, with the words written under: 'None of this allowed here.'"

LUCIVEE

It was the Canada lynx or its pelt. This is a New Brunswick variant of the French and Acadian *loup-cervier*, a direct borrowing from Medieval Latin *lupus cervarius* 'the wolf who attacks deer.' The European *loup-cervier* is not the same species as our lynx. But English did a multiple mangling of the word. It appears as *lucerver*, *lucervi*, *lucifee*, and the magnificently silly and lisp-inducing *lucififer*, a local name on the upper Saint John River at the turn of the century.

LUMBER: ORIGIN OF A WORD IMPORTANT TO CANADIAN ECONOMICS & HISTORY

Lumber is one of the founding mainstays of the Canadian economy, both historically and presently, so this startling history of the English word *lumber* is apt and worth knowing by Canadians.

Lumber harks back to Lombardy, or Lombardia, one of the regions of Italy. A central northern region of the republic with its hub at Milan, Lombardy is bounded on the south by the Po River, and the flat, fertile plain of the Po Valley. On the north, Alpine foothills gently cup in forest hands shining Italian lakes: Maggiore, Como, Varese, Lecco. Lombardy contains in fact most of *la regione dei laghi*, the Italian Lake District whose shores hold lushly gardened private villas and elegant resorts. To the east of Lombardy are Venice and Friuli; to the west lie Piemonte and the bustle of Turin.

The Lombards were a Germanic tribe living in northwest Germany by the first century AD. They skirmished with the imperial legions of Rome from time to time, but were usually peaceful, successful farmers. The Roman historian Tacitus mentions them and calls them Langobardi. The Germanic roots of their name are *lang* 'long' and *Barte* 'axe.' The Langobardi had a characteristically ferocious Teutonic clan name, 'men of the long axe.' Ancient word studies suggest the less frightening Germanic root *Bart* 'beard.' So they might be the Long Beards? And, instead of axes, they carried sickles? Like Father Time? I don't think so. And neither does modern etymology. There is no evidence that they called themselves *Langbarden* ('long-beards'), though you will see this nonsense in some continental dictionaries.

Population growth and pressure from the barbarian Huns forced the Langobardi to migrate during the fourth century into most of what is now Austria. And then they crossed the Alps and invaded northern Italy. By AD 572 they held every major city north of the Po.

The Kingdom of Lombardy lasted for more than two hundred years, and its power extended over much of Italy, including for a time, Rome. In southern Italy they were Langobardi or Longobardi. The word survives today as a Sicilian surname, Longobardo. But in the north the first element of their name was modified and they were Lombardi.

Eventually Lombard greed for new territory forced Pope Adrian I to form an alliance with the king of the Franks. Charlemagne smashed their armies in 774 and became king of Lombardy. In the middle ages the region was a ripped quilt of quarrelsome city states. Then Spain ruled for almost two hundred years followed by a century of Austrian dominance. France had a fling from 1796 to 1814. And finally Lombardia became a part of Italy in 1859.

How Lombard Became Lumber

In the middle ages the Lombards were great bankers. From about AD 1400 immigrants from Lombardy spread through Europe as money-changers and bankers. In London, England, they set up money-changing shops, pawnshops, and banks, and gave their name to Lombard Street in central

London which is still the chief avenue of large British banking firms. Lombard became an English word for any merchant or banker. Geoffrey Chaucer, the first great poet in English, mentions this in his *Canterbury Tales* (c.1386), specifically in "The Shipman's Tale":

> This merchant, which that was ful war and wys.
> Creanced hath, and payd eek in Parys
> To certain Lumbardes redy in hir hond,
> The somme of gold, and hadde of hem his bond.

Chaucer's lilting Middle English may need my prosaic and literal translation: "This merchant who was wary and wise, creanced (had negotiated a loan), and paid also in Paris to certain Lombards ready in their hand (at their Paris bank) the sum of gold he owed, and had of them his bond (the bond he signed on making the loan was returned to him upon his total repayment of said loan).

For several hundred years there was a common saying in British betting slang to indicate long odds, that is, a sure thing. To the question, "What are the odds, mate?" the reply was "Lombard Street to a China orange." Lombard Street was solidly there, steadfast as its banking firms. The first, sweet, eating oranges imported from China to England were popular and not too expensive at the time this saying was coined. Betting the massed wealth of Lombard Street banks against a fruit peddler's orange was to accept insanely long odds.

In Middle English lombard changed to lumber, because English speakers were shortening the first vowel in everyday speech and dropping the final *d*. Lombard and then lumber referred first to a banker, a moneylender, or a pawnbroker. Although the spelling of Lombard Street remained, the pronunciation of the street's name altered. By 1668, the great British diarist Samuel Pepys writes "Lumber Street" for Lombard Street. Soon the meaning of lumber grew to encompass the pawnshop itself, and lumber meant goods stored in pawn, or junk, bits and pieces stuffed into an attic or heaped up in a pawnshop or a spare room at home. Pawnbrokers from Lombardy introduced to England the three golden balls that long symbolized a pawn shop. It is said this trio of gilt orbs was borrowed from the escutcheon of Italy's wealthiest family, and indeed a triad of aureate globosities does adorn the coat-of-arms of the Medici family.

The lumber room in a British house is still a spare room filled with unused wooden furniture and household bric-a-brac. British colonists who immigrated to America took one use of the word with them to the New World. In North America, lumber began to mean exclusively unfinished planks, cut timber, and pieces of wood in general. And soon the medieval Italian word *lombardo* was wearing full Yankee dress as a lumberjack! A jack was a man, as any man jack of the day could have told you.

LUNENBURG PUDDING

This pudding is actually a pork sausage, and, as they say, every part of the pig goes in except the squeal. Sausage casings are now usually bought at a butcher shop or meat packers. Note the original meaning of pudding in English was 'sausage,' which sense survives in terms like blood pudding, black pudding, white pudding. British English still uses a French borrowing, *boudin*, to name a black pudding. It is a curiosity that Canadian French borrowed pudding from English back into the food language of Québec as *poutine* (see the entry in this book on the fascinating story of Québec's most famous food, *poutine*). Remember, too, what Robert Burns called that obscene Scottish nightmare-parody of sausage known as haggis: "great chieftain o' the puddin'-race." Och! Will you no' cease to exaggerate, Robbie! Pudding is an English mangling of the Old French *boudin*, from Latin *botellus* 'pudding.'

The eventual association of sweet pudding and sausage occurred because early dessert puddings were stuffed in a bag and boiled or steamed, the stuffing in the bag reminding cooks of stuffing sausage meat in casings, often made of sheep or pig intestines. Elizabethan cooks began to adapt some of the sweet pudding recipes so that they did not have to be boiled or cooked in a cloth or bag. In modern British English, pudding evolved to mean any dessert: "What's for pudding, luv? Month-old treacle again?"

Your Bowels Are Your Sausages!

Now here is a small detour to discuss another French derivative from the Latin *botellus*, which gives us the English word *bowel*. The etymology looks like this: *botellus* Latin, little sausage > *boel* Old French > *bouel* Middle English > *bowel* Modern English.

Yes, your bowels are your sausages. Bowels, the plain English word for intestines, go all the way back to a Roman battlefield. Roman physicians, who were trying to find out how the human body worked and how it was made, were hampered by religious taboos and superstitions. For example, early studiers of the human body were not allowed to dissect a corpse. Cutting up a dead body was not legal in ancient Rome and Greece. It was thought to be a horrible sin. So those ancient scientists studying anatomy had to rely on looking at the dead bodies of humans who had suffered fatal, body-ripping injuries. One of the places these early anatomists could see cut-open bodies was on the battlefield after a bloody fight in a war. Exposed coils of intestines stuck out from the corpses of slain soldiers. Perhaps these soldiers had fallen when their bellies or abdomens had been slashed open with a sword. Their intestines or bowels, exposed in a wide-open wound, looked like little sausages. So the Roman word for bowels was *botelli* 'little sausages.' More common use of such a word in Latin may have come from soldiers' rough slang: "Got a bellyache, Brutus? Guess your sausages are upset today."

Another word from the same root word as bowel is *botulism*, from another diminutive relative of *botellus*, this time spelled *botulus* 'sausage.' Botulism is a severe food poisoning, first observed in early-nineteenth-century Germany in carelessly prepared sausages, which lay around uncooked for too long after they were made and so germs grew in the raw meat. The toxins in the poisoned food can be fatal if ingested in great quantity. The cause is excessive growth of a poison-making bacterium called *Clostridium botulinum.*

MALPEQUE OYSTER

The succulent viscera of this shuckable mollusc swell to juicy maturity in the waters of Malpeque Bay where they provide Prince Edward Island's most internationally renowned food, highly prized as the world's most flavoursome oyster on the half-shell. Malpeque is an Acadian French rendering of *Mak Paak* 'big bay,' a place name in Mi'kmaq, the language of the island's earliest named settlers. It is an apt descriptive for the large body of water cutting deep into the north coast of the island, rich in oysters and other foods from the sea. Malpeque is also the official name of a federal electoral riding of the province. But the name is often used for any high-quality oysters from Prince Edward Island waters. On Malpeque Bay and at several other island localities, commercial oyster farms abound. Here seed oysters are "sown" into the muddy bottom of the bay and when mature the oysters are removed by long, scissorlike tongs.

MANGEURS DE LARD OR PORKEATERS

Mangeurs de lard, used in English and Canadian French, were, of course, literally porkeaters. Both terms were now-obsolete insults by established local residents and indigenes of any newcomers, any passing voyageurs who depended on pork-fat rations carried in their canoes, with the implication that they could not live off the land like those who had already settled an area.

Porkeaters served as a put-down among the grizzled old interior trappers of the Northwest Company. These tough veterans of lonely canoe routes through interior country scorned new employees of the company who had to paddle only the canoe routes between Montreal and Grand Prairie. These young beginners lived "high off the hog" on salt-pork rations, unlike the interior hunters who ate rougher fare, such as pemmican. So voyageurs came in two classes: raw beginners were porkeaters, while seasoned veterans were winterers or *hivernants* in Canadian French.

In explorer John Franklin's 1823 *Narrative of a Journey to the Shores of the Polar Sea in the Years 1819, 1820, 1821, and 1822* is this little note: "There is a pride amongst 'Old Voyageurs' which makes them consider being frost-bitten as effeminate, and only excusable in a 'Pork-Eater,' or one newly come into the north country."

MANITOULIN

It means 'spirit island,' isle of God, Gitchi Manitou, the Great Spirit in the Sky. Ojibwe legend recounts the creation of Manitoulin. The Great Spirit first dreamed the cosmos, made the elements, then the stars and the earth, and finally the friends, the children of earth, the *Anishnabeg* 'people made of the void.' Now while the Great Spirit was forming earth, he kept aside certain choice morsels of his creation: the most shining water, the fields and woods most abounding in game and food, the most sun-dappled shores, the freshest breezes. He piled these up beside him to delight himself as he completed the rest of the earth. Then he fashioned a great island from his mound of treasured keepsakes and floated it upon Lake Huron where breezes blew it to snuggle against the north shore, the green island set off by the stark, rocky coast. With a thunderbolt and a lightning flash, he fixed the island in the lake forever, and called it *Manitouminiss* 'island of the Spirit.'

MANITOWANING

The best guide book to the island, *Exploring Manitoulin* by Shelley J. Pearen, is published in paperback by the University of Toronto Press. In it,

Pearen gives this origin: "The Wikwemikong Peninsula is separated from the rest of the island by two bays, South Bay and Manitowaning Bay . . . Manitowaning received the Ojibwe name for 'den of the Great Spirit.' The bays are separated by a three-kilometer neck of land containing, according to native legend, a secret underwater passage which the Great Spirit uses to travel between the bays."

MAPLE! THE TOTALLY AWESOME SUPER ENTRY OF THIS ENTIRE BOOK

The maple leaf is *the* symbol of Canada. Every Canadian should know a few of the lesser-known facts about maple trees in order to bamboozle dinner guests and inquisitive Americans, and here is the place to find such lore. In this humongous treasury of nuggets of maple knowledge, you will find more juicy bits of maple trivia than anywhere else in Canadian print. That is my guarantee. By the way, your humble author usually avoids boasting. But, in this article you will find my totally new origin of the word *maple*, hypothetical yes, but reasoned, an etymology accepted by two British authors published by Oxford University Press. You will discover as well how human beings all over the world have named this tree, and you'll find out that neither Canadian Aboriginal peoples nor Canadian immigrants invented maple syrup! Read on to find out who did first tap and make flow the sugary elixir of the maple.

Genus Name of the Maple Tree

Acer < *acer, aceris* Latin, maple < **ac* Indo-European root 'sharp, pointed.' The Latin term has a cognate in the modern German word for maple *Ahorn,* and a direct descendant in Spanish *arce.* The Latin word may refer to the hard wood. Romans used maple, among other hardwoods, to make spear and pike hafts. The wooden base of a Roman child's writing tablet was often a maple board scooped out to hold the wax on which the student wrote with a stylus. But the genus name *Acer* may also refer to the maple's distinctively pointed leaves. Compare a synonym for the usual German *Ahorn*, *Spitzblatt* 'sharp leaf.' Russian has *ostrolistnie klejen* 'sharp-leaved maples.' Turkish borrowed the Latin *acer* to produce *akçaagac* 'maple' where *-agac* is 'tree.'

French gives: *érable* < *acerabulus* Vulgar Latin < *acer* Latin, maple + *-abulus* possible Latin diminutive suffix, but more likely influenced by a Latin-Gallic hybrid word whose last part contains *abolo* Gallic 'rowan tree' ultimately < **abel* Indo-European root, fruit of any tree, tree-fruit. Our English word *apple* stems from this ancient root.

Quebeckers have the standard *sirop d'érable* for maple syrup, but add a near insult to define imitation syrups that are thick with glucose glop. They call this sugary impostor *sirop de poteau* 'telephone-pole syrup' or 'dead tree syrup.'

Word Lore

Maple < *mapultreow* Old English, maple tree

< **mapl-* Proto-Germanic root, maple. This appears to be a compound in which the first *m-* part's meaning is lost, but is likely the nearly worldwide **ma*, one of the first human sounds, the pursing of a baby's lips as it prepares to suck milk from mother's nipple. The **ma* root gives rise to thousands of words in many, widespread world languages, words like mama, mammary, mammal, maia, Amazon, mummy, etc. Here it would make the proto-Germanic compound **mapl-* mean 'nourishing mother tree,' that is, tree whose maple sap is nourishing. For indeed the second part of the compound, *apl-*, is a variant of Indo-European **abel* 'fruit of any tree, tree-fruit.' The primitive, etymological analogy compares the liquid sap with another nourishing liquid, mother's milk. Possibly akin to English maple are Old Norse *möpurr*, Old Saxon *mapulder*, Middle Low German *mapeldorn*, and modern Irish *mailp*.

Maple Syrup Not Unique to North America

The contention of writers like Leo H. Werner in *The Canadian Encyclopedia* entry "Maple Sugar Industry," that maple syrup is unique to North America is nonsense. China has more species of maple than any country in the world. More than one hundred species of maple are native to China, while Canada has ten native maple species. In China, maple sap has been tapped for thousands of years. North America does happen to be home to the sugar maple, the species that produces the sweetest sap and the most abundant flow. But it is likely that Proto-Amerinds who crossed the Bering land bridge to populate the Americas roughly twenty thousand to forty thousand years ago brought with them the knowledge that maple trees held a sugary sap that could be extracted for a brief period in early spring. Maple syrup may have been news to European French newcomers to North America in the seventeenth century, but it was not to Oriental peoples and to northern Europeans.

Another Indo-European Maple Word

The words for maple in the following list are cognates, literally 'born together,' but in linguistics referring to their common origin from the same Indo-European root. They all mean 'maple,' except where noted.

Ancient Greek *glinos, gleinos* (Theophrastos' word for the Cretan maple, *Acer creticum*)

Medieval Latin *clenus*

Russian *kljen*

Polish *klon*

Lithuanian *klevas*

Swedish *lönn*, Norway Maple

Norwegian *lönn*, Norway Maple

Danish *lon*, Norway Maple

In German languages, the root *lehne, lin* was early transferred from maple to Tilia species (basswood).

On Species of Maple

Sugar Maple, *Acer saccharum* (Medieval Latin, sugar or sugary)
Soaring to thirty metres on a good site, bestowing sweetness on the spring tongue and on the autumn eye, the sugar maple grows from Lake Superior to Cape Breton Island. Acid rain threatens all maple trees and has already fatally damaged or killed thousands and thousands of specimens of this symbol of our country. Acid rain is caused chiefly by sulphur dioxide emissions from major polluters, Canadian and American industries not now policed efficiently.

Maple Leaf as Emblem

Long symbolic of Canada, the leaf of a sugar maple has been the heraldic device on our flag since 1965. The Québec and Ontario coats-of-arms granted in 1868 have maple leaves; so does the 1921 Canadian coat-of-arms. But did one event begin this Canada-maple leaf association? Well, some say the maple leaf symbolism began with its use as camouflage! An intriguing suggestion, in the form of a folktale, is repeated in Frank Quance's *The Canadian Speller: Grade 6, Third Edition* (Gage, 1950): "During the war of 1812–1814, the scarlet jacket of Canadian and British soldiers made a perfect target for the enemies. Therefore, when fighting in the woods, each soldier cut slips in his blouse and inserted a twig of maple leaves to bluff the enemy. This was the first time the maple leaf had been specifically identified with Canadians or with Canada."

One day in the fall of 1867 a Toronto schoolteacher named Alexander Muir was traipsing a street in the city, all squelchy underfoot from the soft felt of falling leaves, when a maple leaf alighted on his coat sleeve and stuck there. After it resisted several brushings-off, Muir joked to his walking companion that this would be "the maple leaf for ever!" At home that evening, he wrote a poem and set it to music, in celebration of Canada's Confederation earlier that year. Muir's song, "The Maple Leaf Forever," was wildly popular and helped fasten the symbol firmly to Canada and things Canadian.

Maple Uses

Sugar maple is of great commercial value for its syrup and for its beautiful wood. A favourite of furniture makers, maple wood has several rare grain variations that are especially prized. Birdseye maple has a dotted pattern, while fiddleback maple and curly maple display annual rings in pleasingly undulant waves. Even maple-cured meat is a gift to white settlers' cuisine from peoples of the eastern woodlands like the Iroquois. They tell of the first human who accidentally stuck a knife in a spring maple, collected the "sweet water" and boiled some venison in this maple water.

An Ojibwa Myth

The maple looms large in Ojibwa folktales. The time of year for sugaring-off is "in the Maple Moon."

Among Ojibwa and other Algonquin-speaking peoples the mythic earth-mother and primordial female figure is Nokomis, the wise grandmother. In one story about seasonal change (among other things), cannibal wendigos, creatures of evil, chased dear old Nokomis through the countryside. Wendigos throve in icy cold. When they entered the bodies of humans, the human heart froze solid. So these wendigos represent here oncoming winter. There the evil beings were, chasing poor Nokomis, the warm embodiment of female fecundity who like the summer has grown old, pursuing her to the death. But Nokomis outsmarted the cold devils. She hid in an autumn stand of maple trees, all red and orange and deep yellow. This maple grove grew tall beside a waterfall whose mist sometimes blurred the trees' outline. And the maple trees saved Nokomis. As they peered through the mist of the waterfall, the wendigos thought they saw a raging fire of red, in which their prey was burning. But it was only old Nokomis being hidden by the bright, autumn leaves of her friends, the maples. For their service in saving the earth-mother's life, these maples were given a special gift: their water of life would be forever sweet, and humans would tap it for nourishment. All sugar maples, says the story, are descended from these trees.

Word History of Saccharum and Sugar

The specific epithet of the sugar maple is part of the history of our word *sugar*, one of the great travellers of world etymology. The Roman encyclopedist Pliny has the Classical Latin form *saccharon* for 'a sweet juice distilled from the joints of African sugar cane.' The Romans borrowed the word from Greek *sakcharon*. In the timeline below, one can trace a remarkable series of word borrowings.

Verbal Timeline for the Word Sugar

English *sugar*

Medieval French *sucre*

Italian *zucchero*

Arabic *sukkar* (Spanish *azucar* is directly from *Arabic al-sukkar* with definite article assimilated)

Classical Greek *sakcharon*

Persian *shakar*

Prakrit (language of ancient India) *sakkara*

Sanskrit *sarkara*

Old Malay *singkara* (but perhaps brought there by Buddhists whose liturgy was written in Sanskrit)

Sugarcane native to Asia came to India, then Persia, Arabia, Africa, and the near East, Phoenicia, Greece, Italy, Spain, the rest of Europe, and finally Columbus brought it to the New World of the Americas on his second voyage. The establishment of sugarcane plantations led directly to the capture and enslavement of black Africans. Remarkably, most of the original Asian word clung to this sweet and dangerous gift of the earth to humans.

Maple Medical Terms

Maple Bark Disease
Susceptible persons can get maple bark disease, an inflammation of the lungs from inhaling spores produced by a mould, *Cryptostroma corticale*, which grows in the bark of certain maple tree species. Acute symptoms include fever, cough, difficulty breathing, and vomiting. Chronic symptoms include weight loss, hard breathing during exertion, and coughing up phlegm.

Maple Syrup Urine Disease
MSUD is an inherited disorder affecting the metabolism of certain amino acids such as valine, leucine, and isoleucine. An enzyme needed to break these amino acids down is missing and this metabolic flaw produces urine and sweat that smells like maple syrup. MSUD untreated in a newborn leads to rapid collapse of many neural functions and early death. Treatment includes peritoneal dialysis, exchange transfusion, and controlled intake of the amino acids involved, but even these measures are not always effective. Speed readers please pause long enough to note that MSUD is a genetic defect. The afflicted are born with it. It is not, not, not caused by eating maple syrup!

A Few Other Maple Species

Black Maple
Acer nigrum (Latin, 'black') has darker bark than

Sugar Maple. But Black and Sugar Maple are the woods available at the lumberyard, both sold as hard maple. Southern Ontario and Québec are the northern limits of its range.

Douglas Maple or Rocky Mountain Maple
Acer glabrum var. *douglasii* is a western variety first discovered by David Douglas. See Douglas Fir entry. The specific refers to the smooth bark of younger trees. Douglas Maple, usually a tall shrub that turns an appealing flat red in the fall, often brightens small gardens in British Columbia where it is native to the interior and Vancouver Island. Scattered stands are found in the Alberta foothills too.

Manitoba Maple: Pollen Alert
Many a prairie street sports rows of the fast-growing Manitoba Maple, *Acer negundo*. But tree-picking town councils across Canada ought to consider the pitfall of this tree, or should I say the pollenfall. Recent scientific allergy research has shown that Manitoba Maple pollen has the highest level of allergenicity of all tree pollen on earth! Manitoba Maple pollen has the potential to have more susceptible people allergic to it than to any other tree. The specific *negundo* is a Sanskrit word for an Asian species called the chaste tree or *nirgundi* in Bengali and Sanskrit. An early botanic cataloguer thought the maple and the chaste tree resembled each other. Manitoba Maple grows also in Saskatchewan and Ontario, but its use as an

ornamental has allowed it to spread to many areas of Canada where it is not native. An old American common name is Box Elder or Ash-leaved Maple.

Red Maple
Acer rubrum (Latin, 'red') is native from Newfoundland to Ontario's western border. No specific epithet could be apter: its twigs, buds, flowers, leaf-stalks, and autumn leaves are a bright tunic red.

Samara, the Botanical Word for Maple Key
The dry, winged seeds of maples (and a few other genera like elm) are samaras, from the Latin word *samara* that Pliny and Columella, a writer on Roman agriculture, used to mean 'elm-tree seed.' Samara is a Latin dialect version of an earlier form like **semera* related directly to the 'seed' words in Latin, such as *semen*. Further back in the verbal timespan, samara derives from the Indo-European root **se* and its extension **sem*, roots that mean 'one and the same.' Thus the metaphor behind sowing seeds was basically 'making more of the same living thing.' Children make keen whistles from samaras, best caught on the wing as the seeds helicopter down to spiral themselves into any soft earth below.

My Personal & Favourite Maple Quotation
As the author, I hereby permit myself to include one really corny quotation. This is the first poem I remember memorizing as a child, to be recited in

class at Dunnville Public School. I probably received a good mark. My father, Alfred Casselman, was the principal. I can't find the poem in any anthology and don't recall the title; but two stanzas waft back into what's left of my mind every fall when the leaves turn in Dunnville. Anyone who knows the poet and the full text is asked to drop me a note at the email address given at the end of the preface.

When autumn leaves come drifting down
  upon a country way,
There's nothing half so beautiful, and
  nothing half so gay,
A million merry rainbow groups of maple,
  beech, and oak,
All madly dancing in the wind, like little
  fairy folk.
And then some golden eve'tide, when each
  of dancing tires,
The country people rake them up and light
  the autumn fires.
And, oh! the smell of burning leaves upon
  the frosty air!
There's never a land in all the world holds
  incense half so fair.

Corny? Yes, but a fitting end to our maple trip, because I'm sure it has occurred to many of us that a maple leaf tumbling and scurrying down a Canadian street on a breezy morning late in autumn might be a symbol of every Canadian, might reflect our own chancy path through life in this northern Dominion. We are all maple leaves blown aloft by the high winds of fate. On that bit of poetic piffle, we shall tiptoe out of this maple-leafery and press onward.

MARQUIS WHEAT

"The wheat that changed the West," one journalist called it. Dominion cerealists and brothers Percy and Charles Saunders began crossing and hybridizing spring wheats at the experimental station at Agassiz, Manitoba, as early as 1892. By 1907, they sent seeds of Marquis to prairie fields where the wheat matured much earlier than previous strains, thus greatly extending the area of prairie where wheat could be grown commercially. Marquis made good flour and kept its grains on the head even when stalks were buffetted by the constant wind of the plains. By 1911, Marquis wheat was being exported, and, as exports grew, this wheat improved the economy of our Prairie Provinces. Ninety percent of spring wheat grown in Western Canada during the early 1920s was Marquis, and more than half of the wheat crop south of the border was Marquis, as American farmers learned the advantages of this Canadian hybrid.

MEDICARE

Saskatchewan officials coined the now-endangered word for a now-endangered concept—Medicare—and introduced the world's first universal prepaid medical care in 1962, but only after a bitter strike by Saskatchewan doctors. Medicare is one Saskatchewan word that has been borrowed into American usage. In the United States, medicare usually refers to government-sponsored health care for elderly citizens. Saskatchewan's CCF government under Tommy Douglas had introduced free hospital care in 1947. Douglas was premier of the province longer than any other politician (1944–61), and the nastiness surrounding the introduction of Medicare was one of the factors that cost him the 1961 election. For many Canadians Tommy Douglas remains one of the best men ever called to public office in our country.

Thomas "Tommy" Clement Douglas (1904–86) was one of my heroes. Mr. Douglas was a Baptist minister who became a politician, a Prairies socialist who helped found the CCF, precursor of the NDP, an incisive debater who could be warm and funny, the father of Medicare and the Canada Pension Plan, and premier of Saskatchewan. He was a plain, kind Christian, from the turn-of-the-century social gospel tradition, who had examined in his head and in his heart what exactly such a label might require of a man who found himself in the midst of the twentieth century. What it required of Tommy Douglas was compassionate action, a humane quality in very scant supply among some who throng today's temples and who infest the sleazy television temples of instant salvation.

MI'KMAQ POTATO OR GROUNDNUT

Groundnut, *Apios americana* or *Apios tuberosa*, is a member of the pea family, and its dark red or brown flowers resemble those of the sweet pea. These climbing plants thrive in damp ground from Prince Edward Island to Ontario. Mi'kmaq people prized the sweet tubers of this plant which has a chestnut flavour, and they call it *sequbbun*. Early white settlers in the Maritimes shared the taste, sometimes by necessity—a report from Port Royal in 1613 tells of Biencourt and his followers scattering through the woods around the fortifications searching and digging for groundnuts. The Nova Scotia town and river, Shubenacadie, is an Acadian French attempt at a Mi'kmaq phrase that means 'sequbbun (groundnuts) grow here.' The plant is also called Mi'kmaq potato, bog potato, and travellers' delight. The botanical genus name is Greek *apios* 'a pair,' because the tubers on an individual rhizome seem to grow in pairs. One healthy plant may have ten or twelve tubers.

MINA: THE CREE WORD FOR 'BERRY'

Here's a Cree root that appears in three well-known Prairie place names, two in Saskatchewan. Saskatoon was named by early settlers because the original site had many saskatoon berry trees. The Cree word for these tasty purple berries is *mi-sakwato-min* 'tree-of-many-branches berries.'

The name of the town of Moosomin in southeastern Saskatchewan is from the Cree term *mongsoa minan* 'mooseberries' or 'highbush cranberries' which abounded in the area. In our Western provinces, mooseberry can also be applied to lowbush cranberries. Another Cree phrase for highbush cranberries *nipi-minan*, literally 'summer berries,' was heard by early French explorers as *pembina* and was much used as a place, river, and commercial name. The Pembina River is still an important waterway in southern Manitoba near the Pembina Mountains, and Pembina was one of the settlements founded by Lord Selkirk that did not endure. Alberta has a long and important Pembina River as well. Still heard in the West is pembina berries for highbush cranberries. Many a traveller has entered Winnipeg along the Pembina Highway.

MOOSEBERRY

Here's a loan-translation into Canadian English of the Cree term *mongsoa-meena* 'mooseberry.' In Western Canada, mooseberry often refers to the lowbush cranberry. Elsewhere and among the Cree peoples who named it, this is *Viburnum opulus*, the highbush cranberry, a favourite nibble of moose and humans. The scarlet-to-orange-coloured and pleasantly acidic berries were added to pemmican and used to make pioneer preserves, compotes, jams, and sauces for fowl and game. In *Flora of Manitoba*, Scoggan gives its accustomed sites as "woods, thickets, shores, and gravel ridges throughout the province." Explorer Samuel Hearne in *A Journey From Prince of Wales's Fort in Hudson's Bay To The Northern Ocean. In the Years 1769, 1770, 1771 & 1772* gives this report:

> Cranberries grow in great abundance near Churchill (site of Fort Prince of Wales, a Hudson's Bay Company trading post where Hearne was for a time governor), and are not confined to any particular situation, for they are as common on open bleak plains high rocks as among the woods. When carefully gathered in the Fall, in dry weather, and as carefully packed in casks of moist sugar, they will keep for years, and are annually sent to England in considerable quantities as presents, where they are much esteemed. When the ships have remained in the Bay so late that the Cranberries are ripe, some of the Captains have carried them home in water with great success.

MOOSE MUFFLE SOUP

A moose muffle or mouffle or moufle is the nose and the pendulous, overhanging upper lip of the moose eaten boiled, baked, or fried as a delicacy. It was particularly prized among the Cree who boiled it and cut the muzzle into very thin slices. In 1754, Anthony Henday, exploring for the Hudson's Bay Company, wrote in his diary: "I dressed a lame man's leg. He gave me a Moose nose, which is a delicate dish, for my trouble." Canadian English moose muffle was borrowed from Québec French *mufle*, itself from Standard French *mufle* 'any animal's muzzle.'

Several cookbooks of Aboriginal cooking tips warn of moose nose and lips being "an acquired taste." Beware of any nutriment for which the eater must acquire a taste. Such a phrase implies that the eater must acquire the taste because the food lacks it.

Although highly esteemed of yore, the spectacle of a moose's nose and upper lip from which the large bristles and hairs have been uprooted violently with a pair of giant pliers does not inspire in the novice diner any great confidence. Ditto with moose-muffle soup, although it has one advantage: the moose's muffle has been chopped and diced until no longer recognizable as the flappy-lipped snout of a large, spooky mammal.

MUG UP

A mug up is a quick snack, maybe tea and a biscuit, between meals, late at night, or as a pause during work. The term is widespread in early English dialects for a fast bite and a cup of tea, and it came across the Atlantic to be used extensively along the Atlantic seaboard of North America and all across the northern regions of what would become Canada. Sailors and fishermen have enjoyed mug ups for at least three hundred years.

NANAIMO BAR

Nanaimo bar is a baked treat popular all across Canada, often as little cut squares of biscuit alternating with a sweet cream filling and covered with chocolate. They may have been first concocted in the city of Nanaimo on Vancouver Island. A number of local native bands amalgamated in the mid-nineteenth century, calling their union *sne-ny-mo*, or 'big, strong tribe.' Something sweet about this island place has entered Canadian English, so the appearance of something slightly sour in a Canadian folk saying may balance the scales. If you boat in British Columbian waters, you may someday hear this scrap of dialogue:

> *Rich bully on big yacht:* Did you see what that trash was wearing, Phyllis?
>
> *Wife of rich bully tipping the scales at a pixielike 150 kilos:* Yeah, Full Nanaimo.

Are British Columbian recreational boaters and yachtsmen a trifle snooty? They seem to pay finicky attention to how their fellow mariners dress. "Full Nanaimo" is an insult that applies to a chintzy outfit worn by a boating parvenu. Whitebuck shoes, white belt, polyester pants, and a blue blazer with a spurious yachting crest brand the wearer as a floating yutz of the first water. A similar chop is FDAM, pronounced to rhyme with ram. The acronym stands for First Day At the Marina.

NETTLE SOUP

No, this is not some nightmare decoction from a masochist's kitchen. Many of our ancestors and Canadian pioneers ate nettle soup for years and were glad of the nourishment. The old pioneer name of "Indian spinach" suggests the use of only the young, tender, sprouting leaves of stinging nettle as a soup green. The plant is widespread over Canada and the northern hemisphere and, surprisingly, humans have eaten the boiled leaves for millennia.

The botanical name is *Urtica dioica*, the genus name *urtica* having as its root the Latin verb *urere* 'to burn.' Both the stem and leaf surfaces bristle with tiny hairs that, triggered by the slightest touch, release a stinging oil rich in formic acid and histamines. Touching stinging nettles produces an intense burning sensation and often angry, red wheals. The medical phrase describing this skin reaction is contact urticaria. But the sting of the bristles is removed by boiling in water, which quickly dissolves and dilutes the histamines and acids. Outdoorsy adventurers who wish to try this wild food ought to wear rubber or thick leather gloves and should use a knife or scissors to harvest stinging nettle leaves.

The boiled leaves are a good source of vitamins A and C, and some minerals. To prepare nettle broth, plunge clean young leaves into rapidly boiling water for one full minute. After draining and rinsing the boiled leaves with cold water, boil a few cups of beef or vegetable broth, drop the boiled nettle leaves into the boiling broth and simmer for two minutes.

Although boiling removes the sting of nettles, drying the leaves does NOT do this, as an incident well known to botanists illustrates. During the bombing of Britain during the Second World War, various important specimen collections were vulnerable. The British government called for their protection if possible. One of these was the great herbarium of Linnaeus, the Swedish botanist who founded modern plant nomenclature. This herbarium was the prince of botanists' very own collection of dried herbs, purchased from his native Sweden by British interests. Its mounted specimens were almost two hundred years old. Gladys Brown, a British photographer, was asked to photograph each specimen lest the whole collection be destroyed by Nazi bombing. When she gently removed Linnaeus' stinging nettle specimen from its mounting, she was stung on the arm and had a red blister raised by a two-hundred-year-old nettle. Perhaps, after all, this nettle soup is a bit of culinary lore better tasted on history's page than on a young explorer's tongue.

Stinging nettles have also been deliberately applied to the skin in northern folk medicine, both European and North American, as dubious remedies for rheumatism and arthritis. The skin surfaces of afflicted limbs were rubbed with nettle leaves in the unscientific belief that the pain caused by the nettle sting would relieve the deeper rheumatic or arthritic dolor. This was once called urtication, although the word is now used in medicine to refer to the burning sensation caused by nettlelike skin reactions and the subsequent development of urticaria, the painful red rash and swelling. When ancient Roman legions were marauding through Teutonic and Gallic tribal lands far from sunny Italy, imperial soldiers are reported to have rubbed stinging nettles on their exposed skin to warm themselves in the damp gloom of infidel forests. If such torture did not heat them up, it certainly would have been conducive to keeping alert those posted on watch.

NEWFOUNDLAND CHANGES ITS NAME

When Brian Tobin was elected premier of Newfoundland early in 1996, he promised to seek a constitutional amendment to change the official name of his province to Newfoundland and Labrador. Most Canadians thought that was already the case, that Labrador was legally and undisputedly and forever a part of Newfoundland. Maybe not? Behind the seemingly innocent expansion of the provincial name is a centuries-old territorial squabble. In his speech from the throne on March 20, 1996, marking the opening of the first session of the Newfoundland legislature with Tobin as premier, Lieutenant-Governor Frederick Russell said, "It is time to change the name of our province to reflect the reality that it is made up of two equally important parts, Newfoundland and Labrador." And Labrador is more vital a part than ever before.

With the decline of the fish stocks off our East Coast, the massive find of mineral deposits at Voisey's Bay in Labrador has become a pivot around which the economy of Newfoundland may turn. Begun in 1998, the mining operation taps one of the world's largest caches of nickel, copper, and cobalt. The multibillion-dollar bonanza has the added benefit of being a lode that will be relatively easy to mine. The smelter for Voisey's Bay ore will be in Newfoundland. So will trans-shipment depots for offshore oil finds, like the Hibernia project in Bull Arm, where already five thousand jobs have been created, and the Terra Nova oilfield off Newfoundland's West Coast. These megaprojects will bring new jobs and growth to a province in need of such a boost.

But a long-standing Labrador boundary dispute between Newfoundland and Québec has sizzled on the skillet of history for more than two hundred years. The boundary in contention does happen to be our longest interprovincial border: 3,500 kilometres long, a territorial limit that has never been surveyed or marked on the ground. A timeline of the dispute makes clear its persistent appearance in Québec–Newfoundland relations.

- **1763** Britain acquired Labrador by the Treaty of Paris, and all other French territories in North America except the two little islands of St. Pierre and Miquelon. The vaguely defined area of

Labrador was included within Newfoundland chiefly to cut off Québec from East Coast access and fur trade of eastern origin. Acadia being annexed to Nova Scotia served to isolate Québec too. Also in 1763, Thomas Graves, the governor of the British colony of Newfoundland, was given by royal commission jurisdiction over the coasts of Labrador. Constitutional experts claim that Newfoundland's ownership of Labrador can be traced back to this year. However, a further royal proclamation later in the same year placed Labrador under Governor Graves' "care and inspection" for fishing purposes only.

• **1774** Labrador became part of Québec (Lower Canada) by statute.

• **1783** The Peace of Paris divided up British territories in North America after Britain lost the American War of Independence. While Cape Breton, the Gulf of St. Lawrence, the Labrador coast, and Newfoundland stayed British, Great Britain ceded to the Americans vast fishery rights, not only to the Grand Banks, but also to fishing inside the then-three-mile limit of British territorial waters, and to going ashore anywhere on British territory, including Labrador, to dry their catch.

• **1809** Labrador is returned to Newfoundland by statute.

• **1825** Part of Labrador is returned to Québec (Lower Canada).

• **1902** Newfoundland issued a licence to a

private company to cut timber near Labrador's Churchill River. Québec protested ownership.

• **1904** Québec succeeded in getting the federal government to submit the question of ownership of Labrador to the Judicial Committee of the Privy Council in London, England.

• **1927** After twenty-three years of wrangling, the Privy Council set the present boundary between Labrador and Québec, and decided in Newfoundland's favour, that is, that Newfoundland could claim Labrador as its own territory "inland to the watershed line."

• **1949** Newfoundland joined Confederation as Canada's tenth province. The territory of Labrador was defined in the Terms of Union, now called the *Newfoundland Act*. And this was re-enshrined in the *Constitution Act of 1982*.

• **1971** Québec set up a royal commission to study complaints since 1949 that Labrador's boundary was not settled. Its own commission ruled against such Québec claims.

• **1990** The dispute is still a good way for a federal back-bencher to get some press, and so in October of 1990, a Montréal MP introduced a constitutional proposal that would have divided Canada into five regions, one of them to bear the quaint title Québec and Labrador. Some honourable members objected, among them a Newfoundland MP, Brian Tobin, who rose in the house to denounce any such rejigging of Canada's boundaries.

In one of his literate columns on Canadian affairs, which for years graced the pages of the *Toronto Star* and other newspapers, Dalton Camp, that wily sage of New Brunswick, once wrote: "The awesome perils of reorganizing societies by redrawing maps have been proclaimed through history. It was a mistake, perhaps, to have so much of Labrador made up of what might have been Quebec." Indeed. But striving to unaccomplish any fait accompli is a popular millennial hobby. Therefore it seems unlikely, as we squirm here in the foreshadow of future separation referenda, that Canadians have heard the last of this litigious bickering over Labrador. What's in the new name of Newfoundland and Labrador? Well, mineral wealth and hydro-electric power, for starters.

NUISANCE GROUNDS

From the Alberta–British Columbia boundary right across the Prairies to northern Ontario one can still hear this euphemism for garbage dump. In print since 1889, it popped up in the *Edmonton Journal* in 1958: "In Banff, the best place to see bears is the 'nuisance grounds,' the preferred title for the garbage dump." In the short story "Where the Wind Began" from her collection *Heart of a Stranger* (1976), Margaret Laurence wrote: "The town dump was known as 'the nuisance grounds,' a phrase fraught with weird connotations, as though the effluvia of our lives was beneath contempt but at the same time was subtly threatening to the determined and sometimes hysterical propriety of our ways." Margaret Laurence here pinpoints one of the chief sources of euphemism in her insightful phrase "hysterical propriety."

NUNAVIK & NUNAVUT: DIFFERENT WORDS FOR DIFFERENT PLACES

Nunavik, a useful place name, gained countrywide prominence as the correct term for one-quarter of Québec, the northern Ungava peninsula and an area south of Ungava Bay, where seven thousand Inuit live, and where their ancestors lived and hunted long before whitemen came. In Inuktitut, Nunavik means 'our place,' and the locative suffix *-vik* appears in other northern place names like the town of Inuvik 'place where Inuit live' and Aklavik 'grizzly-bear place.'

That area of northern Québec was part of the Northwest Territories at the time of Confederation, and did not fall under a provincial jurisdiction until the *Boundary Extension Act* was passed by Parliament in 1912. If the Inuit of Nunavik vote to stay in Canada after Québec decides to deconfederate, it will reduce by one-quarter the size of the province.

Nunavik should not be confused with its neighbour Nunavut that lies across Hudson Bay to the west. Nunavut was created by act of Parliament in 1993 as a new Canadian territory, slated to be fully operational by April 1999, and made up of land in the mid-Arctic that used to be part of the Northwest Territories. Nunavut will hold one-fifth of Canada's land. The word is Inuktitut for 'our land.'

ONTARIO HYDRO

The Hydro-Electric Power Commission of Ontario began small in 1910 and grew to a once-efficient monopoly under the bullying promotion of power mogul Sir Adam Beck. His dream of getting cheap electric power from Niagara Falls also influenced Ontarian and then Canadian English. Although the adjective hydro-electric had been coined in Britain by 1832, Beck gave it wide currency in Canada at the turn of the twentieth century. As the giant utility grew, and delivered on its promise of safe, inexpensive electricity, Ontario customers shortened the name to "hydro" (in Canadian print by 1916) and introduced many combinations like hydro bill, hydro power, hydro man, hydro service, and hydro wires. If you ask an Englishman or an American, "Has your hydro ever been turned off?" they may look puzzled. It's a completely Canadian usage which has spread as a name for other utility services to other provinces.

OOLICHAN: A FISH THAT IGNITES

The candle fish or oolichan, a very greasy little Pacific smelt, was an important source of oil for natives and settlers of our West Coast. Oolichan oil had medicinal properties, contained vitamins A and D, and was more pleasant to the palate than cod liver oil. A writer named Molyneux St. John offered one explanation of the common English name, in a book entitled *The Sea of Mountains: An Account of Lord Dufferin's Tour Through British Columbia in 1876*: ". . . candle fish; so full of oil that it can be lighted at one end and used as a candle."

OTTAWA

Minor fur-trading spots, at which French trappers exchanged goods with Algonkian peoples were the first settlements at our capital, Ottawa. In 1800 a small farming community, Wrightsville, was established on the site of the present-day Hull. The first unofficial name in English of the settlement was Rideau Canal. In 1826, Lt. Col. John By of the Royal Engineers, a town planner and administrator, having supervised the construction of the canal, established and managed Bytown, which later took the Englished version of the name of the Odawa 'traders' people.

Gladstone Street

Some Ottawa bus drivers call it Happy Rock. The street was named for William Ewart Gladstone, a prime minister of England.

Mechanicsville

The name of this area in northwest Ottawa derives

from railroad maintenance crews who first formed the community. It was based around a CP Rail roundhouse in which mechanics repaired locomotives. Later the city of Ottawa operated an industrial garage there to fix heavy road-making machines. In the early 1960s and 1970s Mechanicsville was rezoned for apartments and government buildings. This rezoning was part of an urban renewal scheme that saw the replacement of small, older houses with high-rises and office towers. A group of concerned residents, "Action Mechanicsville," formed to try to preserve the neighbourhood's character. It is now known as Hintonburg.

Rockcliffe

Rockcliffe Park, where the highest-paid civil servants, deputy ministers, and assorted upper crust of Ottawa dwell in splendour, received its name from one early house built in 1835 by Duncan Rynier MacNab who called it Rockcliffe after a beloved childhood haunt in Scotland. The original edifice was a Regency-style freestone cottage with verandahs, to which many additions were later made. In 1928 the building was completely rebuilt in the French Directoire style. One of Ottawa's humorous neighbourhood nicknames belongs to Manor Park in the northeast of the city. Rookie Rockcliffe supposedly describes the aspirations of its upper-middle-class residents.

"PACKINGTOWN" IN EDMONTON

This district once had four meat-packing plants. The nickname is passing out of existence as the neighbourhood improves, even to a Spanish rechristening as Santa Rosa.

The stylish, yuppie area of Edmonton now called Lavine used to be called Skunk Hollow, presumably because it is near the river and was therefore attractive to skunks. Edmonton too has a Knob Hill in the residential neighbourhood of Rutherford on the east side of Mill Creek overlooking the downtown. The park area of Cannard Ravine is Rat Creek. An underground tunnel on 109th Street is universally dubbed The Rat Hole.

PEAVEY

This is a lumbering tool invented in the New Brunswick woods where the first important commercial logging in North America took place. A peavey is a long pole (up to seven feet) with an iron point and a hinged hook. Lumbermen used it to guide logs on a drive. Certain Maine etymologists claim that a J.B. Peavey of that state invented the instrument. The only slight fly in the American ointment is the total lack of any printed record that any person of that name ever existed. I don't want to be peevish, but—tough hook, guys.

PEMBINA BERRY

Pembina is a synonym for highbush cranberries, from the Cree phrase *nipi-minan*, literally 'summer berries.' The Cree words were heard by early French fur trappers and explorers as pembina. The word was much used as a place, river, and commercial name. The Pembina River is still an important waterway in southern Manitoba near the Pembina Mountains. There is the Pembina highway. Pembina was one of the settlements founded by Lord Selkirk, one that unfortunately did not endure. Alberta has a long and important Pembina River as well. Still heard in our West is pembina berries for highbush cranberries.

PEMMICAN

This is one of the most surprising of all the Canadian words I have ever studied, surprising because verbal roots similar to the initial one in the word *pemmican* appear in languages all over the world, languages which are said to be utterly unrelated. The very Canadian word *pemmican* thus becomes a small key to the possibility of the monogenesis of language. In other words, what if all our teachers have been wrong, what if there was indeed one single mother tongue from which all the languages of the world have evolved? In the word lore of pemmican, we can see a hint of this. Read on.

Pemmican is a Cree word compounded of *pimii*

'fat' + *kan* 'prepared.' Buffalo meat was dried and then braised over fire for several minutes. Spread out on buffalo robes laid on the ground, this scorched meat was beaten with a stone pemmican-pounder or with hardwood poles until it was tenderized and fine. At this stage it was called 'beat meat.' Then bags made of buffalo skin, called *taureaux* or *parflèches* by the earliest French trappers who watched them being manufactured, were half filled with beat meat. The best-quality tarrow or rendered buffalo fat was poured in, along with dried berries, often cranberries, and sometimes other plant parts. The contents of each bag was sloshed and mixed thoroughly and set aside to cool. To keep the fat from settling to the bottom, the bags were turned while the contents were cooling. Then the bag was sewn up tightly. Pemmican had a shelf life that would make any modern food-packaging company green with envy. It lasted forever and supplied iron and protein on the longest, remotest trips through the wilderness. Canada's fur trade, and hence the opening up of the country itself, was absolutely dependent on pemmican. Tight in its bag, pemmican would keep even if dumped overboard from a canoe.

There were, of course, variations in the ingredients, hence names like deer or moose pemmican. Kinds of pemmican used in Canada included sundry berry pemmicans, such as one that featured the meat, crushed berries, and leaves of wild peppermint. One berry preparation actually bore the name of bourgeois pemmican. In his autobiography, *Beyond the Palisades*, G.S. McTavish writes: "When the Plains Indians put up a specially prepared lot of pemmican by adding native berries, the product was classified as 'Bourgeois' pemmican, suitable only to the palates and supposedly refined tastes of the 'Ookimows' (chiefs) among the pale faces." Among the Inuit, inferior blubber could be made into dog pemmican, fit only for dogfood, but made and packed by the Inuit before long journeys by dogsled. Fish pemmican, sweet pemmican, and after the coming of whites, even sugar pemmican appear.

Other Aboriginal words with the pemmican root include the Canadian term *siskawet* for a Lake Superior lake trout < Québécois French *sisquoette* < Ojibwa *pemite-wiskawet* literally 'oily-flesh fish.'

Pemmican's World Relatives

The word *pemmican* is related to terms in far-flung languages, its relationship surprising and seemingly inexplicable. Naturally, I wouldn't say that unless I had an explanation. And here it is.

Let's take a common English tree name, pine. The word *pine* has the Indo-European root **pi-* or **pa-* whose basic meaning was fat, lard, grease, then any thick, sticky substance like resin or gum. The IE root had extensions like **pit-*, **pin-*, and **pim-*.

Pitys is the classical Greek word for pine tree. Pine then is the gummy tree, the resinous one. In

Germanic languages the IE root gives forms like fat, *fett*, and fetid (originally the bad smell of rancid fat). Note that \p\ to \f\ and \p\ to \b\ transformations are a normal part of consonant evolution in many languages. In ancient Greek, *pion* was an adjective that meant fat and *pimele* was lard.

This **pa-/*pi-* root for fat seems to predate even Proto-Indo-European. It is found all over the world with similar meanings in languages that modern scholarship states have no relationship whatsoever. But let's forget the nagging finger of disapproval wagged by tenured linguists at universities and look at a few of these words ourselves. North Americans might begin with the term *pemmican*, a word common among Algonkian-speaking peoples. Its roots in the Cree language are *pimii* 'fat' + *kan* 'prepared.' Cree *pimii* looks similar to that classical Greek word for lard or fat, *pimele*. Sorry, that can't be, say professorial guardians of linguistic orthodoxy. Yet there it is again in a sister word in Ojibwa, *bimide* 'grease, oil.' The Blackfoot word for dripping fat or lard is *pomis*, and among the Munsee Delaware, an Algonkian-speaking people, there is *pumuy* 'grease.' Chinese could have no relationship whatsoever with Cree or Classical Greek, now could it? Yet there is the **pa* root nasalized in the second part of the Chinese word for fat, *jy-farng*, in a Romanized transliteration. Mere coincidence! scream many linguists. They must be hoarse from the number of times in the last twenty years they have branded as coincidental the growing number of words recognized as related in widespread languages not in the same current language family.

Now this **p(f)(b)im-* root for fat appears in dozens and dozens of languages descended from Proto-Amerind. Oops, I forgot. Proto-Amerind never existed either! Just ask vested-interest academics who study Aboriginal languages at the Smithsonian Institution, linguists who have publicly condemned the very concept of Proto-Amerind. And yet—drat these manifold coincidences—there are all those languages of North and South America with many words whose roots show correspondence and similarity, words that evolved from three language groups recently dubbed Proto-Amerind (first American Indian), a family of tongues brought to the Americas when the First Peoples crossed from Asia by the Bering land bridge and perhaps by other routes over thousands of years.

PICKEREL WEED

Many an angler of eastern Canada has squatted in a boat patiently hoping that a pickerel weed marsh in the calm summer waters of a shallow cove will live up to its name—soon! Canada's sweetest eating fish does frequent stands of pickerel weed, *Pontederia cordata*, with rootstocks that creep through the mud, one large heart-shaped (Latin, *cordatus*) leaf, and many blue florets on a big flower spike that pokes into bloom late in summer. Pickerel lay their eggs on the submerged stalks of the plant. Owners of aquatic and bog gardens use pickerel weed as an ornamental, although the blue flowers are quite short-lived. It's a relative of the much more widely grown aquatic ornamental, water hyacinth. In the American south the plant is called *wampee*, and in Florida, it's alligator wampee, for gators love to lurk and slumber in hideaways of disguising foliage that Pontederia provides.

The botanical name of its genus *Pontederia* commemorates Giulio Pontedera, an eighteenth-century professor of botany at the University of Padua.

PIKELETS

Brought to Nova Scotia and elsewhere in Canada from England and Scotland, pikelets are drop-scones or thin crumpets, made following a standard scone recipe. A beaten egg is added to a cup of milk. Flour, salt, a pinch of sugar, baking soda and cream of tartar are combined and stirred into the egg and milk. To make each pikelet, a generous spoonful of the batter is lopped into a hot frying pan or on a griddle. The pikelet is fipped when the batter bubbles. As always with quick breads, the precise heat of the griddle or pan must be determined by testing. These little crumpetty breakfast quickies are very popular in Australian and New Zealand, where the term pikelet enjoys much broader use than in Canada.

Pikelet entered English from the Welsh term for this scone *bara pyglyd* literally 'bread pitchy,' that is, bread that is sticky like pitch or viscid as pitch, but, the cook trusts, never as black as pitch.

PIPSISSEWA

If you've ever taken a swig of good, homemade, tongue-startling, palate-corrugating root beer (not the homogenized, limp-bubbled suds of commercial root beers), then you know the refreshing, wintergreenlike taste of Pipsissewa. The word comes from the language of a people inhabiting northeastern Canada, the Abenaki. In their language, Abnaki, *kpi-pskw-àhsawe* means 'flower of the woods.' Its name in botany is *Chimaphila umbellata*. The genus *Chimapila* is a compound of *cheima* Greek, winter + *philos* Greek, loving, winter-loving, so named because the leaves of pipsissewa stay green all the year round. The specific name *umbellate* refers to the umbel or loose terminal cluster of little waxy heathlike flowers of pink hue that bloom in the summertime in dry evergreen woodlands. Nowadays oil of wintergreen is synthesized, but its chief active ingredient, methyl salicylate, is found in pipsissewa leaves. Outdoorsy folk still chew the leaves for their minty brio, and this member of the wintergreen plant family is widely used in herbal remedies.

PITCHER PLANT

The official flower of the province of Newfoundland and Labrador is a bog-dwelling, insectivorous, perennial herb and has some delightful common names besides Pitcher plant. These include Indian Cup, *Petits Cochons* 'piggywigs,' and Whip-poor-will's Boots! To the scientists who study plants the pitcher is *Sarracenia purpurea.* The genus name *Sarracenia*, commemorates Dr. Michel Sarrazin (1659–1734), Canada's first professional botanist. He came out to La Nouvelle France in 1685 to become surgeon-major to the colonial army, and later co-wrote one of our pioneering botanical works, *L'Histoire des plantes de Canada*. The species name *purpurea* is Botanical Latin meaning purple, referring to the colour of the mottled pitchers. Pitcher plant is the stout little carnivore of Canada's peat-quilted swamps and jelly-earthed bogs, where it traps insects in leaves modified to hold water, hence pitcher plant. The slippery sides of each pitcher are lined with downward-pointing hairs that help insects slide into the pitcher but prevent them from escaping. Trapped without mercy, they struggle, fall exhausted back into the water, and drown in the liquid to which the plant has added a flesh-dissolving enzyme. The decomposed bodies of the insects provide essential nutrients for the pitcher plant.

PONASK

From the Cree language, westering travellers borrowed the cooking practice and the verb, to ponask, sometimes seen as ponash. Ponasking is splitting a fish or piece of game, sticking it on a spit and roasting it quickly over an open fire. While meat requiring much tenderizing was boiling in a pot hung over a roaring campfire, strips of more delicate flesh might have been impaled on ponasking sticks held by hand or stuck in the earth around the edge of the fire.

PONNUKOKUR

Icelandic palates around Gimli and other centres of Icelandic immigration in Manitoba delight in these traditional Christmas crêpes, often presented to revellers with hot chocolate on Christmas Eve. In *ponnukokur* (pancake) one can see something of the Icelandic language's relationship to tongues in the North Germanic or Scandinavian branch of the vast Indo-European proto-family, as well as its not-too-distant cousins, German and English. Compare *Pfannkuchen*, one of the German words for pancake.

Ponnu is related to German *Pfanne* and English *pan*, and *kokur* to German *kuchen*, English *cook*, and Latin *coquere*. These tasty little pancakes are made with sweet milk and sour cream or buttermilk, along with the usual eggs, flour, sugar, baking soda, and baking powder, and spiced with cinnamon, salt, and vanilla.

PORK & JERK

Here is some Prince Edward Island humour that arose during times when food was scarce. Pork and jerk was a poor meal, at which the pickings were so slim that a small piece of pork was tied with a long string and passed around the table. If any of the hungry became too greedy and tried to eat the whole piece of pork, it could be jerked away from the too-eager eater and passed on to the next starveling. It was also said that one fish was sometimes tied with a long string and passed about a poor man's table in a similar fashion.

POTLATCH

The potlatch was an important ceremony of many Pacific coast and Interior peoples in which magnificent gifts were given and sometimes exchanged, chieftains invested with power, names bestowed on young persons, spirits propitiated, dances performed, and feasts enjoyed. The word came into English from Chinook Jargon from the Nootka word *patshatl* 'a giving, a gift.' But white busybodies did not always understand the complexity of the potlatch and how its sociological strands were woven tightly into band and clan life. Rivalry between clans of one people made obsessive potlatching reach alarming porportions toward the end of the nineteenth century, with heads of clans ordering the extravagant gifting and subsequent destruction of food and property merely to enhance the prestige of the clan-head giving the potlatch. Massive debts were incurred by clans, sometimes resulting in total poverty and actual starvation. Gifts in potlatch required the giving of a gift in return. Some clan chiefs set out deliberately to impoverish rival clans. Finally, the Canadian federal government outlawed the full ceremony in its 1884 Potlatch Law. By the time the ban was repealed in 1951 during revision of the *Indian Act*, serious clan disruption had resulted, permanently skewing tribal identities, ranks, and statuses.

Potlatch acquired many secondary and figurative meanings in Canadian English. It came to refer to a free handout or to any winter festivity including the watered-down "give-away dances" that replaced ethnic potlatches after they were outlawed. Informal use saw potlatch synonymous with party or celebration. During the 1940s and 1950s in British Columbia English a potlatch also named a carnival or fair held by Aboriginal peoples and featuring canoe races and games, sponsored to raise money for local and charitable causes.

POUDING DU CHÔMEUR

Pouding du chômeur is a 'welfare pudding' in which cake batter is baked and then drenched with brown-sugar syrup. *La chômage* is unemployment insurance in Québec. *Un chômeur* is someone on the dole. In France, the French verb *chômer* from which *chômeur* and *chômage* sprang has less pejorative meanings. *Chômer* is 'to take off work during holidays,' and 'to be unemployed due to legitimate lack of work.'

Word Lore of Chômer

The root of the verb *chômer* is intriguing, because, tracing it, we can observe an ancient word rolling down through the millennia to its eventual place in the modern vocabulary of Romance languages. It begins with a term that appears almost three thousand years ago in one of the founding masterpieces of Western literature, *The Iliad* of Homer, where *kauma* means 'the burning heat of the sun.' The same Greek root, found in *kaiein* 'to burn,' gives the English words *caustic* and *holocaust*. However, the Romans borrowed the word into late, postclassical Latin as *cauma* where it meant 'the hot part of the day, siesta-time.' For example, the word was used by St. Jerome about AD 384–404 when he was making a Latin translation of the Bible from its original Hebrew and Koine Greek, to establish a standard edition sanctioned by the early Catholic Church. The name of this translation of the Bible was *editio vulgata* 'common edition.' It is known in English as the Vulgate. St. Jerome used *cauma* in his translation of the Book of Job to render a Hebrew word that meant 'severe heat.'

In later Latin, a verb was formed and *caumare* meant 'to rest during the strong heat of midday, to take a siesta.' *Caumare* evolved into its early French form *chômer* by 1150 and developed meanings like 'to rest in the shade during the heat of the day' (at first said of cattle) and then 'to break off work during the heat.' More modern senses followed: 'to abstain from work during feast days' and then 'to be idle due to lack of work' and finally 'to be on welfare due to lack of work.'

The Late Latin verb *caumare* took one other little pathway into the Romance languages worth noticing. When it entered early Italian a letter *l* was infixed to produce *calmare*. This *l* just made the word easier to pronounce for the earliest speakers of Italian. Similarly, Late Latin *cauma* became *calma* in Italian. *Calma* was at first a nautical term in early Italian and meant 'absence of wind' at sea. This was quite a natural expansion of the original sense of *cauma* as the hottest part of the day, noontide, when the Mediterranean sun burned brightest, when beasts of the field rested, when the winds ceased and the warm air was still, and the very fields seemed—calm. At such a time of day it was only natural that humans, too, would seek the sweet lassitude of repose, an interval of pleasant rest for aching muscles in the shade of trees. In Spain, people would call this midday rest *una siesta*.

POUTINE: THE COMPLETE & FACTUAL STORY

Perhaps first borrowed with the spelling *poutine* from the English word *pudding* by the Acadians, this food term (pronounced poo-TSIN in Canadian French) has acquired many meanings in Québec and Acadia. First we talk about Québec meanings, then Acadian uses of the word *poutine*.

Poutine does indeed derive ultimately from the English word *pudding*. Fascinatingly, it has been borrowed at least four different times into French. *Le pudding* was in French print by 1678 to denote a pudding steamed in a cloth bag. This acquired several variants including *le pouding* and, in northern France, *poudin*. Then again in 1753 French geologists borrowed an English phrase, pudding stone, which named a certain kind of conglomerate of pebbles embedded in a finer matrix. This went into French geology as *la poudingue*. The third borrowing happened along the shores of the Mediterranean. Pudding had been borrowed into Italian by *i nizzardi*, natives of the city of Nice and surrounding territory. In the dialect of Nice, pudding became *la poutina*, but it named a mess of fried sardines and anchovies done in lemon and oil and used to accompany a soup or even to fill an omelette. In the south of France, maritime cooks borrowed the Italian word and named this fishy Italian fry *poutine*. Finally, northern French people immigrating to North America, to become eventually Acadians, reborrowed pudding as poutine and began the evolution of its present pronunciation.

The most recent reincarnation, or should we say re-empuddingment, of poutine happened in Québec in the fall of 1957, and made poutine the most familiar Québec food word in North America, to the chagrin of Quebecers proud of the gourmet delights of their provincial cookery. Why, they wonder, does poutine get all the fanfare while truly exquisite and scrumptious recipes like *pintadine de L'Île d'Orléans aux groseilles* do not receive the attention they deserve? Perhaps more people like junk food than appreciate guinea hen in a red currant sauce?

Today's poutine is a serving of thick-cut French fries, topped with fresh cheese curds and hot gravy poured on top of the curds before serving or, by some cooks, served in a little gravy dish on the side so the fries do not get soggy. Two men claim to have invented this poutine in the fall of 1957 in a region of the province's Eastern Townships called Bois-Francs "hardwoods" just south of the St. Lawrence. In Warwick, Québec, near Victoriaville, halfway between Montréal and Québec City, Fernand Lachance, "*le père de la poutine*," and his wife Germaine operated the Café Ideal. One of the *piliers du café* 'regulars' was truck driver Eddy Lainesse. Now the region of Bois-Francs is dairy country, famous for its fresh cheese curds, and M. Lachance sold little boxes of the fresh curd in his eatery. One autumn day, Eddy Lainesse suggested mixing the cheese curds with fries. *Et voilà!* The gravy was not beef gravy at first, but Germaine Lachance's special recipe of brown sugar, ketchup, and a plop or two of Worchestershire sauce. After interviewing these three innovators for the October 9, 1997, edition of the *Globe and Mail*, reporter Tu Thanh Ha points out just how popular this poutine is in the province: "Burger King's decision to add it to the menu in 1992 generated an extra $2-million in curds business for Warwick's Fromagerie Côté." Wherever Quebeckers travel in numbers, from Alberta to New England, they like to see on distant menus some home dish; for some residents especially that *mets à la maison* is poutine. I've eaten it in a Manhattan restaurant, but the cheese curds had been stored in a refrigerator too long and were rubbery. Restaurants in Florida that cater to vacationing snowbirds from Québec actually fly in fresh curds by air freight.

Acadian Poutines

Poutines râpées are the famous Acadian potato dumplings made from two parts of grated raw potatoes squeezed dry in a cotton bag, and from one part plain mashed potatoes mixed together with the grated potatoes and formed into a ball about—as one Acadian cook told me—the size of the fist of my *petite tante Yvonne*." In parts of New Brunswick, a hole in the centre of each poutine is stuffed with diced salt pork. To cook these poutines, drop two or three into water at a rolling boil then simmer for two and a half hours. *Poutines râpées* may also be plunked into a gently bubbling *fricot* (stew).

Poutine en sac is another of the old European puddings steamed in a cloth bag, so many of which have made their way to Canada with names like son-of-a-gun-in-a-sack, cloutie from Scotland, and figgy duff from Newfoundland. Also called *poutine à la vapeur*, the pudding is some variant of a lard-sugar-eggs-flour-milk-baking-powder mixture to which is added raisins and perhaps blueberries, apples, or cranberries. This doughy delight is mixed together to form a large ball, put in a cotton bag tied up with string, and placed on a wire-mesh rack in a large pot with an inch of water. The steaming takes two hours. A double-bottomed pot may be used, or a double-boiler if you want to forego the bag, but since half the fun of a bagged pudding is the bag, why forego it? *Poutine en sac* can be served with sweet cream, brown-sugar sauce, or even slices of fried pork.

There are also Acadian *poutines* that resemble pies (*poutine à la mélasse*) and bread puddings (*poutine au pain*).

PRAIRIE CHICKEN

The prairie chicken is becoming very scarce. Although we give a pioneer recipe, game wardens plead with prairie visitors not to kill these birds, but to enjoy them alive in their plains habitat.

Potting prairie chickens was only one way of

preparing this wildfowl, but a popular method. Cleaned, plucked, drawn, and trussed birds were dusted with flour and browned in hot bacon fat. Five or six birds were then put in a large stew pot. Several cups of stock, a few onions, spices, and a drift of flour were added to the bacon fat in the fry pan and the mixture was boiled and poured over the prairie chickens. The pot was covered and baked for two hours.

The greater prairie chicken, a member of the grouse family, is native to our southern prairies, and goes by a welter of other names such as heath cock, pinnated grouse, prairie fowl, prairie hen, and squaretail. Zoologically, it is *Tympanuchus cupido*. The genus name, from Greek *tympanon* 'drum' + *ochos* 'possessing,' arises from the deep, hollow booming sound uttered by male prairie chickens during their spring courtship activity when they gather at familiar grounds called leks for elaborate displays of feathers and the drumming mating calls typical of grouse. Male prairie chickens return every year to the same lek. One instance is recorded where a prairie farmhouse was built on ground used as a lek. The next spring, the male prairie chicken returned and did his mating display on the roof of the farmhouse.

The sharp-tailed grouse, *Pedioecetes phasianellus*, a different species that is also called prairie chicken, is the official animal emblem of the province of Saskatchewan.

In the humorous slang of British Columbia lumber camps during this century, anyone born on our Prairies who went west to work in the logging industry might be called "a prairie chicken." But a man so-called might reply, "When you say that, stranger, smile."

PRAIRIE: ORIGIN OF THE WORD

To a visiting botanist, prairie is a vastness of grasses, and of xerophytes, plants adapted to intermittent drought. To a homesteading newcomer in 1876, prairie might have meant "the first land anyone in my family ever owned." Later such a "drylander" might decide to sow a domesticated grass called wheat. To a writer like W.O. Mitchell, born at Weyburn, Saskatchewan, prairie might resound in his heart like the great chord of words that opens his novel *Who Has Seen the Wind*: "Here was the least common denominator of nature, the skeleton requirements simply, of land and sky—Saskatchewan prairie. It lay wide around the town, stretching tan to the far line of the sky, clumped with low buck brush and wild rose bushes, shimmering under the late June sun and waiting for the unfailing visitation of wind, gentle at first, barely stroking the long grasses and giving them life . . ."

Who first applied the word *prairie* to the rolling grasslands in the middle of North America? Canoe-stiff French adventurers dubbed it, early in the eighteenth century. Rough explorers they were,

China-hungry, gold-thirsty, fur-crazy, paddling the continental interior by unknown lakes and rivers. They had no exact French word to label the grassy plains whose immensity and reach had startled their sense of geographic proportion, based as it was on the populated density of their native Europe. But there was a French word for grazing land, sometimes used to describe dry scrub in the south of France. *Prairie* 'grassland' had entered Old French by AD 1180. Its first meaning in French was 'pasturage,' any field with plants that were suitable fodder for domestic animals.

La prairie may have arrived directly from a Late Latin phrase like *terra prataria* 'meadow-land.' Compare such borrowing in other Romance languages where Italian has *prateria* and Spanish *pradera*. The classical Latin root was *pratum* 'meadow.' But *pratum* had come into French earlier as *pré* 'meadow' and so French prairie may simply be an extension of *pré* formed by adding to it *-erie* to produce *préerie*, which is actually one of the early spelling variants. *-Erie* was a French noun suffix, giving *préerie* the sense of 'a considerable area of meadow-like land suitable for pasturing cattle and sheep.'

A few hundred years later, when French surnames began reaching some of their final forms, a person whose house was beside a *pré* might have become known as Jacques Dupré, giving one of the commoner modern French surnames with continental French regional variations like Duprey, Duprat (note retention of the original Latin *t*), and Dupraz. Once the name reached the New World, we see American variants like the original Louisiana spellings Dupree and Dupry. Famous bearers of the name include French organist and composer Marcel Dupré and the American cellist Jacqueline Dupré. These surnames are semantic equivalents of English ones like Meadow and Meadows.

Canadian French produced a diminutive of prairie, *prairillon* 'a small tract of grassland,' which enjoyed a brief vogue in Canadian English, sometimes spelled *prairion*.

In France, Bastille-stormers took up prairie too. French Revolutionists wanted everything ancient and stinking of noblesse to be dumped, including the old calendar. They made up a clumsy new one that lasted a short time. The ninth month of the Revolutionary calendar, which fell between May 20 and June 18, was called *Prairial* 'meadow-month.' In the third year of the Republic June 8, 1795 appeared as *20 prairial, an III*. Oh, it was a really new month name, if you consider one thousand years old to be new. Prairial in fact was a Republican scholar's sneaky translation of one of the earliest month names in proto-Germanic languages. Even among the Anglo-Saxons one name for what became the month of July was *meadmonath* 'meadow-month,' the time when northern meadows throve. How very revolutionary.

Back home, where the buffalo roamed, later Canuck sodbusters were coining a variety of phrases:

Bald-headed prairie—rolling plains with no trees

Prairie itch—a dermatitis produced by contact with nasty micro-organisms called freshwater polyps of the genus *Hydra* found in prairie potholes, ponds, and ditches. In W.O. Mitchell's *Jake and the Kid* (1961) a character "had the measles and the prairie itch once and the mumps on both sides."

Prairie lily—the official floral emblem of Saskatchewan, *Lilium philadelphicum*, the red range-lily

Prairie oyster—a drink used as a pick-me-up or as a so-called cure in the Canadian West for a hangover: Crack open a fresh egg in a small cup, sprinkle with pepper, splash in a taste of vinegar, swirl and add a double shot of rye, drink at once. A better cure might be not to drink alcohol to excess and avoid a hangover. That, of course, might require forethought and self-control. Prairie oyster is also a kitchen phrase where it names calves' testicles fried as food.

Prairie squint—from too many long days in the sun harvesting that yellow grain. Did you know that Estevan, Saskatchewan, has more hours of sunshine than any other city in Canada: 2,537 hours per annum, on average?

Prairie wool—wild fodder for sheep consisting of graminaceous goodies like spear-grass, bunch-grass, and buffalo-grass

Rare Prairie Words Can Be Fun Too

Our little gopher-scurry over the word *prairie* concludes with a question. If you dwell in the south of Alberta, Saskatchewan, or Manitoba, do you ever tire, when asked where you're from, of answering "I live on the Prairies"? Just for fun sometime, raise a listener's eyebrow by responding, "I am pratincolous." Your listener will probably snort and say, "Seen a doctor about that yet?" But stick to pratincolous, with stress on the second syllable and a hard *c*. It's a neat and obscure word. Pratincole was coined by an ornithologist in 1773 and is still the correct name of an Old World swallowlike bird of the plover family, with related species also found in Australia. But it was made up of Latin *pratum* 'meadow, prairie' + *incola* 'inhabitant.' So it can perfectly well be transferred to humans who live on a prairie. You could invent a verb too. Yes, my forefathers came to Canada and pratincolated near Saskatoon. On second thought, maybe not. It sounds more like their buggy broke down coming back from town!

PRAIRIE TURNIP

The prairie turnip, *Psoralea esculenta*, also called biscuit-root, breadroot, buffalo root, Indian carrot, or prairie potato, is the starchy, foot-long root of a legume, a member of the pea family, pounded and used as flour by First Peoples of the Prairies and early white settlers. It was not esteemed for its flavour. The explorer Captain John Palliser, after whom the Palliser Triangle is named, travelled along part of the Saskatchewan River and wrote in his 1857 journal, "the root is very dry and almost tasteless, and even when boiled for a great length of time does not become soft, and is at best but insipid, unnutritious trash." Yikes! I wonder if Cap'n John was sufferin' a patch of canoe-chafing that day? Earlier, French Canadian voyageurs encountering the staple food had dubbed it "*pomme de prairie*."

PRICKLY PEAR CACTUS

One of the cactus family native to Canada, *Opuntia polyacantha* (Botanical Latin < *polys* Greek, many + *acanthos* Greek, thorn, spine) has indeed many spines. On the dry banks of old coulees in southern Saskatchewan and Alberta, on the dry hills of British Columbia's interior, even on some dry islands in Georgia Strait, the prickly pear cactus blooms in early summer. Surprisingly, it also grows on Pelee Island in Lake Erie. Among the cat's cradle of prickly spines sit sensual cups of translucent yellow sepals, seemingly spun of buttery silk. These cactus flowers beckon insects into their bowls with the promise of nectar, and send them on their way with a freight of pollen. But sweet as the flowers are, prickly pear spines penetrate shoe leather quick as steel needles. They also hide under snow and stiletto straight through a ski boot.

But you can eat the flesh of this cactus. If you

skin the stubby leaves and carefully pluck out the spines, you can eat the leaves after roasting them in the bottom of a hot fire. If raw cactus leaves, peeled and despined, are too sticky, just wash them off in cold water. As a fresh vegetable, they can be served marinated in vinegar and lemon juice or raw in salads.

PRINCE EDWARD ISLAND OF MANY NAMES

Abegweit and Minegoo were the first names of Prince Edward Island, both from Mi'kmaq, the language of its earliest named settlers. The Mi'kmaq people trace their ancestry back to Aboriginal hunters and fishers whom anthropologists call "the Shellfish People," and whose sites on Prince Edward Island have been dated as old as ten thousand years. Those ancient people, probably seasonal visitors from the mainland, drawn by good catches and abundant wildlife, could have walked to the island across a flat lowland now covered by the waters of Northumberland Strait. Geologists suggest that as glaciers melted some five thousand years ago, this plain was covered by rising ocean levels. Nowadays, visitors to Prince Edward Island can speed across Confederation Bridge.

Mi'kmaq people have lived permanently on the island for almost two thousand years, and Abegweit has been the affectionate way they refer to Prince Edward Island. Loosely translated from their language, Abegweit means 'cradled on the waves.'

The word is pronounced EPP-eh-kwit, all syllables short. More precisely, the Mi'kmaq root is *epegweit*, 'lying in the water,' or *abahquit* 'lying parallel with the waves.' The first Mi'kmaq hunters paddled to Abegweit even in the wintertime by canoe to fish and take wild fowl; and after drying their catch along the shores of Bedeque Bay, they would return to permanent winter camp on the nearby mainland. The Mi'kmaq divided their ancestral lands into seven parts, which still bear the ancient names, as attested in the Mi-kmak Grand Council for the District of Epekwitk (Abegweit).

Most people who have called the island home have been more than fond of Abegweit, a lovely, watery name. Here is Lucy Maud Montgomery, author of *Anne of Green Gables*, writing in 1939 in Prince Edward Island, "You never know what peace is until you walk on the shores or in the fields or along the winding red roads of Abegweit on a summer twilight when the dew is falling and the old, old stars are peeping out and the sea keeps its nightly tryst with the little land it loves." The island's deep, fertile, reddish-brown soil, now sandy, now clayey, holds abundant deposits of iron oxides that produce the famous redness.

Ships, too, have proudly borne the name of Abegweit. A CNR automobile ferry that used to ply the waters of the Northumberland Strait between New Brunswick and Prince Edward Island was christened MV *Abegweit*. Then in 1962, the body of water crossed by the ferry was officially named Abegweit Passage.

Samuel de Champlain called Prince Edward Island *Île de Saint Jean* in 1604. The British possession of the island in 1759 caused a simple translation to St. John's Island. Then in 1798 the British garrison at Halifax was being commanded by Prince Edward, Duke of Kent, and some local royalist, some cringing, lickspittle toady, thought it might show a pleasing deference to name yet another piece of colonial real estate after yet another imperial poobah. That Prince Edward, the island's namesake, was the father of Queen Victoria.

What became Prince Edward Island was just one of the Mi'kmaq living places, but they revered it and called it *Minegoo* 'the island.' In this word we see the common Algonkian root for water *mine*, which appears in numerous North American place names like Minesing in Ontario (derived from the Ojibwa word for island) and the American state of Minnesota, a Siouan descriptive referring to the river and meaning 'cloudy water.' Minnehaha does not mean 'laughing water' but simply 'waterfalls.'

RAMPIKE

A British dialect word of unknown origin gave us this sturdy noun that names a dead but standing tree burnt in a forest fire. Joshua Fraser, a nineteenth-century Scottish immigrant, in his 1883 *Shanty, Forest, and River Life in the Backwoods of Canada*, gives this description: "In backwoods parlance these are called 'rampikes' and make you think of the crowbars which the Titans may have used to pry up the rocks, with which they tried to pelt Jupiter out of Heaven."

RAPPÉ PIE

A hearty Acadian dish, literally 'grated pie' from Acadian French *tarte râpée* or *pain râpé*, this *tarte à la râpure* was the traditional meal served after a pioneer quilting frolic in New Brunswick. Among the ingredients inside the pastry were potatoes, onions, chicken or black duck or rabbit, lard, salt, and pepper.

REAL McCOY OF ONTARIO: AN AFRICAN-CANADIAN INVENTION

The real McCoy is the genuine article, and there are three origins that all contributed to the spread of the catchphrase. Closest to home and perhaps the earliest to be attested is Canadian and American railroaders' jargon where the real McCoy was the nickname for a railway car coupling invented by an African Canadian named Elijah McCoy who was born in Colchester South, Ontario. McCoy's self-lubricating cup permitted metal joints to be oiled automatically as the machines that contained them worked. Railway cars ran longer and more smoothly with Elijah McCoy's invention. Canadian playwright

Ashante Infantry wrote an entire play about this early African-Canadian whiz. "The Real McCoy" opened in Toronto in 2006. When railroad engineers asked for a lubricating joint after that, they always wanted McCoy's invention and asked for "the real McCoy."

But the phrase was alive in Scotland too, as "the real Mackay," a superior Scotch whisky made by the Mackay company. The phrase appears in print in Scotland by the 1870s and also in a slight variant as "the real McKie." Even in America, Mackay's whisky had brand clout, and was advertised widely as "the clear Mackay" which by prohibition times was whispered in American speakeasies as "the real Mackay," an amber distillate far superior to the illegal, watery rotgut being peddled in most honky-tonk dives of the era.

Both those usages predate the origin that gave wide currency to the expression in the United States. A boxer named Norman Selby (1873–1940) took the ring name of Kid McCoy in 1891. He won the world welterweight championship in 1897 and two years later in a spectacular boxing match that went twenty rounds McCoy knocked out heavyweight Joe Choynski. A headline the next morning in the *San Francisco Examiner* written by their sportswriter William Naughton blared: "NOW YOU'VE SEEN THE REAL McCOY!" The catchphrase raced across American newspapers and stuck in public speech as a synonym for 'the goods, the authentic thing.'

McCoy himself did not last long on the canvas. In 1900 he saw stars the hard way when he was k.o.'d by Gentleman Jim Corbett. In *The Real McCoy*, a racy biography of the boxer, Robert Cantwell traced the man's sad decline. He tried running a saloon in New York City. It failed. He tried showbiz, appearing as a boxer in an early and classic silent film, *Broken Blossoms*, directed in 1919 by D.W. Griffith. He tried marriage, ten times. In 1924 he tried nine years in San Quentin for manslaughter. The judge disagreed, but most people attached to the case figured McCoy murdered his mistress. It seems ten wives did not completely occupy his free time. He committed suicide in 1940 and left a note which he ended with this signature: "Norman Selby." At the end, even the real McCoy was sick of his own moniker.

RED RIVER BANNOCK

Red River bannock differed from true Scottish bannock because wheat flour eventually replaced oatmeal in the recipe. The Red River settlers' original recipe had no leavening agent and was a hard flour-and-water biscuit cooked in an exterior brick or mud oven or on a hearth. Where the Scottish recipe might call for beef drippings, later prairie bannock was likely to use buffalo fat.

The colony established by Lord Selkirk in the valley of the Red River in 1812 borrowed its name from the French name, Rivière Rouge, used as early as 1740. But that, in turn, was a loan-translation either from Cree *Miscousipi* 'red water river' or Ojibwa *Miskwa-gama-sipi* 'red water river,' both Aboriginal names deriving from the red silt frequently carried by the river's current.

Bannock was also called trail biscuit, bush bread, river cake, and galette. The word is Scots Gaelic, *bannach*, for a thin oatmeal cake, ultimately from an Old English word *bannuc* 'morsel, little bit.' As to its taste, it is perhaps best to recall Dr. Samuel Johnson's definition in his famous dictionary (1755) "Oats, n. a grain which in England is fed to horses, but in Scotland supports the people." To the first Canadian settlers of the eastern seaboard, bannock was flour, lard, salt and water, done over an outdoor fire in a frying pan if one was on the trail, and at home pan-fried at the hearth. This rough bread is remembered in the little town of Bannock, Saskatchewan.

RICHIBUCTO GOOSE

Richibucto goose is salted shad (a fish) as prepared in Richibucto, Kent County, Nova Scotia. It's a comic reference to common use of this food; compare Digby chicken.

RIPS

Where New Brunswick rivers ran fast and shallow, white waters were 'rips.' Rips called for deft canoeing, log-booming, and bateau-ing. The more usual English word was *riffle*, and perhaps rip is a shortening of riffle. The Rips is a local tag for white-water rapids at several places in New Brunswick.

ROBIN HOOD FLOUR

In 1909, a miller on the banks of Thunder Creek at Moose Jaw, Saskatchewan, began to make all-purpose, hard-wheat flour that he named after Robin Hood. It first came to market in 100-pound sacks marked "Absolute Satisfaction or Your Money Back Plus a 10% Premium."

ROCK TRIPE OR *TRIPE DE ROCHE*

Rock tripe is a translation of the Canadian French coinage *tripe de roche*, here meaning 'rock guts.' Aboriginal peoples first showed whitemen how to eat this emergency food, which they called *wakwund*. Voyageurs often scraped this edible lichen directly off the rocks from their canoes, and sometimes carved their initials in the blank rock wall so exposed. It is not highly nutritious but does fill the stomach of a starving wretch until he finds his fellows, his fate, or some real food.

Lichen is a symbiotic partnership between a fungus and an alga. The fungus supplies the outer form of the lichen, the alga supplies chlorophyll so photosynthesis can take place. The genera that make up rock tripe are *Gyrophora* and *Umbilicaria*.

Here is explorer Samuel Hearne on rock tripe in his *A Journey from Prince of Wales's Fort (1795)*:

> There is a black, hard, crumply moss, that grows on the rocks . . . and sometimes furnishes the natives with a temporary subsistence, when no animal food can be procured. This moss, when boiled, turns to a gummy consistence, and is more clammy in the mouth than sago; it may, by adding either moss or water, be made to almost any consistence. It is so palatable, that all who taste it generally grow fond of it. It is remarkably good and pleasing when used to thicken any kind of broth, but it is generally most esteemed when boiled in fish-liquor.

Tripe started life at the back of the butcher shop. It is tissue from a cow's first or second stomach used as food. Tripe came into the English wordstock from Norman French after 1066 and all that. The French borrowed it from Provençal *tripa* and cow-stomach-eating troubadours heard it first in Italy as *trippa*. English extensions of the sense followed, and tripes meant guts, then tripe was a worthless person, food, or thing.

ROULEAUVILLE IN CALGARY

This was a French part of Calgary, annexed by the city in 1907, and rechristened with the spiffy name Cliff Bungalo! There is now a park in the district named Rouleauville Park in memory of the city's small but proud French heritage.

RUBBABOO

Rubbaboo was a stew or soup made by chopping up pemmican and tossing it into boiling water. Any other available nutriments lurking in a saddlebag or camp larder might be thrown in as well: a handful of flour, a few wild onions, perhaps a few roots of prairie turnip, and a hunk of salt pork. Because it was a mixture of whatever was available, rubbaboo later came to refer to any miscellaneous collection of things. When settlers and trappers used a mixture of French, English, and Aboriginal words, this mixed bag of jargon could be called a rubbaboo. There has even been an anthology of Canadian stories and poems entitled *Rubbaboo*.

The etymology is complex and obscure. Rubbaboo seems to be a comic attempt at saying the name of another pioneer stew, *ruhiggan burgoo*. *Ruhiggan* was a word in Algonkian languages denoting 'beat meat,' the first preparatory stage of making pemmican. *Burgoo* was a word for stew used by many British immigrants, derived from eighteenth-century British naval slang where burgoo was oatmeal gruel eaten by sailors. Canadian and American English also grabbed the term from British traders who used burgoo to name any unappetizing food, especially a thick stew made from camp or kitchen scraps of meat and vegetables.

But the form rubbaboo was also influenced by Ojibwa and Cree words for soup, namely, *nempup* and *apu*. One must remember the polyglot salad of words that might fly across a prairie campfire when French-speaking voyageurs met up with English-speaking trappers and perhaps with Cree-speaking Métis along with, say, Blackfoot people. It was indeed a verbal rubbaboo, out of which this word emerged.

As usual, the finicky and fastidious palates of some Europeans were appalled by what they had to eat on their travels across the North American continent. A Scottish poobah, one James Carnegie, Earl of Southesk, trekked through our West in 1859–60, and later published his reflections in *Saskatchewan and The Rocky Mountains: A Diary and Narrative of Travel* . . . Among useful comments, the good Earl also had this to say: "Pemmican is most endurable when uncooked. My men used to fry it with grease, sometimes stirring in flour, and making a flabby mess, called 'rubbaboo,' which I found almost uneatable. Carefully-made pemmican, such as that flavoured with the Saskootoom [*sic*] berries . . . or the sheep-pemmican given us by the Rocky Mountain hunters, is nearly good, but in two senses, a little of it goes a long way."

SALAL

This member of the wintergreen genus is a little evergreen shrub native to our Pacific coast. British

Columbians who enjoy wild foods pick the purplish salalberries in late summer or early autumn to make jams. Tart salal jelly makes a grease-cutting accompaniment to servings of game. Aboriginal peoples of our Pacific coast cooked salalberries into a jam between red-hot rocks in ground-ovens. Salal leaves and berries, containing methyl salicylate, the chemical that gives oil of wintergreen its distinctive smell and some of its properties, should not be fed to children who are hypersensitive to aspirin, the common analgesic that is related chemically to methyl salicylate. Otherwise salalberries or young, fresh leaves make a pleasant, fragrant tea. And the glossy, reasonably long-lasting leaves of salal are a favourite of West Coast florists' bouquets.

Salal's botanical name is *Gaultheria shallon*. The genus is named after a botanist who spent most of his life in eighteenth-century Québec City. Jean-François Gaulthier was a royal physician, amateur botanist, and friend to the Swedish explorer of North America, Peter Kalm, who in turn was a supplier of specimen plants to the great Swedish founder of botanical nomenclature, Linnaeus. Thus, after Kalm returned to Sweden with samples of wintergreen collected near Québec by Gaulthier, Linnaeus gladly named the wintergreen genus in honour of the French doctor. The specific *shallon* and the common name salal both derive from the name of this plant in Chinook Jargon, the early trading language of our Pacific coast, which in turn drew it from the wordstock of the Chinook language where the berry is *sálal.*

SALMONBERRY OR OLALLIE

Salmonberry is also known by its common name in Chinook Jargon, *olallie*, although olallie strictly denotes any berry. For example, among several Aboriginal peoples of British Columbia, homemade berry wine is *olalliechuk*, from Chinook Jargon *olallie* 'berry' + *chuck* 'water.'

Salmonberry is *Rubus spectabilis*, a showy shrub of the raspberry family with pretty red flowers and salmon-coloured berries. The specific *spectabilis* means showy. There was a Canadian movie starring Alberta's k.d. lang entitled *Salmonberries*. In *Salmonberries* the frisky warbler of pop songs played a provocative but beguiling role. So too did the sweet red berries of this shrub that belongs to the huge rose family of plants.

Salmonberry's juicy fruits look like big raspberries and are eaten ripe or made into a delicious jam. The common name was used first along the banks of the Columbia River where native peoples had a favourite dish that consisted of the very young, tasty shoots of the plant eaten with dried salmon roe. Indeed, salmonberry's home range is the Pacific coast, and it thrives west of the Rockies. At one of the best dinners he has ever eaten in Canada, a private and delightful affair served at a table overlooking tidal pools on Vancouver Island's west coast, the author has tasted salmonberry charlotte, a dessert that combines sweetness, sin, and regional appropriateness in equal portions.

SASKATOONBERRY

The Cree word for these succulent purple berries is *mi-sakwato-min* 'tree-of-many-branches berries.' They are the fruit of a serviceberry tree, *Amelanchier alnifolia*, and the acidic sweetness of the berries helped cut the fatty taste of pemmican, so that saskatoons were frequently added to the buffalo fat in preparing pemmican. The fruit ripens across the Prairies in June and July. First Peoples on their initial migrations into Prairie regions more than ten thousand years ago would have seen bears eating the tart, juicy berries.

SAW-OFF

This pure Canadianism began in political backrooms where one party agreed not to run a candidate in a certain riding, if the second and opposing party agreed not to run their candidate in a riding where the first party was certain of victory. Saw-off now has broadened its scope to mean any mutual concession or trade-off. In *Our Own Voice: Canadian English and How It Is Studied*, R.E. McConnell shows how it can even refer to a draw in a hockey game, by quoting a *Vancouver Sun* headline: "Canucks Manage Saw-off."

SAW-WHET OWL

This little owl of eastern North America, *Aegolius acadicus*, was named by New Brunswickers (*acadicus*, Latin 'Acadian') who thought its characteristic cry reminiscent of the sound made when filing or whetting a saw. Also known as the Acadian owl, it was dubbed "the sawyer" in pioneer Ontario. A citation from Upper Canada in 1822 states that it was sometimes called the "whetsaw."

SCARBOROUGH

Scarborough means 'Harelip's Fort.' Honest. Now a city, once Toronto's largest borough, Scarborough was dubbed Scarberia in the late 1950s because snobbish downtowners thought of it as a distant barrenland of new housing divisions and no class. Like some other neighbourhood names, its latest nicknames are racist. New Canadians of Caribbean origin in some numbers are moving out of the inner city and into the suburbs of the Torontonian megalopolis, thus one hears anti-black nicknames like Scarbados and Scarlem, punning on Barbados and Harlem. But the original name was no lovely moniker either. Scarborough means Harelip's Fort, a fact no doubt unknown to Elizabeth Simcoe, wife of Upper Canada's first Governor-General John Graves Simcoe, when she named the village because the local bluffs reminded her of cliffs near the town of Scarborough in Yorkshire. Scarborough in England was a Viking settlement. A Norse saga recorded that one Thorgils Skarthi founded the North Yorkshire settlement around AD 965. Viking warriors liked frightening and repellent names. *Skarthi* meant 'harelip' in Old Norse, a language some linguists now dub Old Scandinavian. In Old English the settlement became *Skaresborg* 'Harelip's Fort.'

SCOTCHMAN'S HILL IN CALGARY

From this Calgary lookout at Salisbury and 6th Street, one gets a superb vista of foothills, Calgary's city core, the Saddledome, and the Calgary Stampede grounds. Scotchman's Hill is one of the best spots to view the fireworks set off during Stampede celebrations. The name arose because cheapskates can watch many of the Stampede activities from the hill for free, instead of paying admission. Och, it's a wee libel against the inherent generosity of the true Scot, would you not say then?

SCRIPTURE CORD

Many early New Brunswick farmers took to the woods in winter to work in lumber camps or as independent lumberjacks. When in the spring the trimmed wood was sold, Scripture cord was cut timber that measured more than the invoice indicated. It was the equivalent in local lumber jargon of a baker's dozen, in which the good Christian selling the wood, mindful of scriptural injunctions about generosity, gave the buyer a little extra wood for good measure, perhaps with the practical benefit that the buyer would return for more small bargains.

SCRUNCHINS IN NEWFOUNDLAND AND LABRADOR

A juicy, salivant lip-licker of a word, scrunchings or scruncheons or cruncheons are fried cubes of fat-back pork, sprinkled over fish and brewis, or served as accompaniment to many other dishes. Scrunchins also refer to pieces of any fish or animal fat after the oil has been extracted from them.

SCUT ON PRINCE EDWARD ISLAND

The *Oxford English Dictionary* suggests this opprobrious epithet for dismissing a contempible person—"You dirty scut! You mean old scut!"—is a dialect variant of "scout," itself in use as a term of contempt from 1380 to 1869. In Anglo-Irish a scut was a rabbit's tail or a nasty person. In his *Dictionary of Prince Edward Island English*, T.K. Pratt found it in limited use on the Island among older rural residents. But scut is a fine, spittable, corrosive monosyllable that should be revived and spread about to bolster the tired stock of insult words in Canadian English. "Scut work" for any low, disagreeable task is widespread across Canada.

SHEDIACS

Oysters from Shediac, New Brunswick, suffered a few sea changes when subjected to the metamorphosis of pioneer spelling. Here's how the succulent molluscs saw print in 1835 in the pages of *The Novascotian*, a weekly published in Halifax: "Where have you been all your days, that you never heard of Shittyack Oysters? I thought everybody had heard of them." Shediac as a place was named by the Mi'kmaq people from their phrase *esedeiik* 'running far back,' referring to the bay's indentation from Northumberland Strait.

SKIDROAD IN VANCOUVER

Skidroad and its later variant skid row come from West Coast lumbering slang. The first Skid Road in Canada was in Vancouver in an area presently bounded by Carrall and Cordova Streets. From there the term spread across Canada as the designation of any slummy part of a city or town populated by rubbies and winos. In Vancouver's early days, the area was the terminus of an actual skidroad, a slideway used to drag logs to water or to railway track for transport to a lumber mill.

A skidroad was a specialized kind of corduroy road. Skids were peeled and greased logs, laid transversely across a cleared pathway, so that teams of oxen, horses, or mules could haul rough timber down them. In the first British Columbian lumber camps the grease used was frequently dogfish oil. The men who built such logging trails were called skidders and so were the teamsters who drove the horses. Later on, when motorized vehicles replaced horses and mules, the phrase "skidder tractor" appeared.

How was skidroad altered to Skid Row? Unemployed loggers often gathered at the end of these trails to ask a boss for work. When no jobs were available, it was time for a little logging R & R. In Vancouver and in Seattle, this involved booze, broads, and brothels to which gambling was soon added. Then came cheap lodging houses for the out-of-work loggers, rough hiring halls, beer parlours, mission soup kitchens, and an influx of transients, derelicts, and petty criminals. The apex for a time in Vancouver was Water Street with its rows of saloons and flophouses. Canada can stake a claim to this second Skid Road, but not the first one. That was a street called Yesler's Way in Seattle, Washington, constructed in 1852. When coastal stands of lumber were depleted and logging operations moved inland, the name Skid Road stuck, and was soon altered by folk etymology to Skid Row. "On skid row" became synonymous with down-and-out.

From Canadian lumbering slang sprang several verb phrases: 'to hit the skids' to be broke or unemployed, to fail utterly; 'to grease the skids' to make things easier; 'to pull the skids out from under' to cause to decline, to abandon support for;

'to put the skids under,' to topple, to cause to fail.

Skid is one of the words borrowed into Old English during the Viking raids and settlements toward the end of the first millennium. Old Norse, now also called Old Scandinavian, had *skith* 'stick of wood.' The same root gave us 'ski,' a specialized stick of wood.

SKUNK CABBAGE & ME

In the thick-aired, sepulchral gloom of a rainforest bog on Vancouver Island I once spied the bold yellow sword that is the spathe of Western Skunk Cabbage poking up early in February, emerging in the coolth with its spadix coyly sheathed in a yellow all-covering tunic. This tunic or spathe later opens to reveal the flower-bearing rod of the spadix within. Some plant books label western skunk cabbage as "evil-smelling" and "with a foul stench." I lived in British Columbia for three years in the 1970s, most happily in a cottage on the Beach Grove Road near Tsawassen. One day in early spring I took the ferry to Vancouver Island, and went tromping and swamping for a day or two in Pacific Rim National Park. I certainly saw vast platoons of serried skunk cabbages in fenny glades a few yards from the Pacific waves. They did not smell skunky at all. The odour that *Lysichitum* gives off probably imitates the sex pheromones of several swamp insects that pollinate the plant. The aroma is one of fresh, primal fertility, of the vernal surge of life. Bears wolf down the whole plant, rootstock and all. The root can also be roasted, dried, and pounded into good flour, much like its Polynesian relative, taro.

Skunk cabbage comes in a western and in an eastern Canadian type, and they are swamp plants of similar habit but of entirely different genera. *Lysichitum americanum*, Western Skunk Cabbage, takes its generic name from Greek where it means 'loosened chiton,' referring to the shedding of the giant spathe. Now the chiton was one ancient Greek equivalent of a tunic. It could be made of homespun cotton, of sturdier and more expensive linen, or of the flimsiest gauze. If an Athenian citizen or a slave in the fifth-century BCE wore too loose a chiton, local prudes would tsk-tsk and declare it an outer sign of an inner moral laxity.

Symplocarpus foetidus is the Eastern Skunk Cabbage does stink, as its name makes plain. The Latin adjective *foetidus* gives us fetid in English. The generic means 'with connected fruit' referring to the aggregrate fruit formed from joined ovaries. Eastern Skunk Cabbage often is the first flower of spring in eastern Canadian wet places. The spathe that at first encloses the spadix is not yellow like the western version but a mottled brown-purple.

SKYR

Skyr is a kind of Icelandic yogourt made in Manitoba. A gallon of fresh skim milk is boiled, let cool to lukewarm, and then a cup of cultured buttermilk is stirred into the warm skim milk. The starter for the culture is often a couple of tablespoons of *skyr* from the last batch made. Sometimes a few drops of rennet are added to help the milk set. The mixture is then put aside to let the culture work at a slightly high room temperature, just above 21 degrees centigrade being best. After letting the culture work for about fifteen hours, a big bowl is lined with cheesecloth and the mixture is poured in. The full cheesecloth is lifted to drain another half-day at warm room temperature. The *skyr* is beaten briskly and served. It can be kept chilled and will last for several weeks. *Skyr* was eaten by itself with cream or poured on porridge. Some Icelandic cooks added fruit flavours to their *skyr*, but traditionalists considered this sacrilege.

SLOVEN

New Brunswick carters invented the sloven, a cart with a crank axle and a very low floor that facilitated loading and unloading. Its practicality saw use spread to all of the Maritime Provinces. In his 1941 novel *Barometer Rising*, whose climax is the 1917 Halifax explosion, Hugh MacLennan writes: "Grinding on the cobblestones behind a pair of plunging Clydesdales came one of Halifax's most typical vehicles, a low-slung dray with a high driver's box, known as a sloven."

SMELT STORM

An old Canadian term in our Atlantic Provinces, a smelt storm is a snow- or windstorm, toward the end of April, heralding the spawning run of smelts into tidal estuaries and harbours. It is also called a black storm, a sheep storm, or a robin snow. In spring, smelts are fished using a broad landing net. But much Maritime smelt fishing happens in early winter when rivers are frozen and homemade smelt shacks are pushed out onto the ice, a hole is bored, and a smaller net fastened to wooden poles is dropped through the hole. Those with quick reflexes sometimes spear smelts, but this takes great patience. Being a small fish, the smelt is often not filleted. Most cooks just lop off their heads, and fry them. More fastidious eaters pull the guts out through the gills after decapitation, and snip off the fins and tail with kitchen scissors. Acadians like to poach smelt by simmering them in herbed water.

Etymology of Smelt Words

Smelt came into Old English from a word for small fish in Old Scandinavian, the language spoken by the Vikings. Compare modern Norwegian *smelta*, itself sprung from an Indo-European root like *(s)mel* 'soft, slimy, smooth.'

Acadian French for smelt is *plan* or *pelan*, dialect variants of standard French *perlan*, borrowed into early French from Middle Dutch *spierlinc*. Québec has its very own *Rivière Éperlan* 'Smelt River,' a little stream near Forestville on the north shore on the St. Lawrence. Compare *Spierling* in German, an old synonym for the standard German word for smelt, *Stint*. Spierling probably means 'little spear,' referring either to the shape of the fish or its method of capture. Scottish and northern English dialects still have a synonym for smelt that was also borrowed from the Dutch word, *sparling* or *spirling*. This is the source of some of the English surnames in the Sparling-Sperling-Spurling group.

SOAPOLALLIE, SOAPBERRY, OR HOOSHUM

Best known is soapolallie "ice cream," which is soapberries whisked with water to froth up and with other wild berries like wild raspberry added, along with sugar, to sweeten the naturally slightly bitter soapberry. Earlier in West Coast history, this berry was also called brue, from voyageurs' French *broue*, the old Québec word for the froth on beer. Soapolallie ice cream is a foamy British Columbia treat made by picking ripe soapberries and macerating them with sugar. Then take a broad wooden spoon and whip them briskly until they foam and froth into what is also called Indian ice cream. The word is Chinook Jargon. Soap means soap, because they froth up so. *Olallie* is Chinook for 'berry.' The root shows up in the word for a potent homebrew of our West Coast called *olalliechuk*, which is a berry wine. Chuck is Chinook Jargon for water. Compare the common British Columbia term for the ocean, the *saltchuck*, from Chinook Jargon chuck 'water.' Tribes of the southern Pacific coast also made a berry bread called *olallie sapolel*. Farther north, Athapascan-speaking peoples called soapberry *hooshum*.

Soapberry is a shrub, *Shepherdia canadensis*, whose berries were often dried into flat cakes by First Peoples of our Pacific coast, and packed as rations for travel. The cakes could be whipped into a foamy trailside drink after being soaked in water. A related Shepherdia of our prairies has the popular name, buffalo berry.

SOCKEYE SALMON: A BRITISH COLUMBIA WORD

Once upon a time, I was camping near Pacific Rim National Park on Vancouver Island. One morning as I hunched over a tidal rock pool to observe a starfish lazily lunching on a hapless mollusk, an elderly gentleman (of a type whom I seem to encounter in every natural setting) approached. Let's just call him the World's Foremost Living Expert—on pretty well every topic known to human conversation. We exchanged a bit of amiable lip-flap, and in the course of his palaver, the grizzled old salt asked me if I knew that the sockeye salmon received its name when hearty fishermen of olden days waded into the water and captured the fish by socking it in the eye.

"It's an urge that could overtake any of us," I said, eyeing him.

Then I suggested there might be another explanation, having to do with a local Aboriginal language called Coast Salish; but by then the World's Foremost Living Expert was a hundred feet up the beach where I perceived that he had waylaid another innocent and was busily explaining The Origin Of The Universe as revealed to him one day while he was standing on his head reading upside-down Tarot cards. That way they'd be right-side-up as he read them. Right?

The Salish are a people who live, among other places, on the southern part of Vancouver Island and some surrounding islets. Sockeye is the English version of the Coast Salish *suk-kegh*, "red fish," an apt name for this frisky Pacific salmon. Or it may derive directly from Northern Straits Salish *seqey*, "red fish."

Ichthyology, the scientific study of fish (*ichthys*, Greek "fish"), presents a fascinating word related to this salmon. Sockeye are anadromous (pronounced uh-NAD-ruh-mous). When they are spawning, anadromous fish swim or run (*dromos*, Greek "running") up (*ana*, Greek "up") a river from the sea. The opposite word for fish that swim or run down (*kata*, Greek "down") a river to the sea, to spawn in the sea, is catadromous (pronounced kuh-TAD-ruh-mous).

Ichthyological name of the sockeye: *Oncorhynchus* = *ogkos*, Greek "tumour," "bump" + *rhughkos*, Greek "nose of an animal, snout, beak" so that the sense of the zoological name is bumpy-snout, perfectly describing the sockeye, particularly as it reaches spawning time and turns bump-nosed or hook-nosed and bright red.

Curiously, the sockeye has another common name "blueback," applied to the salmon in its adult migratory phase as it swims in the ocean, so named because the fish at that time in their life cycle have a blue dorsal coloration and silver sides.

SON-OF-A-GUN-IN-A-SACK

Son-of-a-Gun-in-a-Sack is a chuckwagon "pudding." An empty sugar sack was dipped in water and dusted with flour. Pudding ingredients enough to feed twenty cowboys were spooned into the sack and the top sewn up. The pudding sack was plunged into a large cauldron of water and boiled for three hours. To serve, the sack was peeled off and the pudding cut into slices for eating. If it didn't turn out to be quite as toothsome a repast as the cook expected, those nibbling sometimes dubbed it "son-of-a-#!$&*-in-a-sack." At one roundup, the frowsy head of an unpopular and generally unclean cook was covered with an empty sugar bag and he was plunged into the water pot "to clean him off." Itinerant kitchen workers, take due note.

SONSY

The author of *Anne of Green Gables* loved this

word. One of Lucy Maud Montgomery's cherished Prince-Edward-Islandisms describes a full-figured, healthy woman, a lady of proportion, the Edwardian ideal of womanhood, big and buxom. In *Anne of the Island* (1915) Montgomery writes of "Mrs. Lynde . . . sonsy, kindly, matronly, as of yore." Sonsy came over as a Scots-Gaelic adjective and may be related to Erse *sonas* 'luck' so that the sense extension is 'lucky, thriving, healthy, robust.' Sonsy is a fine figure of a word.

SOUNDS

Sounds are the air bladders of a cod that regulate the buoyancy of the fish, permitting it to swim up to the surface or to sound, to go deep. These hydrostatic organs lie along the inside of the cod's backbone, which some fishermen call the soundbone. The air bladders are removed when splitting cod and then they are dry-salted and stored in a wooden tub, sometimes for months. To make a dish of cod sounds, the coarse salt is washed off and the sounds are soaked in cold water for a day. Then their black lining is scraped off, and they are boiled and simmered until the cook decides they are "done." Sounds are then fried in pork fat with chopped onions and home-fried potatoes. Some say cod sounds make the zingiest breakfast served in Newfoundland Labrador. Since the collapse of the Maritime cod fishery, sounds are of course an increasingly rare treat.

SQUATUM

A term invented by Newfoundlanders, squatum is homemade berry wine, made by crushing wild fruit such as blueberries or partridgeberries, adding sugar and letting it ferment. The word arose from a verb no longer used in Standard English, a dialect verb, to squat, that meant to squeeze, crush, or flatten. The verb disappeared from Standard English early in the eighteenth century, but not before immigrants using it had come to Newfoundland, where the word has been kept alive and useful as part of islanders' unique vocabulary. If the squatum made from local berries does not seem potent enough after fermenting, there is no harm in adding a splash of grain alcohol to the mix, no harm until one attempts to get up the morning after.

ST. JOHN'S, NEWFOUNDLAND

We could speak of many colourful neighbourhood names, both current and historical, like The Cribbies, Maggoty Cove, and Tarahan's Town, but we shall make do with Signal Hill, the highest point of St. John's, called Ladies' Lookout, either because sailors' wives climbed to the spot to look out anxiously for their husbands' ships making home for the harbour, or because sailors and soldiers liked to "walk out" with their ladies fair to take the breeze of a gentle evening long ago.

STOG YOUR FACE

It's a slangy way to say "go eat" on Prince Edward Island and in some parts of Newfoundland. The British dialect verb *stog* meant 'to stuff.' It was brought to Newfoundland and Prince Edward Island by immigrants and used in the original sense there, as shown by a definition in *Devine's Folk Lore of Newfoundland*: "Stog: to chinse moss between the logs of a log house to keep out draughts." But stog developed extended meanings in our Maritimes: "to stog (stuff) the Christmas turkey" and "to stog your gob (to stuff one's mouth full of food)." On Prince Edward Island one can also hear, "Stog the cattle with grain." I think it makes excellent high school slang: "Watcha doin', dude?" "Goin' home to stog my gob."

TAR SANDS OF FORT McMURRAY, ALBERTA

Tar sands is an Alberta coinage, a phrase known by every Canadian and by all oil specialists throughout the world. The Canadian phrase has been borrowed into many foreign languages just as it is, as an intact loan word from Canadian English.The vast Athabasca tar sands appear in print by 1897 as "tar sand-beds." One scientific estimate suggests that by the year 2020 Alberta's tar sands deposits will comprise the world's largest reserve of oil. The tar sands lie under more than 31,000 square kilometres of the north and contain a cache of recoverable synthetic crude oil estimated at more than 4 billion cubic metres. A Canadian chemist named Karl Clark pioneered the hot-water process for recovering oil from tar sands that was used successfully in 1967 at Fort McMurray by Suncor Ltd. and later by Syncrude.

These extensive deposits of oil sand containing bitumen are quite close to the surface around Fort McMurray and the extraction plants there on the banks of Alberta's Athabasca River helped turn the little village that began as a post of the North West Company (a syndicate of fur trading firms absorbed into the Hudson's Bay Company in 1821) into an important economic centre. By the late 1960s, Fort McMurray had become "a company town" which is a phrase totally Canadian in origin, describing a settlement built and controlled by a business to house its employees. It is likely that "company town" originated as a description of the outlying buildings around early Hudson's Bay Company posts. But the term has not always been music to the ears of Canadian workers' unions. Some company towns live in infamy, like Murdochville in Québec. Even certain residents of Fort McMurray were not entirely enamoured with life under company rule. During the slump in world oil prices in 1987, bitter strikes and lockouts produced unrest there. But as the only game in town, the oil industry managed, even in a year beset with labour strife, to increase levels of production. Some in Fort McMurray claim there can be too heavy and too wide a hand laid upon the lives of employees when one or two corporations have the final say about almost everything that happens in one locality. But Fort McMurray is now a thriving city of more than thirty-five thousand inhabitants, and the diversity of aims its citizens have brought to this northern Alberta outpost, have made company town less applicable a label.

TEDDY OF SHINE

In the dry times of Prohibition on the Island, bootleggers used long-necked green beer bottle empties to hold homebrew illegally sold to the public. A teddy of (moon)shine might cost a dollar in those days. T.K. Pratt, editor of *Dictionary of Prince Edward Island English*, says some of his linguistic informants claimed a teddy of shine was the bribe used in certain election shenanigans which from time to time besmirched the honesty and fair name of Prince Edward Island politics.

TILLEY HAT: CANADA'S MOST RENOWNED HEADGEAR

Here we examine the surname Tilley, most famously carried today by Alexander Tilley, the inventive Canadian designer of outdoor and travel clothing and originator of the Tilley hat. But there were Tilleys who came to the fore before the hat.

Leonard Percy de Wolfe Tilley (1870–1947)
The New Brunswick lawyer and politician was premier of the province from 1933 to 1935. He was the son of the Father of Confederation listed next.

Sir Samuel Leonard Tilley (1818–96)
Born at Gagetown, New Brunswick, he began in the drugstore business and rose to political fame as a staunch advocate of New Brunswick's inclusion in Confederation. He was Macdonald's politically astute point man in the province and held many cabinet portfolios in both Macdonald governments.

Source of the Tilley Surname
The origins of Tilley as an ancient British surname are complex. The earliest form of the name appears as Ralph de Tilio in the *Domesday Book* of the English county of Derbyshire in AD 1086. This man was of Norman-French extraction and a recent arrival from France—remember the Norman Conquest of 1066 a few years before. The founding ancestor of this family took his name from the place he lived in France. There are five little towns in northern France that may be the locality of origin: Tilly-sur-Seulles in Calvados, Tilly in Eure, Tilly in Seine-et-Oise, one in Meuse, and one in the Pas-de-Calais. Only a rigorous genealogical search might determine the precise locative origin of the family.

This Norman Tilley has many spelling forms both in England and in France, among which are: Tillie, Tilly, Tiley, Tily, Tylee, Tyley, Tilhet, Thillet, and Thiellet! Why is this particular name and its variants so widespread over northern France? Because it belonged to a Teutonic tribe who controlled much of the area, even long before the Romans conquered northern Gaul. The area was known to Gallo-Romans as *Tilliacum* and that term was based on the tribe's name in Old Germanic *Tielo*, short for *Theod-ilo*, and that word contains a Germanic rootword *theod* that means 'the people.' So Tilley harks all the way back to a word at least two thousand years old and means 'the people.'

Is that it then, for Tilley? Unfortunately no. Several hundred years later in England, Tilley was coined as a new matronymic surname based on the nickname of an ancestral mother. Till and Tilly were pet forms of Matilda. Some English Tilleys also stem from Middle English *tilie* 'one who tills the fields,' a forebear who was a husbandman.

TOGUE

The popular name of a tasty lake trout of our Atlantic provinces, also seen as "tog," well illustrates one of the trade-offs people make in using common names. For togue can refer both to a freshwater fish (also called gray lake trout, mackinaw trout, mountain trout, and salmon trout) and also to a saltwater fish, an Atlantic wrasse, the tautog (*Tautoga onitis*). Tog and togue all stem from an eastern Algonkian plural *tautauog* 'black fishes' which gives an American common name for the saltwater species 'blackfish.'

TOONIE: BIRTH OF A CANADIAN MONEY WORD

Ducats. Louis d'or. Doubloons. Pieces of eight. Arrr, matey. Pirate terms for money have the aura of adventure seemingly built into their very names. But, to Canadians, our own money terms like loonie and toonie may seem everyday, pedestrian, far too common to have an interesting story behind their creation. Wrong! Here's the tale from the middle 1990s of how toonie became the name for our two-dollar coin.

Hissy Fit over the Toonie

"The word 'toonie' has too much of the nursery about it, but commends itself on grounds of accuracy (two loonies) . . ." wrote Warren Clemens, the *Globe and Mail's* 'Word Play' columnist. At least Warren Clemens was interested in the names we might give a new coin in this coign of the realm. Quite testy was the same paper's art and architecture critic, John Bentley Mays, who pouted in print that he was "bored silly by the wacky squabbling over what nicknames to give it." Nevertheless, there was bickering about what to call our new coin back in 1996.

Is the Toonie Really Bimetallic?

The first two-dollar coin was, stated the Mint, also Canada's first bimetallic one, with an outer ring made of nickel, and a centre made of aluminum-bronze. But bronze is an alloy of copper and tin, which seems to indicate that the toonie is made of four metals. Therefore, the more cumbersome neology of quadrimetallic is fitting. In any case, on the very first toonie, one side of the centre featured a bust of Queen Elizabeth the Second. On the other side was a polar bear. So, ran an early joke, it should be called the moonie, since it shows the Queen on the front with a 'bear' behind.

Pssst! Spot Me a Borden, Dude?

What were we to call this new coin in popular speech? Throughout Canadian history, our paper currency and coinage have attracted nicknames both proper and improper. I heard a tangy one not so long ago at a used car lot in Hamilton, Ontario, where the salesman, looking remarkably like Oilcan Harry from the old Mighty Mouse cartoons, was about to foist a rattle-trap of a used car on some innocent buyer: "So, good-lookin' set of wheels, eh? Tell yuh what. Four thousand dollars is the list. I'll knock off a couple of Bordens. You'll take it." Former Prime Minister Robert Borden appears on the Canadian one-hundred-dollar bill. A 'Borden' meaning a one-hundred-dollar bill is still common at Canadian racetracks among bettors who play the ponies and their touts to tip them off to sure winners for a share of their winnings, hopefully not delivered in toonies.

Birth of the Toonie

The Royal Canadian Mint officially introduced the toonie on February 19, 1996. A year earlier when plans to discontinue the two-dollar bill hit the media after Finance Minister Paul Martin announced it in his 1995 federal budget speech, the most popular name for the planned coin was doubloon, for "double loonie." But that did not stick. Neither did bloonie. Apparently both were too piratical.

Doubloon?

But a minor doubloon rush did occur at the Canadian Intellectual Property Office in Hull, Québec, where new brand-names must apply to be trademarked. The federal registry then publishes them so that any objections to new brand-names may be stated. In the August 2, 1995, issue of the *Canadian Trademarks Journal*, Hagemeyer Canada Inc., maker of candies and chocolates, filed an application to trademark "Doubloon" and "Double Loon." Imperial Oil Ltd. sought to trademark "Dubloon," also as a chocolate and candy. A few weeks later in the *CTJ* an enterprise called Triple-C Inc. applied to trademark "Toonies" as a chocolate confectionery. "Twonies" was listed in the *CTJ*, too.

That'll Set You Back Three Polar Bears, Pal!

In late February and early March of 1996, newspapers were referring to it formally as the polar bear coin. In the streets one heard "bear, bear buck, bearback, bear butt, Teddy, Yogi, and Winnie." The loonie weighs 7 grams and the toonie 7.3 grams.

This extra burden had fussbudgets fretting that their pocket seams would burst. They dubbed the weighty newcomer “Unbearable” and “Pocketbuster.” In fractured franglais one waggish Montrealer offered “deuxbear” because it was too heavy to bear.

Greenpeace Objects? Now There's News!

At the February launch of the toonie in Montreal, federal Public Works Minister Diane Marleau was tuning her tonsils in an introductory address when a Greenpeace protester costumed as a polar bear drowned her out by screaming: “Help me, help, I'm an endangered species.” Other Greenpeacers at the ceremony passed out pamphlets pointing out the decline in the polar bear population and predicting that the new polar bear coin, with a life in circulation of twenty years, just might outlive the polar bear itself.

In Ottawa the Commons heritage committee heard a proposal in mid-March from Jack Iyerak Anawak, the MP from Nunatsiaq, a riding in the eastern Arctic, to bestow the official name of *nanuq* on the new coin. *Nanuq*, or in the older and less precise spelling nanook, is one Inuktitut word for ‘polar bear.’

Oh No, Not Deuxsy!!!

Deuce, deuxsy, doozie, double burden, double loon, doubloon(ie) were slangy monikers. So was doughnut, because some of the toonies, fresh off stamping machines at the Mint's Winnipeg production facility, popped their centres and thus had a hole like a doughnut. In a brief attack of late-winter cabin fever, frenzied Canucks took to bashing and smashing the toonie. People dropped it off skyscrapers, plunged it into liquid nitrogen, blow-torched it, and whacked it with hammers and chisels.

Toonie Denounced as Dangerous to Children

In Mississauga, Ontario, a nine-year-old boy popped a toonie into two parts and used the doughnut-shaped outer ring as just that, a ring for his middle finger. The boy could not remove it. Alarmingly, his finger began to swell. The boy's father went to the school and cut the toonie off with tin snips. Said the inquisitive lad's mother, "The government recalls dangerous toys. What about dangerous coins?" At another school, firefighters carefully hacksawed a toonie's outer ring from the pinkie of a junior scientist and restored his digital dignity.

Keep Your Pinkies Off That Coin!

While the toonie was designed to withstand 60 to 80 pounds of pressure per square inch, it is quite illegal to tamper with, damage, or deface Canadian coinage or paper currency. The *Criminal Code* offence provides for the convicted miscreant a $2,000 fine and/or six months in the slammer. Is that, milord, payable in toonies?

Splittoonie?

Popping the coins in two brought forth a new nickname too: the splittoon. The smallest change, even in small change, is still change, and seems to unsettle some people momentarily. A new piece of pocket change jingle-jangles the nerves. Novelty and damp armpits go together. So even at the birth of a new coin, strident midwives were everywhere. “It’s a monstrosity!” yelped some bank tellers who opened toonie rolls to find the occasional blank. Now the Mint did issue 55 million toonies by March 31, 1996. As with any new mass-produced object, a few blanks occurred as quality control in the manufacturing process was fine-tuned. So the numismatic neonate was imperfect.

Gadzooks! It was not in mint condition. Heaven forfend! The brouhaha abated in the following weeks as the Mint’s publicity department gushed bumf explaining the toonie’s raison d’être.

How Ottawa Makes Big Bucks from Coins

Foremost were government savings and profits on the coin. The gain to federal coffers by March 31, 1996, was estimated to be $100 million! Not too shabby a wad in these times of deficit reduction mania. Over the next twenty years, soothed the Mint, replacing two-dollar bills with the coins could save us $250 million, maybe $500 million. This will happen partly because the issuance of paper money and coins are treated quite differently in government account books. For example, a two-dollar paper banknote is in fact a promissory note issued by the Bank of Canada payable to the bearer on demand, and must therefore show on their account books as a liability.

Coins, however, are bought by the federal Finance Department, at cost from the Royal Canadian Mint. A toonie costs 16 cents. Finance sells them to chartered banks for the face value of $2. That's a whacking good profit of $1.84 each. This profit has an interesting name derived from feudal times: seigniorage, the margin between the face value of coins and their production cost. In late Middle English, seignorage or seigneurage (these are variant spellings) was any prerogative claimed by a feudal lord or monarch. Then in England it referred to the Crown's right to keep a certain percentage of any gold bullion purchased by a mint to make coins. Now seigniorage is the technical financial term for profits on coinage.

Designer Short-changed?

The toonie is a bonanza for the government but less of a windfall for the artists who designed it. The portrait of Queen Elizabeth the Second, stamped on all Canadian coins since 1990, is by Canada's most honoured medalist and medallion designer, Dora de Pédery-Hunt. The winning polar bear motif on the two-dollar coin was commissioned in a closed competition from Brent Townsend, a wildlife painter from Campbellford, Ontario, who received the semi-measly sum of $5,000. It seems the Mint only invites submissions from draughtspersons who draw and paint in a "magic-realism" style, with emphasis on the realism, and less on the magic.

Reviews Are In: Toonie is Artistic Failure

By April 1996 it was clear the toonie for most Canadians was an esthetic flop. It was "plain, boring, unexciting." Christopher Hume, the art critic of the *Toronto Star*, had said in a March 21 column, "The latest addition to our currency has gone from a state of abuse to indifference." Hume thought the new coin looked like "a souvenir" or "a locker token." After a month in circulation, "the new coin has failed to grab the public consciousness. It's not so much a question of ugliness as emptiness. The proportions are wrong and the imagery not large enough." The Queen's head and the polar bear were too tiny, Hume decided, having been confined to the core piece. There was a lack of detail. Even the current and much-hated penny had more numismatic verve than the toonie. "Without the accumulation of such elements [of design], no matter how small, to fill the surface, add texture, reflect light and, ultimately, to impart value, the toonie falls flat," wrote Hume. Canadians polled at random agreed with him.

Racism Exists: But What About Dollarism?

Another reason for replacement of the Canadian two-dollar bill is that the average deuce banknote of late has looked tattered and rather ratty, because it has been used more frequently since 1987 when our one-dollar bill went bye-bye and the loonie was introduced. The Canadian two-dollar bill also had some historical opprobrium attached to it, especially in our Prairies where in yearning days of yore it was the standard wages of sin, being the fee paid for the services of a prostitute. Some businesses in our West used to refuse to take a deuce note at all. The deuce was also the devil. Other Prairie establishments sneered at the two-dollar bill as a "B.C. buck." Early in their history, many Americans had disliked their two-dollar bill so much that it was discontinued. A deuce was vulgar. It reeked of the racetrack tout and the cheap bet in some iniquitous den of Las Vegas.

Toonie, Don't Drive Me Looney!

Such were the ephemera attendant on the creation of the toonie. The spelling "toonie" was in print early in 1995, long before the debut of the fissionable fiasco. There were variants. On Tuesday, February 27, 1996, a front-page headline in the *Toronto Star* spelled it "toonie" while that same night CFTO-TV in Toronto supered it as "twoonie." In less than two weeks, the orthographical variants largely disappeared, and most media used "tooney" to conform with "looney" in both sound and spelling. Will tooney suffer the same sea changes as looney which one stills sees as loony and loonie? Perhaps. But the acceptance of new slang is severely practical. If a new word is short, easy-to-remember, easy-to-spell, not likely to be confused with a word already in use, and based on a past word, it quickly gains favour. The potency of all of the puns and one-shot, cheap jokes waned with repetition. "Twosince" rhymed with nuisance, and disappeared.

Twoonie or twooney could be mistakenly pronounced tuh-woony. Those in favour of the spelling t-w-o-o-n-i-e point out that we don't say tuh-woo for two. Nevertheless, twoonie was too complicated, and gave way to tooney. But not in the pages of the *Globe and Mail*. As a national newspaper, the *Globe and Mail* plays a legitimate and major role in determining the spelling of new Canadian words. When there are variant spellings of a new word, what the *Globe* chooses often becomes the standard. By March 23, the *Globe and Mail* style mavens had decided on the clumsy but clear twoonie and put it in a subhead. Leaving the *w* of twoonie in the word is logical, but many other newspapers and print media selected tooney to jibe with looney. Then on March 30, a *Globe and Mail* editorial sniffed that twoonie was "an alloy so cute it makes us [Canadians] sound like a stuffed puppet kingdom at the end of the miniature railroad in Mister Rogers Neighbourhood. Money is not funny. Money is grand and solemn, serene, sublime." The editorial concluded by bestowing its approval upon *nanuq*, Inuktitut for 'polar bear.'

And for the future? The government of Canada is considering the introduction of a five-dollar coin. When I heard that, my heart *cinq*.

Other Canadian Money Terms

Although they are not Canadian, we use words like coin, dollar, mint, money, and penny every day, and they have interesting sources.

The $ Sign

Most contested is the origin of $, the dollar sign. Officially the dollar sign has one vertical stroke, but it is often written with two. Print a capital U and then print a capital S directly over it. It began as a bankers' short form, so that US 10.00 became $10.00 with the bottom of the loop of the U being dropped to speed the writing of the superimposed form. A Boston newspaper printed this explanation as early as 1847. Some claim it was Thomas Jefferson's personal abbreviation for denoting American currency. Others guess that it was a fancy figure-8 modified from the way it was struck on old Spanish coins called in English pieces of eight.

Coin

Coin derives from Old French *coing* 'angle, corner, wedge, metal stamp' and referred first to a die used for stamping money that did resemble a wedge, then the meaning was transferred to the stamped impress on the money, and finally to the piece of money itself. Old French coing came from Latin *cuneus* 'wedge.' When the ancient Assyrians wrote in unbaked, wet clay they impressed their letters in wedge-shaped strokes that later linguists called cuneiform.

Mint & Money

Both mint and money stem from the same Latin root. The queen of the gods in the Roman pantheon was Juno. Greek and Roman gods had many by-names; one of hers was Juno Moneta, which the Romans glossed as Juno the Warner, seeing in *moneta* their verb *moneo* 'I warn.' Admonish and monitor hold the same root. In the Roman mythological scheme of things, Juno did warn women and girls of various dangers. To later etymologists, it appears that Moneta may be the remnant of an Etruscan name that predates even the founding of Rome.

In any case, around 384 BC a worthy gent named Camillus had cornered the silver bullion market in ancient Rome. He paid for a huge temple to be built to honour Juno Moneta, and just coincidentally attached the first Roman mint to the temple. Ever accommodating in the goddess responsibilities she would take on at the drop of a toga, Juno became guardian of Rome's finances. On some Roman medals and coins, Juno carries the tools of the coin-maker: hammer, anvil, pincers, and dies.

Several hundred years later, certainly by the time of Cicero, *moneta* was the Latin noun for 'place where coins are made' and then for 'coinage.' The Latin word became *moneie* in Old French, and English borrowed it around AD 1290 as money. But earlier Anglo-Saxon monks knew *moneta* directly from their Latin studies, and put it into Old English in the eighth century as *mynit* 'coin, money,' which by Middle English was mynt 'place where money is coined' and the spelling evolved into the current "mint."

Penny

A penny is a mere flash in the pan. Old Norse *panna* 'cooking bowl' and Old High German *pfanne* 'broad, shallow, and usually open cooking vessel' probably are ultimate sources of the German word *pfennig* 'a penny' which itself has cognates like Old Norse *penningr*, Dutch *penning*, Old Frisian *panning*, and Old English *penig*. The etymological sense is likely 'something made in a pan' (like an early coin-maker's tray) or 'shaped like a pan.' Some linguists dispute this origin. But I think it's correct. Betcha a toonie!

TORONTO STREET SLANG

Two scraps of street lingo heard in Toronto are new to me. One was a synonym for petty theft: "the five-finger discount" and the other was similar to "take shank's mare," the very old English phrase to describe walking somewhere as opposed to another means of transportation. "Goin' by subway?" asked one student. "No," came the reply, "I'll take the shoelace express."

TORONTO WORDS & PLACE NAMES

The rest of Canada loves to loathe TO. Was it dubbed Hogtown due to a slather of piggeries and meat-packing plants makin' bacon, or, as invidious non-Torontonians claim, because Toronto hogs everything for itself? No one knows. Due to pioneer bad roads, it certainly was Muddy York when Upper Canada's first governor-general, John Graves Simcoe, laid out a little hamlet in 1793 by the harbour and called it York. The city was incorporated as Toronto in 1834. Now some residents say Trawnuh. As early as 1898 its Methodist piety and Anglican reserve earned it the nickname Toronto the Good. A vast block of the original site, some 251,000 acres from the Scarborough Bluffs west, had been purchased from the Mississauga people for 10 shillings, giving early credence to its reputation as a community of sharp dealers. The Wendat (Huron) place name Toronto was first applied to what is today Port Hope. Toronto probably means 'meeting place' in Wendat, because it was the trail-head for a land-and-canoe route that Aboriginal peoples used to get from Lake Ontario up to Lake Huron. Explorer Étienne Brûlé knew this trail as *Le passage de Terounto* in 1615. The first buildings were called Fort Rouillé, burned down in 1759. Its ruins were excavated on the present site of the Canadian National Exhibition on Toronto's lakeshore.

Bloor Street

Trendy, toney, and expensive shops line Bloor Street west of Yonge in Toronto. It's called the Mink Mile. A few blocks west is my favourite Toronto place nickname: a block of Hungarian restaurants that students from the nearby University of Toronto dubbed The Goulash Archipelago in the late eighties. An older tag was the Schnitzel Strip. Not to be confused with The Strip, which is Yonge Street's sleazy pinball haven between Gerrard and Dundas Streets. And don't confuse Toronto's Mink Mile with the Miracle Mile, which is cabbies' slang for a stretch of Danforth Avenue from Victoria Park to Coxwell, so named because, if cab drivers time their speed just right, they can get green lights for many blocks.

Cabbagetown

From 1860 to 1880 poor immigrants from Ireland and England lived in small garden lots in central Toronto. They grew cabbages and boiled them to eat, giving the area an aroma and a nickname. A perusal of old deeds makes clear that there were far more British newcomers than Irish ones in the first Cabbagetown. The greatest concentration of poor Irish was farther south in an area of Toronto once but no longer called Corktown.

Between the two World Wars, Cabbagetown became a slum. One native who wrote about working-class lives there was Hugh Garner. His novel *Cabbagetown* was published in 1950. Canadian painter Albert Franck put on canvas many scenes from Cabbagetown backyards and alleys during his career. Then, in the 1960s and 1970s, yuppie white-painters moved in and renovated with a passion, boosting real estate prices in the neighbourhood and changing forever the aura of the word *Cabbagetown*. Some urban professionals who work in the high-rise canyons of Bay Street live here and chuckle at their cohorts who must endure long traffic jams every morning as they drive in from the suburbs. Cabbagetowners can stroll to the office, hop a bus, or take a subway to work.

Other Toronto Nicknames

Ryerson Polytechnic University in central Toronto is widely ribbed as Rye High. York University's chilly setting farther north is The Tundra, while The University of Toronto's controversial Robarts Library building looks to many students like the place where Arnold Schwarzenegger's Terminator would live, had he been a medieval prince. The library has accumulated labels like Fort Book, The John, and Robo-Monster.

Parkdale in Toronto's west end has been christened Perkdale, because the prostitution and street drug trade once made Percodan pills a common medium of exchange.

A few street corners in TO have playful, alternative names. Young businesspeople thronging Yonge and Eglinton earn this yuppie crossroads the title of Yonge and Eligible. Queen and Roncesvalles in Parkdale is a hangout for prostitutes, so it's Queen and Raunchy. The most notorious road in Toronto for motorists is the DVP, the Don Valley Parkway, but widely known as the Death Valley Parkway, due to traffic fatalities and many serious vehicle accidents.

TOURTIÈRE

A *tourtière* is a shallow meat pie with onions, often flavoured with the traditional French medieval spice combo of cinnamon and cloves. In kitchens along the majestic Saguenay River, a *tourtière* can be quite a production, consisting of cubed meat, potatoes, onions baked in many layers in a deep, pastry-lined casserole: in other words, what would have been called a *cipaille* or *pâté de famille* in older days is here a *tourtière de Saguenay*. In 1836 in Québec, a *tourtière* was a pork pie. One local *tourtière* became a favourite of Scottish and British soldiers posted to the citadel at Québec City who then stayed on, buying outskirt farms and growing oats. Thus, in one Québec City *tourtière* oatmeal thickens the ground pork filling instead of the traditional French potatoes.

The food *tourtière* took its name from the utensil in which it was baked. The original *tourtière*, in French print by 1573, was a pie pan for baking *tourtes*. In old French cookery, a *tourte* was a round pastry pie with a pastry top and filled either with meat and vegetables if it was a savoury or with fruit and cream if it was a dessert *tourte*. This word stems from the street Latin phrase *tortus panis* 'a round of bread.' The word *tourtière* also names the mould used to make these pastry *tourtes*. This *tourtière* has an expandable circumference, can be made of porcelain, clay, or glass, and can serve as a pie dish, a tart mould, or a flan ring.

TOUTIN

Toutins, toutans, toutens, toutons, or towtents, are still on the home breakfast menu of some Newfoundlanders. Bread dough is made and set to rise with yeast at night. The next morning the dough is cut into small pieces and fried in pork fat. Hot molasses with a pad of butter melted in it might top the toutins that are served at breakfast to children off to school on a frosty winter morning. There are many varieties. Bits of bacon can be sprinkled on top. One toutin is flattened into a pancake form and wrapped around a sausage or a slice of bologna. Toutin may also refer to a pork cake, a bun made by mixing diced pork with flour, water, baking powder, and molasses. Toutins were common fare from a sealing ship's galley or done over a wood fire in a hunting camp. Sometimes molasses toutins and fat-back toutins would both be served at the same away-from-home meal.

TREE NAILS OF NEW BRUNSWICK

Eighteenth-century homesteaders did not have a ready supply of iron nails unless a blacksmith had set up a forge nearby. So, early New Brunswick building timbers were fastened together with wooden pegs dubbed in pioneer lingo "tree nails."

TRILLIUM, A.K.A. MOOSE-FLOWER OF NOVA SCOTIA

The great white trillium, *Trillium grandiflorum* (Botanical Latin, 'big-flowered'), is the floral emblem of Ontario. A common colonial name was wake-robin, because it blooms in spring. But much more frequently, in earlier diaries and pioneer letters home, the trillium was simply called a lily. In Nova Scotia, settlers dubbed it Moose-flower, according to the 1868 *Canadian Wild Flowers* by Catharine Parr Traill. One species on our West Coast is *Trillium ovatum*, or western wake-robin.

The Genus *Trillium* has more than thirty species, all of them with three-part leaves and flowers, hence the first root in the botanical name, namely *tri-*. The great Swedish botanist and founder of systematic botanical taxonomy, Carolus Linnaeus (1707–78), may have named the genus; and so the *Oxford English Dictionary* suggests that trillium is a Latinizing of the Swedish word for triplet, *trilling*. Maybe. There's no written proof of that. My informed etymological vote goes to this explanation. A member of the lily family, trillium might also be a shortening of *tri + lilium* (Latin, 'lily'), in other words a 'three-part lily.' It is certainly not, as many American botanical books state, from *triplum*, Latin for triple.

VENT-VIEW

This noun names a product first used in the Prince Edward Island potato business and now something most of us see every time we buy a bag of potatoes at a supermarket. A vent-view is a potato bag with plastic mesh covering a hole so that customers can see and palpate through the mesh the potatoes inside the bag.

WANGAN & WANIGAN

New Brunswick lumbermen used this raft or scow to transport to a new site personnel and camp supplies. The cook shack could be on the wagnan too with a floating mess hall, until facilities on shore were set up. Whites borrowed the term from local Algonkian-speaking peoples. In Ojibwa *wa'nikka'n* was a storage pit containing a cache of odds and ends that might be useful for trade. Montagnais has *atawangan* 'trade storage' related to *atawan* 'to trade.' The same Algonkian root appears in the name of the Ottawa people, the 'trading band' that gave its name to our capital city. In the Abnaki language *waniigan* is a 'pit trap' or 'a container for sundries.'

"Running the wangan" was taking a loaded boat downriver. In *Seven Rivers of Canada*, Hugh MacLennan writes of lumbering on New Brunswick's Saint John River: "Within three weeks the Wangan boat men clear the river of stray logs all the way from Beechwood to Maugerville."

A wangan box was a large chest in which New Brunswick lumberjacks kept clothing, pipes, tobacco, and other camp necessities. Out west, logging company stores were called wanigans where the logger could buy bush clothes and supplies. During the gold rushes wanigan was used to name a one-room shed on skids that was used as instant accommodation in boomtowns. Up north, huts mounted on sleds with runners and towable by Bombardiers were called wanigans. And the latest use of this all-purpose term can be found in a 1966 Western edition of *Eaton's Fall & Winter Catalogue*: "Natural sheepskin wannigans for wear under overboots." This wannigan is a short-laced, leather-soled boot. Adaptable wear. Adaptable word.

WEATHER RHYMES OF CANADA

Please note, readers, that these are weather rhymes here. Part Two of this book also contains the best printed sample to date of folk sayings about Canadian weather, expressions about weather quite different from these weather rhymes. Rhymes are meant to convey information about predicting weather. Weather folk sayings are often comic or satiric comments on how weather affects us adversely. Enjoy both!

1.

A summer fog for fair,
A winter fog for rain,
A fact most everywhere,
From Canso right to Maine.

2.
Red sky at night, sailors' delight.
Red sky at morning, sailors take warning.

The first weather rhyme is from Nova Scotia. The second is familiar to most Canadians. But how old is the latter one? Well, Jesus knew it! The Gospel according to Saint Matthew (King James' version, 16:2–3) reports that Christ began his rebuke of the Pharisees with these words: "When it is evening, ye say, it will be fair weather: for the sky is red. And in the morning, it will be foul weather today: for the sky is red and lowring. O ye hypocrites, ye can discern the face of the sky; but can ye not discern the signs of the times?" With no wish to profane Holy Writ, we today might fling that line at a TV weather person after some spectacularly inaccurate forecast.

How Old Are Weather Rhymes?

Just how old is the Gospel According to Saint Matthew? Some scholars say Matthew attained its present form, the koine Greek version, about AD 70. But we can find that very same red-sky weather saying more than four hundred years earlier, in fragments of the West's first book of weather forecasting written around 340 BC by the Greek philosopher Theophrastus. Although the text was composed in classical Greek, what now remains of the work is known by its Latin title *De signis tempestatum* or "Concerning the Signs of the Weather."

Check Out This Neat Tongue Twister Weather Rhyme & Say It Fast

Whether the weather be fine
Or whether the weather be not,
Whether the weather be cold
Or whether the weather be hot,
We'll weather the weather
Whatever the weather
Whether we like it or not.

Are Weather Rhymes Accurate?

So this red-sky weather rhyme is old. Are this and the Canadian weather rhymes we're going to examine precise and accurate? Sundry professors who teach meteorology and climatology dismiss most proverbial bits of weather lore. The rhymes have no general scientific validity because the weather rules they state have no universal application. Many a red-faced twilight has turned to rain. Many a rosy-fingered dawn has been the herald of a sunny morning. Yet the true believer in weather folklore, almanac predictions, and plant-and-animal weather signs will reply that sometimes these sayings hold true. Sometimes. Somewhere. The difficulty, especially for professional prognosticators like climatologists at Environment Canada, is that weather systems are too complex to predict accurately and fully in every instance.

Chaos Theory & Our Weather

Much of our natural world, including weather systems, is turning out to play by rules that are not linear, not always obedient to the laws of Newtonian physics. Chaos theory and the new science of complexity brand such systems as non-linear. The millions of variables that help make up these systems obey strange rules which scientists who study complexity are just barely beginning to understand. In chaos theory one such factor is called "sensitive dependence on initial conditions." It is impossible to measure weather conditions without some small errors. But in non-linear systems, as the equations play out in time, the magnitude of the initial small errors increases exponentially. M. Mitchell Waldrop, in his book *Complexity: The Emerging Science at the Edge of Order and Chaos*, gives this memorable example: "The equations that governed the flow of wind and moisture looked simple enough . . . until researchers realized that the flap of a butterfly's wings in Texas could change the course of a hurricane in Haiti a week later." Chaos theory forces home the truth that everything is connected, small changes don't stay small; the uncertainty of complex systems like world weather can make them quickly chaotic. Even powerful computer simulations of weather patterns, with thousands of variables fed in as data by the second, cannot produce totally accurate forecasts. Nor do weather systems behave in tidy obedience to all previous meteorological observations.

Have we roved too far from simple weather rhymes? I don't think so. For now we can be more sympathetic to the hapless TV weather guru whose computer-animated maps help but never tell all. Although casting a mildly skeptical eye on weather rhymes, we can still enjoy them for their tang and folksy resonance.

How Canadian Are These Rhymes?

Few of the rhymes in this chapter are Canadian in origin; all are Canadian in use. As the ancient roots of the red-sky saying show, some of the rhymes are thousands of years old. Others still heard in Canada were brought here by emigrants from the British Isles, although English cannot claim to be the originating tongue. Consider this weather maxim: "Under water, famine. Under snow, bread." In the temperate zone of the northern hemisphere where this truism holds, variant expressions include: "A year of snow, a year of plenty" and "A year of snow, crops will grow." David Phillips, senior climatologist at Environment Canada, in his November 1994 "Weather Wise" column in *Canadian Geographic* magazine, comments: "These [sayings] are pleasant ways of pointing out that a snowy winter provides enough moisture to assure good crops, and that a good covering of snow insulates against killing cold and the cycles of thawing and freezing, especially ruinous to winter grains." But the saying did not originate in English. We have it in medieval Italian and in this current Italian form too: *Sotto la neve pane, sotto l'acqua fame*. Earlier still is the Late Latin version: *Sub nive panis, sub aqua fames*.

These folkisms are remembered and passed down to sons and daughters because people who depend for their livelihood on weather, principally farmers and fishermen, have found them useful and psychologically comforting. In a world of climatic turmoil, even false surety propels the sower to cast his seed and the sailor to cast off. So shall we go now on a weather-rhyme tour of Canada.

Newfoundland

Nautical aphorisms abound on the bounding main. These are my favourites.

> A high dawn, look to your reef points.
> A red sun got water in his eye.
> When rain comes before the wind,
> Halyards, sheets, and reef-points mind.
> When the rain comes from the south,
> It blows the bait in the fishes' mouth.

> Mackerel sky and mares' tails,
> Warning sure for reefing sails.

The rhyme above is a variant of the British one below.

> Mackerel sky and mares' tails
> Make lofty ships carry low sails.

A "mackerel" sky is blotched with altocumulus and cirrocumulus clouds in patterns resembling the dorsal scales of that fish; "mares' tails" are long, slender cirrus clouds.

Sea birds keeping near the land,
Tell a storm is near at hand.
But flying seaward out of sight,
You may stay and fish all night.

When a snipe bawls, the lobster crawls.
When herring rush to the shore,
The wind will blow some more.

When caplin eat sand,
Their bodies to ballast,
Then heavy seas stand,
And the fisher's hand—is callused.

When the sun is drawing water,
Bide home with wife and daughter.

Patrick Devine in *Devine's Folklore of Newfoundland* explains the last maxim: "When the yellow streamers called 'sun hounds' surround the sun after its rising and extend right down to the surface of the ocean the fishermen say: 'The sun is drawing water and a storm is pending.'"

Prince Edward Island

Some of the weather rhymes I first heard from Islanders are of course found in other parts of Canada. This holds true for most of these widespread sayings.

From Rustico to Summerside,
A moon-ring will rain betide.

When the wind is west, the fish bite best.
Even from away, put a boat in the bay.

The gull comes against the rain.

When the wind is in the north,
The fisherman goes not forth.

If the sun goes pale to bed,
'Twill rain tomorrow, it is said.

A fair day in winter is the mother of a storm.

Nova Scotia

A summer fog for fair,
A winter fog for rain,
A fact most everywhere,
From Canso right to Maine.

Rainbow to windward, foul fall the day.
Rainbow to leeward, damp runs away.

Snails on the road, water for the toad.
(It will rain tomorrow.)

When the mist creeps up the hill,
Fisher, out and try your skill.
When the mist begins to nod,
Fisher, then put up your rod.

Evening grey and morning red,
Make the sailor hang his head.

Rain before seven,
Lift before eleven.

If the goats come home in files,
Get your fish in covered piles.

New Brunswick

Pale moon rains,
Red moon blows,
White moon neither rains nor snows.

Compare the rhyme above with this non-rhyming one from nineteenth-century Italy, still heard in the Italian countryside:

Luna bianca, tempo bello;
Luna rosa, vento;
Luna pallida, pioggia.

Translation of the Italian:
'A clear moon, nice weather;
A pink moon, wind;
A pale moon, rain.'

Onion skins very thin,
Mild winter coming in.
Onion skins thick and tough,
Coming winter cold and rough.

When the stars begin to huddle,
Soon the earth will be a puddle.

This implies that when a high mist obscures the smaller stars and makes the large ones blurry, almost like a cluster of stars, then rain is on the way.

Sound travelling far and wide,
A stormy day will betide.

Québec

These are not rhymes but are Québec sayings about the weather.

Le diable est aux vaches.
'The devil's in the cows' portends a change of weather.

Il fait si froid que quand je crache par terre, le crachat gèle avant d'arriver!
'It's so cold when I spit, it freezes before it reaches the ground.'

Chez moi l'hiver y fait tellement froid que la flamme des bougies fige!
'Where I live, winter's so cold that candle flames freeze.'

Chez nous, y fait tellement froid que la neige émigre vers le sud!
'Around here it's so cold the snow takes off for Florida too.'

Il fait tellement froid chez nous qu'on est obligé de coucher dans le congélateur pour se réchauffer!
'It's so cold we gotta sleep in the fridge to warm up.'

Ontario

When the woods murmur, and the Great Lakes roar,
Then close your windows, and stay on shore.
When poplar shows its underwear,
The clouds do rain and thunder bear.

On the approach of a storm, aspens and poplars do turn their leaves up due to changes in barometric pressure that cause alterations in water pressure within the vascular system of the leaf. I first heard that little scamp of a rhyme at a United Church summer camp in Muskoka.

When the dew is on the grass,
Rain will never come to pass.

Where the firefly lights his lamp,
The air is always warm and damp.

But this saying is disproved by dry midsummer nights in Ontario when the winged nocturnal beetles of the *Lampyridae* family produce their flickering flashes by the intermittent oxidation of the biochemical luciferin. They flash to attract mates.

When the glass falls low,
Prepare for a blow.
When it rises high,
Let kites go fly.

This barometric ditty has meteorological truth on its side. Perhaps that's why it is so obscure and infrequently quoted?

If you don't like the weather in Toronto,
blame Queen's Park.

(Queen's Park in Toronto is the location of the Ontario legislature.)

Manitoba

If you don't like the weather in Winnipeg,
you're out of luck.

When the grasshopper sings near,
The weather will be hot and clear.

When fleas do very many grow,
Then surely it will rain or snow.

All signs fail in dry weather.

Saskatchewan

If twilight's ducks and rabbits,
Don't let them bring bad habits.

Fluffy cumulonimbus clouds (ducks and rabbits) in the late afternoon sky make the harvesting farmer stop work early (a bad habit), because ducks and rabbits foretell a glorious day tomorrow. But the weather proverb reminds us how quickly changeable Prairie weather may be. Is it valid for Saskatchewan? I can't say except to note that this rhyme was first quoted to me in the cafeteria at CBC Regina.

Calm weather in June sets corn in tune.
No weather's ill if the wind be still.

Alberta

When Chinook blues above the foothills show,
Then soon warm winds will melt the snow.

Chinook "blues" are the archlike cloud formations, often seen as a bright blue strip over the Rockies that stands out from the darker, overcast conditions that surround it. The Chinook is a dry, moderating, westerly wind, common in winter and spring, especially in the eastern foothills of the Rockies from Peace River country all the way down to Colorado, and occasionally over much of our Prairies. The word pops up in Canadian English all over the west. Recent arrivals in Calgary who experience their first balmy spell may succumb to Chinook fever. Following a long tradition in the expansion of the English wordstock, the noun has become a verb. "It chinooked last night, went up 40 degrees in two hours. Had to toss all my blankets off. She was blowin' warm as summer."

The higher the clouds, the fairer the weather.

Yukon & Nunavut & The Territories

When the wind is blowing in the North
No fisherman should set forth,
When the wind is blowing in the East,
'Tis not fit for man nor beast,
When the wind is blowing in the South
It brings the food over the fish's mouth,

When the wind is blowing in the West,
That is when the fishing's best!

Rain before seven, fine before eleven.

British Columbia

If you don't like the weather in Vancouver, wait a minute.

If God had really wanted people to live in the Lower Mainland, we'd have been born with umbrellas sticking out of our heads. (Heard on the street in Richmond, British Columbia.)

Rain, rain, go away,
Like a B.C. premier in a day.

So ends our scamper across the fields of weather-rich Canada. If you have local weather rhymes and sayings to share with fellow Canadians, please email them to me at canadiansayings@mountaincable.net

To conclude, here is a general rhyme to keep in mind:

Some are weather-wise, some are otherwise.

WHORE'S EGG

Something no lobster fisherman or any commercial fisherman wants to see in his nets, a whore's egg is a type of sea urchin, a sea-thistle, a spiny shellfish also called Aristotle's lantern. In his *Dictionary of Prince Edward Island English*, T.K. Pratt ingeniously suggests a derivation from French *oursin* 'sea urchin' combined with English sea egg. *Oursin* stems from Latin *ursinus* 'bearlike' possibly from the bristly nature of a sea urchin's spines, which resembled stiff, matted hair in the fur of a bear cub.

WHY I'M NOT A WORD COP: AN ESSAY AGAINST NITPICKERS

I'm a word-nut, not a word cop. Nothing spoken or written in English is alien to my linguistic interest. Word-nuts want to describe, not prescribe, how humans use language. Some readers of my books urge me to include long lists of bad grammar and words misused by Canadians. But quarrelsome language pedants have their ordained venue. Their fretful quibbles appear in letters-to-the-editor in many of our newspapers. You know their peevish tone: "Proper English is in decline. I have been much troubled of late about the wanton use of the semi-colon in the novels of Jane Urquhart. If only everyone would write and speak precisely as I do, the virginal purity of our noble tongue would be preserved in its ancient and pristine form." Well, first, virginity is something most healthy human beings don't want to preserve forever. Second, there never was, nor is there now, a pure English. Our language began as a West Germanic dialect transported to England around AD 450. Over the next fifteen hundred years this dialect grew into a language as it borrowed and was influenced by Old

Scandinavian loan words, Norman-French vocabulary, and scholarly Latin and Greek. English was—may it always be!—the great thief of tongues. It grabbed new words and concepts whenever they appeared useful.

Word cops pine for an English mummified in amber, like some Jurassic mosquito. They pine for a golden age of unchanging literacy where perfumed verbal dandies exchanged exquisite ripostes in Shakespearean blank verse, while outside their mullioned windows the profundum vulgum trudged to its loathsome chore of growing the dandies' food, serving it to them, and cleaning up after the dandies consumed it. Word cops would like to stop language from changing. In a world where social change is fast and frightening, so they seem to say, we'll carp and cavil and try to prevent English, at least as we learned it, from any alteration. But words don't work that way. If the spirit of a living language could give tongue to its quintessence, it would shout: "Alive from lips to lips of humankind I go awinging!" In that translabial exchange, living language "morphs" and "polymorphs," in a rich sea change caused by usage through time by smaller and larger groups of speakers, often separated by geographical, political, and social distance.

That change produces dialects and varieties, hybrid speech and writing whose diversity is its glory, whose Protean habit makes it a joy to study.

Language change is not shoddy slippage. Change

is programmed into the complex systems that comprise a language. It is inevitable, natural, linguistically healthy. The languages we can study through their history begin with small vocabularies and complex syntax and grammar, and then evolve toward larger vocabularies and simpler syntax and grammar. English has been so evolving for a thousand years. The only languages that do not change are dead languages. Word cops want English to be dead. For when a language is all rouged and lip-sewn and pickled in formaldehyde like some glum stiff in a funeral parlour, why, then it will never alter and present new words and grammatical ploys to the horrified eyes and ears of the word cops. These fussy pontificators would enjoy life much more if they would embark on a study of some dead tongue, not Latin and Classical Greek which can be studied to see how "dead" languages can be "alive" in modern vocabularies, no, but, say, ancient Egyptian. Learn hieroglyphics instead, you defenders of English against change, and then curl up for a comfy evening with *The Book of the Dead*.

Here is a letter bitching about someone who has had the effrontery to use a new verb. The miscreant had written: "We'll brainpick in the morning session, and present formal reports in the afternoon." "Brainpick" is a fresh, terse verb formed, like many in the history of our language, by compressing a longer verbal phrase 'to pick one's brain' into tighter form. Delightful! But not to the letter writer who "could find it in no dictionary." Awww. Maybe, if it gains wider usage, the dictionary will have to include the vivid brainpick in a futute edition? Might that be the chief function of a dictionary? To describe how we currently use our language? A dictionary is not some immutable linguistic pattern-book against which all speech and writing must be measured. Unfortunately, that is how word cops use dictionaries, as a Procrustean bed. In Greek mythology Procrustes was a sadistic bandit who kidnapped travellers and made them fit into his special bed. If they were too tall, he cut off their feet. If they were too short, he stretched them on the rack that was his bed. Word cops like to do this to other people's varying use of English.

But the word cops are wrong. English glories in variety. To paraphrase the Bible, in the house of language there are many Englishes. Only the impaired are deaf to the delight of Cockney, the honey of Jamaican English, the word joy of Newfoundland talk, the humorous practicality of Prairie phrases, the peculiar lilt of Ottawa Valley speech, the local words like "skookum" that sometimes brighten chat with a person from British Columbia's Lower Mainland.

Word cops are snobs too. What their shrill complaints hide is their prejudice against all whom they perceive to be not of their class, and often not of their race. These elitist moaners huddle together in the warm certainty that they alone use correct

English, and all the other, lower orders write and speak twaddle. One of my tests for word cops is to read their plaintive missives and see if I can imagine the writers of such letters throwing down their pens, turning off their emailing keyboards, and going to volunteer at literacy programs in their neighbourhoods that teach basic reading and writing to the functionally illiterate. Ha!

Consider this dialect phrase: "Is you is or is you ain't usin' English?" Did you understand what it means? Yes. Is it grammatical? In spite of what word cops might answer, it is grammatical. In Ebonic grammar, a subset of English. A basic grammar may even be genetically inherited. We may be born with a neurological "grid" that predisposes humans to think grammatically. "Is you is or is you ain't" happens to be a dialectical use of the verb "to be" in certain interrogative instances. Now, certainly, it is not the grammar of Standard English. But SE began as a dialect too, as the speech and writing of a group of powerful, educated Londoners centuries ago. There is a complicated, binding relationship between dialect and snobbery, as George Bernard Shaw pointed out at the turn of the century in his drama *Pygmalion*, later turned into the Broadway musical *My Fair Lady*. Shaw had fun with the fact that even a Cockney flower girl could rise to the heights of British society if she did one small thing: switch her verbal codes from Cockney to those of the ruling British elite. The lesson of *Pygmalion* is still valid.

Use your natal dialect, but beware. If you or your children wish to advance into the ruling, professional elite, you will have to learn Standard English. If school does not make you a graduate literate in Standard English, you may well be doomed to flip burgers and push mops. A life will be lost, not only a life of earning, but also a life of learning. You must acquire Standard English in order to learn what the modern world most values: the ability to keep learning, because most knowledge worth having will be expressed in a formal standard variety of your native tongue. The average person is capable of, and usually does learn at least two dialects: his home speech and his standard language.

I remember being made painfully aware of my own southern Ontario rural dialect on my first day of college. I promised to meet someone on Saturday night. But I said, according to her, "Sair-dee" night, using a rural Canadianism, quite common too in British dialects, wherein intervocalic *t* is replaced first by a glottal stop and then sometimes the stop disappears completely in a glide as the two, now contiguous, vowels blend into each other. Nowadays I still occasionally say "Sair-dee," but instead of blushing, I smile. That's me and that's my idiolect, my own private mixture of dialect and standard language.

Insulting a person's dialect is snotty and often racist. On the other hand, a dialect speaker who wants to better his or her chances is foolish to remain ignorant of Standard English. All social, ethnic, and regional dialects of English have their validity. I draw the line at schools that preach total freedom: no spelling, no grammar, no reading—just let the pupils speak in whatever dialect they brought to school in the first place. But, even that is permissible, as long as the teacher points out to pupils and parents that this refusal to master SE will handicap their children. In *Paradigms Lost*, critic John Simon wrote: "Everyone has a right to his ignorance and no one is compelled to become educated. But everyone is then also entitled to suffer the consequences of choosing not to become educated."

Dialects suffer many prejudices. Dialects are branded as rural, old-fashioned, substandard, corrupted, and ignorant. They are not. But they won't help you get a job at IBM.

Of course, human nature being what it is—an urge to power—users of dialect can also be crafty in exploiting the guilt of SE speakers. I once attended a public lecture at Convocation Hall on the central campus of the University of Toronto in order to hear a famous British writer talk about her work. A few minutes into her fascinating talk, a member of the audience rose to interrupt her with these exact words: "You oppressin' me by using big words I don't know." The writer looked down from her podium with a friendly smile and replied: "The solution to your problem is the use of a book called a dictionary." I applauded.

Language is rules. But language is also play, and from playful use of language arise neologies. Dialect is a lush seed-bed of new words, from which the standard language often plucks fresh terms to invigorate its vocabulary. I coined a clumsy neology today: "deficitcation," an act of excretion on an entire country and way of life in order to rid that country of a deficit. It won't last. But neither did "lunain" coined in 1971 when man landed on the moon. Lunain was the lunar surface, as terrain is the earthly one. The word cops among us would banish all such playfulness and variety from English. To thwart them, I shall remain a word-nut. Although grim rule-keepers armed with nutcrackers pound at the gates of linguistic diversity, let us keep them in their place, forever outside, envious noses pressed to the bars, while, inside, the noisy dance of words rings forth, until the day lights and the shadows flee away.

WINNIPEG

The sometimes cold centre of this windy city is Portage and Main and is often nicknamed Portage and Pain. At the corner of Corydon and Osbourne in "the Peg" several roads intersect causing great confusion for bus drivers and pedestrians, and earning the crossroads the moniker "Crazy Corners." The Granola Belt of Winnipeg along Wolseley and in Osbourne Village was home to hippies and vagrants in the sixties and early seventies, but now it is yuppified and waspy. The Forks of the Red and Assiniboine Rivers where local settlement began are a must-see part of Winnipeg with museums and markets and pleasant walkways along the riverbanks.

WINNIPEG JAMBUSTER

This is a term for any jelly doughnut consumed in the vicinity of Portage and Main. On numerous field tests, your humble deponent, the author, has consumed coffee and jelly doughnuts in this very locale. While the repast was a pleasant interval of repose amidst the lip-flapping, book-flogging whirl of radio and television interviews, no discernible particularity of taste in the said jelly doughnuts was detected.

That's our tromp through some lively Canadian words. Just around the page in the second part of this book is a joyous and funny field of folk sayings and snappy Canadian one-liners.

PART TWO
Canadian Sayings

1. ABLE TO ENJOY LIFE

1. I'm so happy I could break out in cartwheels and roll all over myself.

   — *Loretta Sherren, Fredericton, New Brunswick*

2. The puck is going my way. *La rondelle roule pour moi.*
3. She's riding the gravy train with biscuit wheels!
4. Dance me out the window and we'll boogie on a moonbeam.
5. Grinnin' like a butcher's dog.
6. I got five shots on goal and bad luck's penalty box is full.

2. ADVICE TO A PERSON PICKING THEIR NOSE

1. When you hit grey matter, stop.

- Grey matter would be brains and that could get really sticky.

3. ALL IS NOT WELL

1. There's something black in the lentils.

- Heard in Toronto and Vancouver, this is a literal translation of the Hindi colloquial idiom '*daal mein kuchh kaala hai,*' which is an Indian way of saying there's something fishy going on. The earliest use of the phrase I remember is from the 1975 film *Prem Kahani*, which featured an Anglicized character who was fond of pointing out that there was 'something black in the daal.' The phrase is sometimes rendered in English as 'something black in the lentil soup.'

4. ANGER

1. She was some choked off.

- In our Maritime Provinces, this saying means that she was very angry.

5. ANNOYANCE

1. Go tell your mother she wants you.

- This is one of the classic public school dismissal lines when you are trying to get rid of a mouthy geek or a creepy nerdlet. If a nerdlet is a little nerd, then we know what a geeklet is!

2. Oh, that really gives me the double-edged pip!

- Elizabeth Creath of Thessalon, Ontario, writes, "My dad came from Ireland and my mother was born in Manitoba to parents who had come from Germany in the late 1800s or early 1900s. These were sayings in our family. 'That just gives me the pip' would be said of any annoying situation. My mother would embroider this as 'the early morning pip,' 'the double-edged pip,' or 'the everlasting pip.' Once when mother was particularly put out, one of us kids said, 'I guess this gave you the double-edged, starts-early-in-the-morning-and-lasts-forever pip, eh, Mom?'"

The origin of this particular use of the word *pip* is startling. It refers to a disease of chickens which veterinarians call infectious coryza of poultry. It also affects members of the hawk family. Pip produces thick white mucus in a chicken's throat and white scale on its tongue, so the bird eventually cannot ingest food properly and simply pines away.

A version of this word for this specific disease of chickens appears in almost every language of Europe. In Middle Dutch it was *pippe,* in Middle English and Middle Low German *pip*. 'To give a person the pip' meaning 'to annoy that person' has been an expression in English for at least four hundred years! In Spanish, it's *pepita*, in French *pepie* or *pépie*, in modern German *Pips*, in older German the delightfully plosive *pfipfs*. In Late and Popular Latin and early Italian it was *pipita*, derived from standard Latin *pituita* 'slime.' So pip has the same root as our modern anatomical term *pituitary gland*. That story belongs to the next paragraph.

The Romans inherited from ancient Greek medical theory the belief that the brain produced snot (Latin, *pituita*) which was discharged from the nose when one sneezed. The Greek philosopher and scientist Aristotle thought the brain produced this mucus to help cool the inside of the head! A sixteenth-century Belgian Andreas Vesalius, a great pioneer of anatomy, first named the organ the pituitary gland because he thought that's where nasal mucus was made.

Two other common English expressions feature the word. To get the pip is to contract any vague malaise or depressive illness. To have the pip is to be low in spirits, morose, or depressed.

3. I have one nerve left and you're on it.

- A mom might say this to a pestering child who is "getting on her nerves."

4. That noise annoys an oyster.

- Sometimes sayings are almost like tongue-twisters. They are made up because they sound really cool. This is one. It means: Be quiet! I'm thinking and possibly conceiving pearls of wisdom.

6. ATHLETES—HOCKEY VERSUS FIGURE SKATING

1. Too much Barbara Ann Scott and not enough hockey!

- Patti Stockton of Victoria, British Columbia, writes: "This was an expression I heard my late father, Sam Stockton, use when we were at hockey games in Drumheller, Alberta. I understood him to mean the players were spending too much time skating around in a fancy manner and not enough time hustling the puck."

Barbara Ann Scott was one of the first great female sports stars of Canada. Barbara won gold in the 1948 Olympics as the champion figure skater of the world. Scott won her gold medal on a puck-dented outdoor rink in St. Moritz, Switerland. The night before, the men's gold-medal hockey game between Canada and Czechoslovakia had seen Canada win big. But the ice surface the next morning was a mess. In 1948 there was no Zamboni to shave the blade ruts and smooth the ice. Barbara Ann Scott skated superbly anyway.

Barbara was born in Ottawa and started skating at the age of six, training eight hours a day at Ottawa's Minto Club. Her Olympic victory made her the most famous and most admired woman in Canada, both for her athletic and balletic skating skill and for the grace and charm and Canadian humility with which she conducted herself after her amazing wins. She was the first living Canadian woman to have a toy named after her. The Reliable Toy Company brought out a Barbara Ann Scott doll, and it sold in the thousands all across Canada at the end of the 1940s and well into the 1950s. So, this expression may be mocking, but the reality of Barbara Ann Scott's physical talent shines through our Canadian sports history. Barbara is in the Canadian Sports Hall of Fame, the American Sports Hall of Fame, and the International Hall of Fame.

7. BAD AIM

1. He couldn't hit a bull in the behind with a handful of wheat.

- Used south of Riding Mountain National Park, in Rossburn, Manitoba, this saying described bad stickhandling in a local hockey game. In other parts of the prairies, it is often a jocular insult among hunters. I picked this up from a listener when I was a guest on Bill Turner's radio show on CKLQ in Brandon, Manitoba.

8. BAD LUCK

1. The chances are slim and none, and slim is visiting Alberta.
2. *Comme la misère sur le pauvre monde.*

- "When misfortune falls hard upon anyone, it falls 'like misery on poor folk,'" writes Lucie Lafontaine of St-Joseph-du-Lac in Québec.

3. You're a day late and a dollar short.
4. Darn! If it's not fleas, it's worms.

- A dog's life awaits many of us.

5. If it ain't the Devil, it's his brother.
6. That's life in the putty factory.

- Fate is fickle. It bends and turns just like putty in your hands or when it's being manufactured in the putty factory.

9. BE CAREFUL!

1. Either look where you're goin' or go where you're lookin'.

• Stacey B. writes, "When I was a child my father, who grew up in Winnipeg in the 1920s, had a saying that has stuck with me to this day. If someone (usually me) was looking in one direction while walking in another, and inevitably would bump into something or someone, he would say 'Either look where you're goin', or go where you're lookin'.' This saying still makes me laugh, and I use it with my kids now."
— *Anastasia Brockbank, Burlington, Ontario*

10. BEAVER FEVER OR BUSH SICK

1. Question: What happened to Mike up north?
Answer: He got beaver fever real bad.

• Beaver fever was Canadian pioneer slang for giardiasis, a usually not-too-serious invasion of the human small intestine by a creepy little parasite called *Giardia*, a protozoan with a slimy sucking disc on its stomach by means of which it attaches itself to the microvilli that protrude from the epithelial lining of its host's intestine. The host of the *Giardia* parasite is usually one of the higher vertebrates, including humans.

Microvilli are little hairlike cylinders, protoplasmic projections sticking out of some cells on our inner intestinal lining. Microvilli increase the surface area of the cell and thus make it a more efficient absorber of food nutrients passing over the gut lining on their way through our intestine.

Giardiasis can also be spread by contaminated water, contaminated food, and by personal contact. Washing of the hands with good strong soap after every trip outdoors prevents most people from ever getting beaver fever.

If one does succumb to giardiasis, symptoms include mild to severe diarrhea, nausea, anorexia, and weight loss. In otherwise healthy people, the symptoms last for two to six weeks. Some patients have no symptoms. Backpackers, hikers, and campers who drink unfiltered, untreated water may contract beaver fever. You know the type. It's their first day at camp and they see their first mountain stream gurgling merrily down a hillside. Hey, it's country water! It must be fresh and clean and pure! No, maybe not. So don't drink it.

Some people recover with bed rest and by drinking plenty of fluids to counteract the loss of water during severe diarrhea. Or, your doctor may prescribe one of several prescription drugs available to treat giardiasis, including metronidazole and tinidazole. Nitazoxanide is used too in the management of giardiasis in children.

11. BEHIND THE TIMES

1. *Ce gars-là est tellement con que l'autre jour sa blonde lui a demandé d'acheter une télé couleur pis y a répondu: De quelle couleur?*

- "That guy is so stunned that the other day when his girlfriend asked him to buy a colour TV, he asked, 'What colour?'"

12. BIG & TALL

1. He could go moose hunting with a gad.

- This expression from Newfoundland implies that he is a big man, big enough to hunt a moose with a little twig. A gad is a twig thin and pliant enough to be used as a tie. In Newfoundland, caught trout were strung on gads. A fisherman might tie a gad to a seal's flipper to haul it from his boat to his home.

13. BIRTH ORDER

1. Second clutch.

- This referred to a child born very late in the family. Laura Lee Life of British Columbia writes, "In the pre-pill era, women nearing or just entering menopause not infrequently found themselves pregnant for one last time, when the rest of the kids were either heading out on their own or very near it. 'Second clutch' was a commonly understood term in our district. A hen that set her eggs early in the spring was quite capable of rearing her chicks, sending them off on their own at the appropriate time, say, around eight to ten weeks, then laying and hatching a second clutch of eggs in the late summer or early fall. As farm chickens, especially in the temperate climate of Vancouver Island, were free range, if not semi-feral, it was a common enough scenario. Bothersome too; the chicks would be too young to butcher or start laying until midwinter, and in the spring, the young roosters were liable to get ideas above their stations and become a real nuisance to the flock rooster, and to the owner as well."

— *Laura Lee Life, British Columbia*

14. BLABBERMOUTHS

1. He'd talk a hole into an iron kettle.
   - This lively old folk saying is still heard today in the province of Prince Edward Island.
2. Save your breath to cool your porridge.
   - This sounds like the sort of dour injunction that might waft across a Scottish kitchen on a damp morning.
3. He's like a teapot—all spout and steam.

   — *Loretta Sherren, Fredericton, New Brunswick*
4. The cow that bellows most, forgets her calf quickest.
   - This is a loan translation from German heard in the Kitchener-Waterloo area of southwestern Ontario.
5. He'll talk your ear off, and then ask you how you lost it.
6. A closed mouth catches no flies.

15. BOONDOCKS OR WAY OUT IN THE WOODS

1. Q: Where do they live?

A: It doesn't have a name. It's a wide place on the TransCanada highway.

- You can't find a Canadian hamlet much smaller or more remote than that.

2. *Traverse des bourgots.*

- This neat dismissal in Québec French describes a tiny community as "a place where moose-callers cross the road." *Bourgot* is the object itself used to make a mooselike call. But here, in a rhetorical figure called metonymy, the meaning of the word itself is transferred from the object to the persons who use the object, in this case, moose calls. The comic place name implies a location far out in the bush.

3. *Paris du bois.*

- Translation: 'Paris out in the woods somewhere.' I heard this in Québec, referring satirically to a very small town in the region of *la Beauce*.

4. You know you're in the boonies, if you cut your grass and find a car.

5. He lives so far back in the woods, he has to come out to hunt.

   — *Paula Steeves, New Brunswick*

6. They lived so far back in the woods, they used to get the Saturday night hockey game on Wednesday.

7. They live so far back in the woods, they have to pump daylight in through a pipe.

   — *David and Moira Parker, Calgary, Alberta*

8. You're in the boondocks if your father walks you to school because he's in the same grade.
9. He was born north of the checkerboard.

- Bert Spencer of Bowmanville heard this around Wiarton, Ontario, and says it harks back to the recent past when the local snowplow did not go beyond a checkerboard sign posted by the side of a road. These checkerboard signs were a common sight on the Ontario roads of my own youth in the early 1950s. The expression could be used to suggest either an isolated, rural upbringing or to hint that the subject of the sentence was inbred.

10. They roll the sidewalks up in this town every night at 7 p.m.

16. BOREDOM

1. Been there. Done that. Got that maple-leaf T-shirt.
2. I already had an apple out of that bag.

17. BUCK TEETH

1. She could chew an apple through the back of a hockey net.

— *Jason Charlebois, Sault Ste. Marie, Ontario*

18. BUMPKIN OR HICK

1. *Amène pas tes vaches en ville.*

- This Québécois saying from the Gatineau Hills advises the listener not to be such a hayseed and means "don't bring your cows to town."

— *Wes Darou, Cantley, Québec*

19. CALM DOWN

1. Cool your jets!
   —*J. Kipp, Waterloo, Ontario*
2. Don't get your teakettle in a tizzy.
3. Don't get your bowels in an uproar.
4. Don't get your knickers in a knot.

Variants: Don't get your knickers in a twist; don't get your knickers in a bunch.

Knickers were originally knickerbockers, loose-fitting breeches gathered at the knee and worn by men and boys playing sports and worn informally too. American author Washington Irving invented the word as a playful nom de plume in his *History of New York* published in 1809 and attributed to one Diedrich Knickerbocker. Knickerbocker was already in use in New England slang as a mildly racist term for any descendant of the original Dutch settlers in New York State. After Irving's book enjoyed great popularity, knickerbocker was applied to men's sports baggies, and then to bloomerlike nineteenth-century undergarments for women. After that, the term found its way to England where knickers is still a common general term for women's underwear.

—*Jane A. Corbett, Ottawa*

5. Don't get your bloomers in an uproar.

- The word *bloomers* was once a slangy synonym for knickers. But true bloomers were loose-fitting women's trousers cinched at the ankle, later at the knee, worn like Turkish trousers with a short jacket and a full, knee-length skirt. They were part of a daily costume for women advocated by a nineteenth-century American women's-rights reformer, Amelia Jenks Bloomer (1818–94). She called her system "Rational Dress," a common-sense reaction to excesses of both frippery and discomfort in female fashions of the mid-nineteenth century.

20. CANADA OUTDOORS

1. How big are the mosquitoes in Quebec?

Au chalet de ma grand-mère, les maringouins sont tellement gros qu'ils doivent se mettre à genoux pour nous piquer dans le front!

- "At my grandmother's cottage, the mosquitoes are so big they have to get on their knees just to bite us in the forehead."

21. CANADIAN ACQUAINTANCE

1. We've ehed but we ain't shook.

- We have exchanged comments like "Cold, eh?" but we don't know each other well.

22. CANADIAN ADVICE

1. Love many; trust few; always paddle your own canoe.

23. CANADIAN ARMY SLANG

1. Black Cadillacs.

- These are combat boots. For example, "Our vehicle broke down but we reached our objective via Black Cadillac. That is, we walked." *—Dave Harris, Petawawa, Ontario*

2. Don't be a dentist with those.

- "This refers to cigarettes when a soldier takes a smoke out of his pack. Someone will use this expression to suggest the soldier not be stingy like a dentist who takes only one tooth out per visit. Instead, the soldier ought to pass the cigarettes around. I've had this used on me while buying a beer at the mess," writes Dave Harris of Camp Petawawa, Ontario. Of course, if the author as fussbudget may intrude, it would be better not to smoke any of them, since cigarettes are cancer-causing tubes of poison that turn your teeth yellow, your lungs black, and your future cloudy.

3. Seen.

- *Seen* is a term used a lot and simply means 'I understand.' Dave Harris writes, "The expression comes from determining arcs of fire in a defensive position. The section commander will gather his group and pick out a readily available landmark on the horizon. He will then hold up his hand and measure left or right, to a smaller landmark and announce the range. It will go something like, 'Tall white birch at twelve o'clock (directly in front) 400 yards, four fingers right at pile of rocks.' The group will mimic his actions and

when they find the rocks, they will shout, 'Seen!' It is now used for any conversation in which someone is explaining something to you and you say 'seen' or 'understood.' Civilians (civvies) get totally confused when this comes up in conversation, and they start looking around for what they think you are looking at."
— *Dave Harris, Petawawa, Ontario*

24. CANADIAN COFFEE

1. I'm going to go grab a dead Tim's.

- This is Winnipeg slang for buying a cup of coffee at Tim Hortons. The chain of coffee, doughnut, and sandwich shops bears the name of a famous NHL hockey player. I heard this saying on the Winnipeg campus of the University of Manitoba and found its use by some students to be a healthy, skeptical counterbalance to the oceans of coffee advertisements that wash over us all day long on Canadian media. It's smart to be a bit cynical about advertising. If you want the company's side of things (and it's only fair to offer it too) you'll find the full story of the founder and the franchising at this website: http://collections.ic.gc.ca/wentworth/timhorto.htm

25. CANADIAN DIRECTIONS

1. She'll be up the line a tad.

- Usually this Ottawa Valley locution means some place is located farther west or northwest of

Ottawa, well into the Ottawa Valley. It might refer to a survey line, concession line, rail line, but most probably is a direct reference to the fabled Opeongo line, a modest roadway, a settlement road that begins at Farrell's Landing on the Ottawa River. It was planned to end at Opeongo Lake in Algonquin Park, but never stretched that far. The road, today no more than a pleasant country lane, fades away near Whitney, Ontario. In the middle of the nineteenth century, such roads were built to lure pioneers to settle the remoter parts of Ontario. Like so many Victorian lures to Canadian immigrants, exaggeration was involved. For instance, "free land for magnificent farms" was promised to newcomers. How this farming bounty was to occur on the thin rocky soil of the Opeongo Hills remains a mystery. The many ghost towns now drooping sadly beside the Opeongo Road attest to these false promises and to the fact that gung-ho folks tried to farm or provide services for lumbermen but failed, packed up, and moved away forever. Yes, a few Ottawa Valley lumber merchants found valuable stands of white pine in the forested hills of Opeongo. But after the pine was harvested, nothing much remained to keep people tied to this hardscrabble stretch of Ontario.

— *Sarah Elvidge, Yarmouth, Nova Scotia*

26. CANADIAN FRIENDLINESS

1. Canadians are so friendly they'll loan you their behinds and never sit down again.

- Friendship can be carried too far.
  — *Len Ross, North Bay, Ontario*

27. CANADIAN NAVY EXPRESSIONS

1. You're a waste of perfectly good rations.

- Several correspondents remember this from basic training at HMCS/CFB Cornwallis in Nova Scotia. The main function of Cornwallis was the training of new entry seamen in the Canadian Navy. Due to a convenient political decision, the base at Cornwallis was closed in 1994. It's now an industrial park with approximately fifty-two businesses operating on site. The only military presences are the Pearson Peacekeeping Centre, Sea Cadet Training during the summer months, and the HMCS/CFB Cornwallis Military Historical Association.

28. CANADIAN POLITICIANS

1. *Jean Chrétien a la bouche tellement croche qu'il parle en italique.*

- This very common insult to our beloved former prime minister cannot be translated word for word. The gist is this: Jean Chrétien's mouth is so 'slanted' when he speaks it comes out in italics, you know: *italics*.

29. CANADIAN PRIDE

1. Eagles may soar but beavers don't get sucked into jet engines.

   — *Len Ross, North Bay, Ontario*

30. CANADIAN REAL ESTATE

1. That property is moose pasture.

- In Northern Canada, moose pasture is swampy land. Moose love to eat aquatic plants. Beware any real estate even whispered to be moose pasture.

  — *Denis Tremblay, Ontario*

31. CANADIAN SPORTS

Curling

1. Q: How do you stop the bacon strips from curling in the pan?

   A: You take away their little brooms.
2. You never miss a shot when you are behind the glass.

- Second-guessing from afar those who are involved in an activity is easy. This is a rebuke to the fan who sits behind the glass partition that separates the ice rink from the spectators' stands at most curling rinks, a put-down of the mere watcher who criticizes every move made by those playing the game.

32. CANADIANA

General

1. *Aussi Canadienne qu'une vache folle.*

- 'As Canadian as a mad cow.' This was a Quebec saying that Canada's beef farmers did not want spread abroad, but it circulated widely in Quebec from 2004 to 2006.

2. Being a Canadian is like having one foot on shore and one foot in the canoe.
3. The National Bird of Canada is the mosquito.

- This was heard from an American just returned from a trip to Canada. Antoine Minard whose family hails from Nipawin, Saskatchewan, picked it up in San Diego.

4. Expecting Canadian politicians to be honest is like hoping that buzzards will say grace before meals.

Alberta

1. The Rockies are fine, but they spoil the view.

Edmonton

1. There's a lot of deaf elephants out there today.

- Good luck trying to guess the precise meaning of this saying—if you are not a frequent visitor to the Edmonton Folk Fest. Somewhat similar to the Ottawa Beaver Tail, the Edmonton Elephant Ear is a broad, vaguely circular piece of dough, deep fried, slathered with butter or margarine, then dusted with icing sugar and cinnamon, and perhaps topped with blueberry, strawberry, or apple jam. Some enjoy a squeeze of lemon juice on their fried elephant ear. Edmonton pastry entrepreneur, Rick Bussière, may have invented the Elephant Ear. His booth does sell thousands of them every year at Edmonton-area venues like Big Valley, the Fringe Festival, and the Street Performers Festival. Rick may also have originated the deaf elephants line in answer to the question most frequently put to him when he's on the job: "How many elephant ears have you sold in total?" My thanks for bringing attention to the elephant ear go to Helen Burchnall of Valemount, British Columbia.

British Columbia

Salt Spring Island

1. Put on your Fulford dancing slippers.

- That is, get to the wet work where you'll need to wear rubber boots. "I used to live on Salt Spring Island, British Columbia. There gumboots or rubber boots are known as 'Fulford dancing slippers' after the south end community of Fulford Harbour where most of the hippies and farmers live," writes Patti Moran of Ottawa.

Vancouver

1. Get on your Vancouver parka.

- It's a light jacket or windbreaker that would be the heaviest outer garment required on the West Coast to ward off their modest winter temperatures.

2. Albino grass.
   - Snow lying on a Vancouver lawn is a rare sight. Some Vancouverites, in a joking reference, call such snow "albino grass."
3. A tourist in Vancouver asked a child if it rained there all the time. The child replied, "I don't know. I'm only six."
4. In Hell, in a heap right beside the burning fiery furnace is a pile of Vancouverites. Why? Too wet to burn.
5. Is Vancouver wet? Well, the official city flower is mildew.

Labrador

1. Mosquitoes in Labrador are so big and so uppity, they don't just bite you. Our mosquitoes rip off a piece of your flesh, buzz to a nearby stump, tie on a linen bib, and dine in style at their leisure.
   — *Loretta Sherren, Fredericton, New Brunswick*

Manitoba

1. They're just Gappers.
   - This collective noun was used along the Manitoba/Saskatchewan border. Those on the Manitoba side of the border thought Saskatchewan folk were braggarts. They got back at them by suggesting that Saskatchewan was just a gap between Manitoba and Alberta, and hence, girls in one Manitoba border town called uppity Saskatchewan boys "gappers."
2. It's snowing in Winnipeg.

- A Canadian rock musician and member of a band that formed at Queen's University called The Arrogant Worms spent some time in Australia. There he was surprised to hear this expression frequently. Aussies toss it into their conversations to indicate how commonplace a previous utterance was. For example, a guy says, "I got a bad sunburn at the beach today, mate." His friend replies, "Right, mate. And it's snowing in Winnipeg." So it is the equivalent of "Tell me something I don't know."

3. Manitoba has two seasons: Black Flies and Snow Flies.

   — *Grace Watson, Calgary, Alberta*
4. Winterpeg, Manisnowba.
5. Windypeg, Maniblowba.

- Numbers 4 and 5 are playful self-criticisms by Manitobans heard in Winnipeg.

6. Hittin' the Sals for a nip.

- This is true Winnipeg argot. The Salisbury House restaurant chain, once partially owned by rock great Burton Cummings, among others, is a Manitoban tradition and so are their nips, or hamburgers. The term *nip* is the coinage of Ron Irwin, founder of the Salisbury House restaurants. It's been around as 'Peg slang for hamburger since 1931.

Newfoundland

1. I was screeched in.

- That is, I became an honorary Newfoundlander.

According to some correspondents, the phrase originated at Trapper John's Pub on George Street in St. John's. Screech itself is much older, although the word meaning cheap Newfie hootch is not attested in Newfoundland before the early-twentieth century. One will hear many colourful origins in a Newfoundland tavern, but this term for low-quality hard liquor, often rum, does derive from the drinker screeching after he or she has consumed enough of it. A noun and verb meaning screech in Scottish dialect *screigh* or *skreigh* was also used to refer to cheap liquor. So one has to ask the impertinent question, Could this use have begun in Scotland and been brought to the island by early immigrants?

— *Ray Bélanger, St. John's, Newfoundland*

Northern Canada

1. After five years in the north, one is an expert; after ten years, a novice.
   - This saying, more proverbial than folksy I grant, is nevertheless apt for this collection.

Nova Scotia

1. With Scottish Highlanders, it takes three generations in Canada before they're civilized.
   - This is said humorously by some Canadians of Highland descent in Nova Scotia.
2. I came from Scotia's Nova where they talk the two talks. Now I speak Gaelic, and the English twice as more.

- M. McKenzie of Neepawa, Manitoba, remembers a mother born in Pictou County in 1888 boasting thus of her heritage to her children.

Ontario

Arnprior

1. Head over to the Braeside Mall.

- This refers to the garbage dump in Braeside. Braeside is a very small village outside of Arnprior.

London

1. More fun than the Western Fair.

- The Western Fair used to be held in London, Ontario, every September.

Sudbury

1. He's wearing his Sudbury dinner jacket.

- A Sudbury dinner jacket is a long-sleeved wool-plaid shirt worn unbuttoned over a T-shirt. "Think Bob & Doug McKenzie at their sartorial scruffiest," writes Denis Tremblay of Ontario.

Toronto

1. The best thing that ever came out of Toronto was the train to Thunder Bay.

   — *Brendan J. O'Byrne, Regina, Saskatchewan*

2. I like the looks of Toronto—in my rear-view mirror.

3. She's wearing a Hogtown gown.

- A "Hogtown gown" was any mail-order dress from Eaton's catalogue. This expression from 1934 referred to Toronto, the distribution centre for Eaton's catalogue operation. Hogtown was applied as a nickname to Toronto early in the nineteenth century when it became increasingly the chief livestock trading centre and later the meat-processing hub of Ontario.

— *Robert Deavitt, Toronto*

4. A trip on a Toronto street car was "riding the Red Rocket."
5. He got a close shave on tech stocks from that Bay Street barber.

- A Bay Street barber is a greedy investment broker who shaves too much off in management fees.

  — *Robert Deavitt, Toronto*

6. That's like going downtown by way of Ward's Island.

- A roundabout route indeed, for Ward's Island sits out in Toronto Harbour. Robert Marjoribanks of Ottawa heard this in the 1950s from Torontonian Paul J. Courian.

Québec

1. She's shopping in Montreal.

- People who dwell beyond Canadian borders do not notice us often. So when we are recognized, it behooves us to take note. This saying originated in Philadelphia, Pennsylvania. It describes people who are distracted, vague, daydreaming, or who suffer more serious abbreviations of their attention spans and are therefore "not all there," "a little weak in the head," or "not in the sharpest mental focus." For example, "Aunt Tillie can't be trusted to go downtown by herself. She's shopping in Montreal, you know." What's the reason for the saying starting in an American city? Montreal is a common destination for middle-class Philadelphians seeking a weekend trip or short holiday. Thanks for this gem go to Lorne Elliott, star of CBC Radio's *Madly Off in All Directions*.

2. *La rivière est tellement croche que les poissons ont des pentures.*

- The river's so winding, the fish have hinges.

  — *Wes Darou, Cantley, Québec*

Saskatchewan

1. It's so flat in Saskatchewan you can watch your dog run away from home for a week.
2. It's so flat in Saskatchewan if you stand on a tall milkcan and look west, you can see the back of your head.
3. It's so flat in Saskatchewan you can see a train coming for three days.

   — *Dick Swarbrick, Sylvan, Alberta*

4. Saskatchewan is the only place in Canada where a woodpecker has to pack a box lunch.

- And this one is said in French too: *Y'a tellement peu d'arbres que les pics-bois se promènent avec leur boite à lunch!*

5. Crop's so short this year in Saskatchewan gophers have to kneel down to eat.

6. You can always tell people from Saskatchewan. When the wind stops blowing, they fall over.
7. Q: Why is it so windy in Saskatchewan?

   A: Because Alberta blows, and Manitoba sucks.
8. Saskatchewan is so flat you can stand on a rain barrel and see the Gulf of Mexico.

Regina

1. Enjoying your first week in Regina? Got buffalo rubbing stones in your pocket?

- This was said by a Cree friend to someone newly arrived in the windy city of Regina. Buffalo rubbing stones were large boulders worn smooth by buffalo rubbing against the stones to rid themselves of their thick winter hair and also to help dislodge ticks and fleas. The implication is: so intense is the Regina wind that one needs pockets stuffed with large stones to weigh one down. Otherwise the strong winds will carry one away!

Yukon Territory

1. Yukon mosquitoes are so big that two skitters can carry away a horse.

   — *Shirley Dobie, Dawson Creek, British Columbia*

33. CHECKING UP

1. Take a quick boo.

- A cursory glance will suffice to inform you of something. Boo here is said to be short for peek-a-boo. But it may also derive from the exclamation

"Boo!" Laura-Lee Balkwell of Toronto writes that this is a Winnipeg favourite to describe a quick look. "I'll just take a quick boo in this store."

34. CHILDREN

1. *Petit rien tout nu.*

- 'A little naked nothing.' This is a response to a child's question "What am I getting for Christmas?"

  — *Angelle Cloutier, Fort McMurray, Alberta (formerly from Lac La Biche, Alberta)*

2. You can't grow apples off a poplar.

- Dennis Kowal of Rossburn, Manitoba, writes, "This was one of my father's favourites and referred to a son who did not turn out as well as his father, possibly because of genetic flaws."

35. CHILDREN & FOOD

1. You might as well have a sickener.

- A mother rebuke to a child's question, "Can I have a treat?" Elizabeth Creith writes, "This was my mother's sarcastic invitation to enjoy oneself thoroughly, usually used of edible pleasures like ice cream."

36. CLOSE

1. Close only counts in grenades, horseshoes and dancing.

   — *Cheryl Wrishko, Saskatoon, Saskatchewan*

37. CLOSE EXAMINATION

1. I'll have to give that a good coat of looking at.
   - Moe Sherman emails, "A colleague at work who came over from Ireland about 1965 used an expression that became popular. When faced with a problem or ticklish situation he would solemnly say 'I'll have to give that a good coat of looking at.' We've extended that to apply to action taken, as in 'I gave it a good coat of looking at.'"

38. CLOTHES

1. You're all dressed up like a Christmas beef.
   - Butcher shops used to deck out a holiday cut of meat with ribbons and sometimes wrappings.

Sent in from Minnedosa, Manitoba

2. All duded up in a Winnipeg jacket.
   - This is an ironic statement, since a Winnipeg jacket was part of cold-weather working wear. Les Robinson of Winnipeg writes, "We used to call them a trail jacket, but I've heard it called a Winnipeg jacket too. It's a heavy cotton checked shirt, black and red, or black and green, tailored like a dress shirt with buttons and fold down the collar." This is the garb of those SCTV hosers, Bob and Doug McKenzie.

39. COFFEE

1. There's too much blood in my caffeine system.
2. Strong enough to grow fur on your tongue.

3. Blacker than the bowels of hell.
4. Thick enough to tar the roof.
5. Black juice from hell.

• These are all descriptions of strong coffee heard in a Manitoba truck stop near Brandon on the TransCanada highway.

40. COMMON-LAW MARRIAGE

1. Third bushel.

• This Canadian Prairie way of referring to common-law marriage originates from the fact that farmers would rent out their land for a third of the crop grown on the rented field, or a third bushel. 'Third bushel' then denotes a renter rather than an owner.

— *Dennis Kowal, Rossburn, Manitoba*

41. CRANKINESS

1. Who wee-wee'd in your cornflakes this morning?

42. CRAZINESS

1. He ain't all coupled up.

• This is Canadian railroaders' slang. The railway cars in his train of thought are not connected. In fact, his train of thought may be derailed—permanently.

2. Nutty as a fruitcake with the fruit left out.
3. *Avoir des bébites dans la tête* 'to have bugs in your head,' to be a little crazy.

4. Crazy as an outhouse mouse.
5. Crazy as Joe Blow's dog—jumped in the river to get out of the rain.

   — *J.H. Toop, Windsor, Ontario*
6. Two fries short of a Happy Meal.

Deborah Laakso of Thunder Bay, Ontario, suggests this indicates the person is just "a little crazy or weird."

7. Daft, but goin' about.
   - This means 'crazy but not locked up' according to Mary Rogers, Peterborough, Ontario, and was a favourite saying of her Scottish mother.
8. She needs her sleeves lengthened so they can be tied in the back.
   - She is crazy and might need the medieval restraint of a straitjacket.
9. She hasn't got all her ducks in a row.
10. He's half a bubble off.
    - From surveying slang: he's not level-headed, hence looney.
11. The porch light is on; there's nobody home; and the guy that used to live there moved.
    - This implies some calamitous collapse of mental acuity that is obvious to everyone who knew the subject when he was more alert.
12. The rocks in his head fit the holes in hers.
    - This expression recalls the young couple who met and fell in love in their psychiatrist's office when

they discovered they had mutually compatible psychoses.

13. He's only got one oar in the water.

- Therefore he's going around in canoe circles. He's crazy.

14. There goes one hamster who fell off his wheel once too often.
15. All her cups are not in the same cupboard.
16. He's crazy as a pig in a peach orchard.
17. There's a hole in her bag of marbles.
18. He's loonier than a junior June bug.
19. She knits with one needle.
20. Crazy as a bag of hammers.

- The hammers would point in different directions, like a crazy person's train of thought. This may be a development of a British catchphrase recorded as early as 1750 that describes someone who is walleyed: "He has a squint like a bag of nails."

43. CRIMINAL—PRAIRIE VARIETY

1. He's so crooked he could crawl up a grain auger.

- A grain auger looks like a giant corkscrew put inside a metal cylinder. When the cylinder revolves, grain can be moved as the blades of the corkscrew turn. The saying suggests the dude in question is a mighty twisted piece of work.
  — *Tom Lowe, Moosomin, Saskatchewan*

44. CROOKS, THIEVES & BAD GUYS

1. Walrus on an ice floe.
- Watch out! He's a pretty slippery dude.
2. Every time I finish a meeting with him, I need a shower.
3. Honest as the day is long? Hmmm. After you shake hands with that dude, count your fingers.
4. He could sell a drowning man a glass of water.
5. He could talk dogs off a meat truck.
6. He could talk the legs off an iron pot and then tell it to roll itself back into the shed for shame.
7. He could charm a tick off a stray dog.

45. CYNICAL KNOWLEDGE

1. Eat right. Stay fit. Die anyway.

46. DARKNESS

1. Blacker than a coal mine with the lights out.
   — *Andrew P. Nimmo, Edmonton, Alberta*

47. DECISIONS, DECISIONS

1. When in doubt, punt.
- "My friend, Leslie Gwozdz (nee Stilling), used to give this advice to us when we were struggling with a decision. We all knew that was what the Saskatchewan Roughriders of the early 1980s would do!" writes Cheryl Wrishko of Saskatoon.

A punt in football is when the ball is kicked without letting it hit the ground first—in contrast to a drop kick. It is a play in Canadian football and American football in which the football is kicked downfield to the opposing team.

If an offensive team has the ball too far away from the end zone to attempt a field goal, and is facing a third down in Canadian football, and too far away from the first down marker, they may choose to punt the ball. This involves kicking the ball from a standing position after it has been snapped (usually a long snap). The purpose is to increase the distance that the opposing team must advance the ball in order to score a touchdown or a field goal.

48. DISDAIN

1. Colder than a ticket-taker's stare.

49. DRINKING ALCOHOL

1. I got rum dumb.
2. I'm "ryetarded."

- That is, I drank too much last night. A pun on "my movements were retarded by alcohol."
  — *Karen Ostoforoff, Saskatoon, Saskatchewan*

50. EXAGGERATION

1. I've told you children a hundred million times, don't exaggerate!

51. EXCESS

1. Hang the expense! Give the cat another canary!

- This sarcastic invitation to wild generosity was borrowed into English from French slang in Sudbury, Ontario.

52. EXCUSES

1. Yeah, and if the fox hadn't stopped to recharge his laptop battery, he'd have caught the rabbit.

- This is said to chastise someone who is late or incomplete in performing a simple task.

53. EXECUTIVE SLANG

1. Let's eat that elephant one bite at a time.

- The boss says this, trying to appear bright and snappy, when he means "this is a big project so we'll do it in stages." Exec blat consists of bad metaphors used by executives, industrial managers, and "the suits" in a company. You've heard some of their gems. When the executive presents a new plan to a meeting: "Let's run this up the flagpole and see who salutes." Yeah, right. Let's not, dork. Or "Let's slap this on the altar and see who worships it." Great! Blasphemous and stupid. Well, with leadership capable of spouting that kind of verbal claptrap, the company is certain to prosper.
  — *Cathy Hellyer, Etobicoke, Ontario*

54. FAMILY

1. The gene pool around here could use a little chlorine.

2. She didn't get that off the wind.
- It's a family trait; so it's best not to blame her.
3. My grandfather's dog ran through your grandmother's backyard once.
- We are distant relatives.

55. FARMING

1. We're growing apples on the fence posts!
- The fields are fertile, the crop's a big one, and the harvest will be bounteous, according to this rural boast reported from Beaver Valley near Clarksburg, Ontario.

  — *Grant and Nida McMurchy*

56. FAT

1. *Ma belle-mère est tellement grosse que quand elle porte des talons aiguilles elle trouve du pétrole.*
- My mother-in-law is so fat that, when she wears stiletto heels, she strikes oil.
2. That's no Buick. That's my wife.
- But, one wonders, for how long?
3. She looks like she got poured into her dress and someone forgot to say when.
4. He's got more guts than a sausage.
- Diane Reid of Kingston, Ontario, remembers this expression as a favourite of her father, Mr. J. Cooney.
5. Imagine the money he'd bring if they still made glue from animal fat.

  — *Loretta Sherren, Fredericton, New Brunswick*

6. *Ma belle-mère est tellement grosse que l'autre jour en passant devant la télé elle m'a fait manquer les quinze dernières minutes de mon film.*

- "My mother-in-law is so fat that the other day when she walked in front of my TV, I missed the last fifteen minutes of a movie I was watching."

7. He's so fat it's quicker to go over than around.

— *Chris Wouters, Morrisburg, Ontario*

8. She's beef to the hoof.

- This is a loan translation from German.

9. He looks like a wootsy pig.

- This means he is dishevelled as well as fat. But I can find no printed reference to the meaning of *wootsy*. Can any reader help? It is apparently not a dialect spelling of *woodsy*.

10. Legs by Steinway, body by Fisher.

- Legs like a piano on a body the size of a car. The last three words were an advertising slogan used by General Motors for decades and were usually printed in several places on their automobiles.

11. *Sa blonde est tellement grosse qu'elle peut se tricoter un chandail avec la mousse de son nombril!*

- An obesity report from one house in Quebec: 'His girlfriend is so fat she could knit a sweater with her own bellybutton lint.'

57. FATIGUE

1. My butt is right dunch.

• This Canadian Maritime expression is appropriate when your bottom is numb after a long car ride or from sitting too long on a chair in front of a computer monitor. Laura-Lee Balkwell of Toronto adds, "To describe mental fatigue or the effects of a hangover, I've also heard 'My brain is right dunch.'"

Dunch is an adjective brought to Canada by British settlers. In several English dialects of Great Britain dunch as an adjective means "stiff, cramped, dulled by a blow, numbed, slow in recognition or comprehension, even hard-of-hearing. Dunch is the adjectival offspring probably of the Middle English verb *dunchen* 'to nudge with the elbow, to bump,' itself a Viking import akin to Icelandic, Swedish & Norwegian *dunka*' to strike,' to Old Norse *dynkr* 'noise' and *dynr* 'din.' Even today in Scottish dialect a dunch is a blow or a push. Dunch bread is heavy, unleavened bread. In Newfoundland English, bread can turn out dunch if it fails to rise.

58. FIXED IN THEIR WAYS

1. He's like concrete – all mixed up and permanently set.

59. FOOD

1. North End steak.

- This is a Winnipeg slang synonym for bologna, based on the fact that North Winnipeg once housed poor immigrants who may have eaten cheap processed meats.

  — Jack J. Eyer, Winnipeg

2. Sit down and put your ears back.

- That is, get ready for a good feed.

3. I'm filled to the what-nots.

- Said after a really satisfying meal.

4. What's for supper? A jam sandwich—two pieces of bread jammed together.

   — Darrell Brown, Centre Burlington, Hants County, Nova Scotia

5. Mix that with wheat and you could poison gophers with it.

- Gopher poison was commonly mixed with wheat and then spread on Canadian Prairie farms. This saying could also refer to cheap, harsh liquor or bad homebrew.

  — Dennis Kowal, Rossburn, Manitoba

6. House out them pizza bones.

- This wonderful bit of creative Ontario slang—check out that new-fangled compound verb—refers to tossing the thin, leftover crusts of pizza out the kitchen door to the dogs.

7. She got a good scald on that grub.

- The meal was certainly well cooked, wasn't it?

8. Tough as an old shag.

- Peggy Feltmate of Toronto reports this Canadian

saying still heard in our Maritime Provinces. "Shag," writes Peggy, "is a common local word in Guysborough County, Nova Scotia, for a cormorant. This put-down of hard-to-chew meat was muttered over a meal by Arthur Rhynold, of White Head, Nova Scotia. When times were especially bad and the larder was desperately empty, coastal residents might hunt and eat cormorants. Shags had little meat and were quite oily too—not a gourmet experience at all!"

Etymology of Shag

British immigrants brought the word *shag* to Canada very early. It appears in print as early as 1566 to label *Phalacrocorax aristotelis*, the common crested cormorant of Europe and North African coasts. Shag may even have been one of the words for cormorant among the Anglo-Saxons. In one Old English glossary written around AD 1050 is *sceacga* and here *shaguh* (as it was approximately pronounced) has its primary English meaning of rough, matted hair, from which all of the later uses of the word derive. For shag can mean the nap of cloth, a rug or garment of rough material, coarse-cut tobacco leaves, etc. Its use to name the crested cormorant may have arisen to describe the crest of long curly plumes developed by the male of this species during breeding season. But it now is used throughout the English-speaking countries of the world to name any of the dozens of species of cormorants, including of course those that nest in our Maritimes. They could all have been named shag because, although their black feathers are lustrous with protective and insulating oil, the oil is often thick and sticks the feathers together, giving the bird a shaggy look.

Etymology of Cormorant

Cormorant as a word entered Middle English from Old French *cormaran*, itself from Medieval Latin *corvus marinus* literally 'sea crow.' The zoological name of the bird, *Phalacrocorax*, appears first in the writings of the Roman encyclopedist whom my old Classics professor liked to call "Uncle Pliny." Gaius Plinius Secundus, knight, public administrator, polymath, charming Roman trivia collector and wandering gasbag, usually dubbed Pliny the Elder in English, wrote thirty-seven books of a *Natural History*, a digest of facts about botany and zoology and the natural world. Pliny's name for the cormorant—which name he may have invented—was *phalacrocorax*, a clumsy Latin word made from two Greek words: *phalakros* 'bald' and *korax* 'crow.' As it happens there is a European subspecies of cormorant, *Phalacrocorax carbo sinensis*, whose breeding plumage includes whitish head feathers. So the bird might well have appeared to a Roman landlubber as a bald, white-headed, sea-going crow. *Carbo* is the Latin word for charcoal (black in colour like our birdlet) and *sinensis* in Late Latin means 'Chinese.' Brisson, who gave the subspecies its modern name in ornithology, must have thought this subspecies of Far Eastern origin.

Other Shaggy Sayings

In Australia, something or someone isolated is said to be as exposed "as a shag on a rock." Captain Frederick Marryat, the English sailor and popular novelist (1792–1848) has a character in his adventure yarn *Jacob Faithful* (1834) utter the following complaint: "I'm as wet as a shag, and as cold as charity."

(Food sayings, continued)

9. She's digging her grave with her teeth.
- That is, she has unhealthy eating habits.

10. Better belly burst than good meat lost.
- In the 1930s, depression-era mothers chided children who did not eat everything on their plates with this line. It was often a response to a child's plaintive "But, Mommy, I'm full!"

11. Oh, take a cold potato and sit on it.
- In other words, dinner will be served soon.

12. Let yer vittles shut yer gob.
- Eat up and be quiet.

13. Stubbed his toe on the salt, I see.
- That guy ate a lot of salt, so much that he was licking off the salt block set in the field for the cows. It is that block he stubbed his toe on.

14. Q: What's for dessert?

    A: Desert the table.

- Moira Parker of Calgary recalls a punning expression of her mother, Muriel Howe of Bloomfield, Ontario, given when her children pestered her about sweets at the end of the evening meal.

15. What doesn't kill will fatten.

- This was said, often to children, in times of scarcity when food was dropped on the ground or floor. It means, "A little dirt won't kill you; it's still good food; pick it up and eat it."

16. Best grub I ever hung a lip over.

17. You have to eat a bushel of dirt before you die.

- Parents used to say this to children who found a speck of dirt on, say, a boiled potato.
  — *The Billingsley family, McGregor, Ontario*

18. I'm full as a tick.

- A tick is an acarid, a member of the spider family. Ticks attach themselves to the skin of many mammals and suck blood until they swell and look ready to pop, like one who has eaten too much.

60. FUSSY

1. *Il est tellement minutieux qu'il corrige les Alpha-Bits avant de déjeuner.*

- "He's such a fussbudget that he corrects the spelling in the Alpha-Bits cereal before he eats them for breakfast."

2. *Mon oncle est tellement téteux en auto que les mouches s'écrasent dans la vitre d'en arrière.*

- The sense of this delightful Quebecism is: "Driving his car, my uncle is such a sensitive, fastidious little twerp that bugs squish themselves on his **rear** window, just so they won't upset him."

61. GOOD WISHES TO A CHILD

1. Bless your little cotton socks.

- Heard in Thessalon, Ontario.

  — *Elizabeth Creith, Thessalon, Ontario at www.hedgehogceramics.ca*

62. GOSSIP

1. She's got a mind like a vacuum cleaner. It sucks up dirt.

63. GREETINGS

1. How's yer feet and ears?

- This greeting means 'how are you doing?'

64. HAIR

1. Q: Did you get your haircut?

   A: No. I got all of them cut.

- This is a smart-ass yokel's response to a simple question.

  — *George Karle, Peace River, Alberta*

2. Tomorrow morning try a hair dryer instead of a Mixmaster.

- Bad hair day big-time!

3. You're having a bad hair day? Think of Walter. He's had a bad hair life!
4. I got bed-head.

- Helen Burchnall of Valemount, British Columbia, writes, "This refers to one's hair being all over the place upon waking up in the morning, sticking up at impossible angles, and being impossible to get back in place. Bed-head affects women more than men, naturally."

65. HAIRCUTS

1. Woman: I see you got your hair cut.
   Man: No, I just had my ears lowered.

66. HAPPINESS

1. Whatever floats your boat.

- Meaning whatever makes you happy, content, or satisfied, this maritime expression can also suggest that you try whatever method will work in a current work project.
  — *Tyler B., Corner Brook, Newfoundland*

2. Does that melt your butter?
3. Does that cream your Twinkie?
4. Happier than a gopher in soft dirt.
5. Whatever shucks your corn.

- Implication: do it and be happy.

67. HEALTH

1. How's your belly for spots?

- Or, how are you? Spots on the stomach may have been the symptoms of an outbreak of some disease that prompted the first use of this playful greeting.

68. HEAT & WARMTH

1. Warm as bats.

- Peggy Feltmate of Toronto writes: "My great-grandparents, Harry Quick Snuggs and Emma Drew Snuggs, immigrated to Ontario from Windsor in England around 1875. They stopped in Collingwood, Ontario, to have a baby and then continued by ox-cart to Spence Township near Magnetawan where they settled. Their daughter, Lucy, said that whenever her mother, Emma, told the story of their trek, Emma always said that on their trip "we were as warm as bats, but our teacups froze to their saucers." It's an extraordinary, Early Canadian image: the two Brits sitting beside an ox-cart piled high with their belongings in the winter wilds of Ontario, drinking from delicate teacups with saucers. "No tin mugs for my ancestors!"

Are bats warm? Yes! If you have occasion to handle one of these toasty wee mammals—little furry cuties—they are warm to the touch due to their high metabolic rate. Most bats are lice-ridden too.

69. HELP

1. I need your help like a kangaroo needs a purse.

70. HELPLESS OR FORLORN

1. There he stood winking and blinking like a toad under a spike-toothed harrow.

- This saying may be a Nova Scotian improvement upon—by my lights it is indeed—or an updating of an old British metaphor for helplessness. The figure of speech has been hopping around our language since 1817, where it appears in a famous novel by Sir Walter Scott, namely, *Rob Roy*. Toad under a harrow is "the comparative situation of a poor fellow whose wife—not satisfied with the mere henpecking of her helpmeet—takes care that the world shall witness the indignities she puts upon him. The expression is also applied to any other similar state of misery, if such there be." This saying was then quoted a few years later in a collection entitled *Glossary of North Country Words* compiled by John Brockett and published in 1825.

71. HOW ARE YOU?

1. Roasty-toasty!

- Donna Green of Toronto emails: "My dear father, Russell Lee, used to say this in response to anyone who inquired about his general health. My father's other answer to 'How are you?' was 'Still able to sit up and take nourishment.'"

72. HUNGER

1. *Mange ta main et garde l'autre pour demain.*
   - 'Eat your hand and save the other one for tomorrow.' Angelle Cloutier, who grew up in the largely francophone community of Lac La Biche in northern Alberta, writes, "This one was passed down from my maternal grandmother. We were told this whenever we nagged Mom just one too many times about being hungry and wondering 'what's for supper?'"
2. We never went to bed hungry. We stayed up.

This is a classic 1930s joke about food scarcity during the Great Depression.

— *Chris Wouters, Morrisburg, Ontario*

73. IMPOSSIBILITY

1. It's like trying to sew a moonbeam to a wish.
   - It's a matter of some delicacy then, if not impossibility. I first heard this said by a surgeon rejecting a medical procedure that had a bad prognosis.

74. INDECISIVENESS

1. Up in the air—like a dog between two trees.
2. Didn't know what to do—like a blind dog in a meat locker.
3. He was quaving.
   - To quave is a lovely slangy verb that means to

shift one's weight from one leg to the other in an anxious dither of indecision.

75. INJURY

1. It's far from the heart.

- Spoken to a child complaining about a minor injury, this saying means it is unlikely to be a mortal wound. This was collected in Iron Bridge, Ontario.
  — *Elizabeth Creith, Thessalon, Ontario*

76. *IN VINO VERITAS*

1. I am going to the pub to get a little lip-loosener.

- A few glasses of beer can make one talkative. The Latin title of this category means "truth resides in the wine," suggesting that when one has drunk alcohol, one will speak truthfully. I don't think there is much solid clinical evidence for this assertion. But at least one member of the Birch Hills, Saskatchewan, Snow Posse Snowmobile Club disagrees with me.
  — *Karen Ostoforoff, Saskatoon, Saskatchewan*

77. INSIDE MORE IMPORTANT THAN OUTSIDE

1. Silk on a sow is still only a well-dressed pig.

- This also repeats the meaning of its more famous related saying, namely, you can't make a silk purse out of a sow's ear. Of course, the moment one utters that old cliché a couturier's seamstress will step out onto the Champs Élysées to present a leather *porte-monnaie* made of exquisitely sewn pigs' ears.

78. INTELLIGENT

1. *Vite sur ses patins.*

• In Québec this saying from girls' hockey and figure skating means literally, she's 'quick on her skates,' that is, she's clever.

79. LAZINESS

1. He's dead but he won't stiffen.

• This worker is not perhaps the model of efficiency.

2. He ain't took a lick at a snake.

• He hasn't done any work at all.

3. Got a piano tied to your back?
4. That feller's been called for, wouldn't go, and wouldn't do if he got there.
5. Born on a Wednesday, looking both ways for Sunday.
6. He wouldn't rise up to scream suee! even if the pigs were eating him.

80. LEARNING TO DRIVE

1. Where'd you get your licence? From a Cracker Jack box?

— *Judy Brooks, Brandon, Manitoba*

81. LIES

1. Reads like a Bre-X prospectus.

All-Canadian synonym for "a pack of lies," this was first said about a suspiciously worded document by Preston Manning during the federal spring election of 1997. Bre-X Minerals Incorporated owned an Indonesian gold mine near Busang, which company officials claimed held the largest reserve of gold known in the world. But it was alleged that ore samples had been altered and made to appear more gold-bearing than they were, after which Bre-X collapsed and Busang was declared a fraud. Hundreds of Canadians who had invested in the company lost money.

82. LOSER

1. When his ship comes in, he'll be at the airport.
   — *Lyn McEachern, Thunder Bay, Ontario*

83. LUCK, DUMB LUCK!

1. Even a stopped clock is right twice a day.
2. Even a blind hog finds an acorn once in a while.

84. MARRY HIS BROTHER?

1. One slice off that loaf of bread was enough for me.

- This is a wonderfully feisty comeback to someone who suggested to a recent widow that she could marry her dead husband's brother.

85. MEN'S CLOTHING

1. Your violin case is open.

- Your fly is undone.

  —Edward L. Coleman, Mesachie Lake, British Columbia

2. XYZ.

- This is a sort of acronym standing for the words 'eXamine Your Zipper,' offered to one whose pant's zipper was down.

  — Dennis Kowal, Rossburn, Manitoba

86. MESSY DRESSER

1. Did you get a look at her? She looks like Annie fresh off the pickle boat.

- She's a mess obviously. But one question? Have you ever even seen pickles carried in a boat?

87. MINOR PROBLEM

1. Many a greater loss at sea.

- Craig Russell of Winnipeg emails, "When something bad would happen, my mother-in-law Margaret Shaw would say this. Her family was from Scotland and, in times gone by, many young men were lost on sailing ships. The intent of the saying, of course, was to put minor problems in perspective."

88. MOCK PRAISE

1. Do you want a medal or a chest to pin it on?

   — Cheryl Wrishko, Saskatoon, Saskatchewan

89. MONEY PROBLEMS

1. This won't buy the baby's boots or pay for the ones she's wearing.

90. MOPING

1. Who stole your wee scone?

- A small child who is sulking might receive this gentle admonishment. A scone is a little bun or quick bread often served with jam.
  — *Elizabeth Creith, Thessalon, Ontario*

91. NAÏVETÉ

1. Hey, pardner, this isn't my first Stampede.
   - I'm not naïve. I've been to Calgary twice.
2. Careful now, cows'll eat you.
   - That is, you are green as grass, a neophyte, so be careful.
3. You don't fatten frogs for snakes.
   - Don't be so gullible: everyone is not your friend.

92. NASTINESS

1. Mean as a poisoned dwarf.

93. NEATNESS

1. Pick up your riggin'.

- A New Brunswick or Nova Scotian mother might say this to children who have left their clothes lying around the house. It obviously harks back to British naval injunctions to sailors to keep the

decks clear and stow gear that was not being used.
— *Irene Doyle, New Brunswick*

94. NEVER

1. When chickens grow teeth.
   - Québec has the same expression: *quand les poules auront des dents.*
2. Yeah, yeah, I'll get it done—sometime between now and Shavuot.
   - This Anglo-Yiddish expression suggests the chore may never be done. Shavuot is the Festival of Weeks, a Jewish harvest celebration held fifty days after the second day of Passover, so it's at the same approximate time as Christian Pentecost. But it's tricky to figure the exact date of Shavuot; and it's a small joke among some North American Jews that nowadays not everyone knows the precise date of this, the least extravagantly celebrated of Jewish festivals; hence it's use in this saying. In Yiddish, Shavuot is pronounced sh-VOO-es. Please, even in English, never make it rhyme with shave-a-lot. In Hebrew *shavuot* is a plural noun meaning 'weeks' referring to the time between Passover and the festival.
3. *Pendant la semaine des trois jeudis.*
   - In the week of the three Thursdays, that is, never. Continental French goes it one better and says "*la semaine des quatre jeudis.*"
4. When pigs fly.

95. NOSE PICKING

1. You can pick your friends; you can pick your nose; but you can't pick your friend's nose.
2. The man you're rolling those pills for is dead.

- In other words, quit picking your nose. This expression is probably one hundred years old at least, and harks back to the days when a pharmacist had various pill-making contrivances in the dispensary at the back of his drugstore. Some prescribed pills were rolled by hand while the patient customer waited.

96. OBSTRUCTION

1. You make a better door than a window.

- Cheryl Wrishko of Saskatoon writes, "My parents, Ron and Virginia Wrishko, used to say this to us as children whenever we stood in front of something they were trying to view."

97. OBVIOUSNESS

1. You're as subtle as a dump truck, Martha.

- You are coming on too strong or too obvious. But there is an echo here of the thirty-year-old American high school slang term for any unattractive, obese, unpopular girl. "She's a real Martha Dumptruck." The expression above may come from the 1989 teen satire movie *Heathers* where a character named Martha "Dumptruck" Dunstock takes plenty of insults. I believe there

was also a short-careered female rock band named "Martha and the Dump Trucks."
— *Laura-Lee Balkwell, Toronto*

2. No need to connect the dots on that one.
• This refers to newspaper puzzles in which one connects a series of dots with a pencil to reveal a "secret" image.

98. OLD AGE

1. How old is the principal of our school? We don't know. But he held the camels for the Three Wise Men.
— *Len Ross, North Bay, Ontario*
2. When God said, "Let there be light," it was Fred who hit the switch.
• Fred is quite old.
3. It's the old dogs for the hard road and the pups for the path.
• Ms. Beau Gabiniewicz of New Westminster, British Columbia, writes, "My granny, born in 1894 in Bobcaygeon, Ontario, used to say this to me when she thought that I, as a younger woman than she, had things easier than she ever did."
4. *Mon grand-père est tellement vieux qu'il est né en Ancienne-Zélande.*
• "My grandfather is so elderly that he was born in Old Zealand." This is a child's reversal joke, but is to be encouraged, because it displays a playful attitude to words and language.

5. Her head has worn out two bodies.

- She looks much older than her age.

6. He's been around since Hell was a grass fire.
7. How old am I? Nine days older than God.
8. I'm so old, I fart rust.
9. In old age you become a prune on the outside and a peach on the inside.

— *Loretta Sherren, Fredericton, New Brunswick*

10. He is older than footprints.
11. So old he could have been a waiter at the Last Supper.
12. They'll never comb grey hair together.

- Said of a newly married couple who fight on their wedding day.

13. There's many a good tune played on an old fiddle.
14. You know you're gettin' up there when your back goes out more than you do.
15. He's older than dirt.
16. He's two years older than God.
17. Don't pull a granny. Don't do a granny.

- This accuses the listener of shamming a hearing or memory loss.

— *Colleen Saunders, Norman Wells, Northwest Territories*

18. As old as water.

- Maritime variant of "old as dirt."

19. I'm as old as my tongue and a little older than my teeth.

- This is one playful answer when a child asks an elder his or her age.

  — *Merrilee Ashworth, West Vancouver, British Columbia*

20. I have so many wrinkles, I can screw on my hat.

  —*Colleen Farrell, Head of Chezzetcook, Nova Scotia*

21. Mutton dressed as lamb.

- Said of an overly madeup older woman.

  — *Reino Kokkila, Etobicoke, Ontario*

22. Old as the hills of Gowrie.

- This expression is still heard on Cape Breton Island. Gowrie is a town in Scotland.

23. I'm so old I sold tickets to the Last Supper.

  — *Ken Ruller, Calgary, Alberta*

24. Rebuke to youthful co-workers by a woman of a certain age: I have shoes older than you!

25. Grey as a badger.

- "My husband's grandmother used this saying to refer to people with extensive grey hair," writes Shirley Miller of Regina. "Gram was born in Scotland and lived the majority of her life in Saskatchewan."

99. OLD AGE: WHITE HAIR

1. I look like a dandelion gone to seed.

100. OLD JOKES

1. Funeeee! Last time I heard that, I fell off my dinosaur.

   — *Laura-Lee Balkwell, Toronto*

101. OTHER FORMS OF LIFE

1. Support bacteria; they're the only culture some people have.

- This stems from the language of the scientific laboratory where bacteria may be "cultured" (that is, grown) in a Petri dish in some nutrient like agar-agar.

102. OVERCROWDING

1. We were packed in tighter than lint in a flea's bellybutton.

   — *Lyn McEachern, Thunder Bay, Ontario*

103. PESSIMISM

1. One rabbit makes a lot of tracks.

- There may be less reason for optimism than you think. If hopes soar too high, this glum bring-down might be uttered.

104. PILL-POPPERS

1. *Ma grand-mère est tellement bourrée de pilules que quand elle éternue, elle guérit quelqu'un.*

- This comic but apt comment on how so very many of Canada's elderly people are overmedicated is translated: 'Gran is so stuffed with pills when she sneezes she cures a bystander.'

105. POOR

1. I'm so broke I'd have to buy a postage stamp on the installment plan.
2. When our shoes wear out, we'll be on our feet again.

- Here's a grim pun of typical, resilient Canadian humour, remembered as heard in Winnipeg during the Great Depression of the early 1930s. *—Stuart Calberry, Peterborough, Ontario*

3. We were so poor we couldn't buy a hummingbird a vest.
4. We were so poor there was nothing to eat but bread and scrape.

- Phoenix Wisebone of Vancouver heard this around Middlesex County in the 1960s said by residents recently arrived from England. Scrape is drippings from the bottom of a roasting pan.

5. I'm so broke I couldn't afford a down payment on a penny match.
6. We were so poor I had to wear a hat to look out the window.

   — Len Ross, North Bay, Ontario

7. Too poor to paint, too proud to whitewash.
8. I'm so poor I couldn't buy a louse a shootin' jacket.

- Paul Bell of Ontario writes, "When as a small child I asked for a penny for candy, my grandmother in Owen Sound used to say this."

9. His shoes were so thin he could step on a dime and tell whether it was heads or tails.
   - This is Depression-era humour from 1930s Saskatchewan.
10. I'm so poor I couldn't buy a ticket to a free lunch.
11. Poor as Job's turkey. Couldn't raise more than three feathers, and had to lean against the barn to gobble.
12. They were so poor there was nothing on the table but elbows, and the mice in the cellar had tears in their eyes.
13. You'll find it mighty dry chewing.
   - This is an experienced person's advice to poor youngsters planning to get married and live on love.
14. *Arm wie a Kirchemaus* 'poor as a church mouse.'
   - From the German of Mennonite and Amish farmers near Kitchener, Ontario (in standard German *arm wie eine Kirchenmaus*).
15. I'm so broke I can't afford to pay attention.
16. Crime doesn't pay, and neither does farming.
17. He was always crying poor-mouth, like a farmer with a loaf of bread under each arm.

   — *Wilhelmine Estabrook, Hartland, New Brunswick*
18. I've never been broke, just badly bent.

19. So poor they get their shoes half-soled one at a time.

— *Charlie Corkum, Summerside, Prince Edward Island*

20. Every time I go into a store, my purse thinks my hands are crazy.

- From the Great Depression of the 1930s.

21. We were so poor we never had decorations on the Christmas tree unless Grandpa sneezed.

22. I've seen times so bad the river only ran once a week.

- This is a nice parody of oldtimers' talk about bad times in the past that were always far worse than any modern bad times. A common error of humans is to think everything in the past was worse than today . . . and better!

23. There's not enough food in their house to feed a nun on Good Friday.

- This saying is still heard in southern New Brunswick

24. I'm so broke, if it cost a dime to go around the world, I couldn't afford to get out of sight.

— *Bert Spencer, Bowmanville, Ontario*

25. We're going dump-diving.

- Not at all a sign of poverty or being a cheapskate, rummaging through local garbage dumps for items still able to be salvaged for further use is a common and even ecologically honorable activity in some parts of the Canadian countryside.

— *Helen Burchnall, Valemount, British Columbia*

26. I couldn't buy a peanut for a starving monkey.
27. We were so poor back then I ate my cereal with a fork so my sister could share the milk.
28. They couldn't buy oats for a nightmare.
  - This pun stems from Brandon, Manitoba. A mare is a female horse that might be fed oats. But the *-mare* in nightmare is no horse. It's from Old English *mære* 'evil spirit.' A thousand years ago our ancestors thought that a fiendish incubus came into your bedroom at night and sat on your chest as you slept and brought you evil dreams. The Latin word for the creature, *incubus*, means 'something in bed with you.'
29. What's for supper? Nothing but push and grit.
  - That is, push your feet under the table and grit your teeth.
30. They're from a long line of far-downs.
  - This Irish saying arrived in Canada early in the twentieth century. It suggests that several generations of the family under discussion have been poor and shiftless and are as worthless as blight on a potato. This is probably an unfair analysis of the reasons an individual family might be impoverished.
31. If train engines were a dime a dozen, I couldn't buy the echo of a whistle.

106. POVERTY IN QUÉBEC

1. *Chez nous les murs sont tellement minces, que quand j'épluche un oignon, mon voisin se met à pleurer.*

- "At our house the walls are so thin that when I peel an onion, my neighbour gets tears in her eyes."

107. QUANTITY

1. They were thicker than horse buns at a country schoolyard.

- In days of yore, contrary to the myth that your grandfather walked to school through three continents and over six mountains, in fact many farm kids were driven to the schoolhouse in a horse-drawn buggy, or in the winter, delivered cozy under a rug in a sleek cutter pulled through the snow by sturdy draught horses. Of course, equine droppings would pile up, as sleighs and cutters and buggies arrived to deposit at the schoolhouse their loads, in both senses of the expression.

108. QUÉBEC'S NATURAL BOUNTY

1. *Y'a tellement des poissons dans le lac près de chez nous qu'y faut les tasser pour prendre une chaudière d'eau.*

- Concerning the fishing bounty of Quebec, the gist of this saying is: there are so many fish in the lake near our house that you have to shore-fish for an hour just to fetch a pail of clear water.

109. RAIN

1. You're not made of sugar; you won't melt in the rain.

- Laura-Lee Balkwell of Toronto writes, "My grandmother used this in urging us children to go outside in wet weather."

110. RELIGIOUS CEREMONIES

1. Timing has an awful lot to do with the outcome of a rain dance.

111. RELUCTANCE TO ACCEPT A THING

1. I wouldn't take that if you gave me all of Cape Breton Island with a chicken on top.

- Professor Jennifer MacLennan at the College of Engineering of the University of Saskatchewan in Saskatoon sent this maritime saying and added, "According to my mother, Margaret Thomson MacLennan, this is something that her mother-in-law, my grandmother, Annie MacKillop MacLennan, used to say when confronted with some phenomenon that she didn't think much of. She was, of course, born in Cape Breton, in the small village of St. Ann's, where the Gaelic College now is located. It is similar in meaning to "not for all the tea in China."

112. RESTING

1. We're just cooling our hoofies.

- We are resting. The comic diminutive of hooves is cute.
  — *Dennis Kowal, Rossburn, Manitoba*

113. SADNESS

1. You look like you lost a quarter and found a dime.

114. SEARCHING

1. If it had legs, it would get up and walk away.

- A mother might say this to a girl looking for something that was right in front of the girl's face. — *Judy Brooks, Brandon, Manitoba*

115. SHODDINESS

1. You put the *k* in *quality*.

- In other words, you are not only a shoddy sleaze-bag but you can't spell either.

116. SICK

1. Seen Tom lately? Looks like Death nibbling a stale cracker.
2. How sick was he? Peas and carrots and Number 11.

- Peas and carrots suggest that he vomited. Number 11 is nasal mucus running down from both nostrils in two lines like number eleven. One correspondent in Manitoba tells me this is a direct translation from Ukrainian. If you know the original, please email me.

117. SMALLNESS

1. It's fly bait.

- In northern Alberta in the seventies and eighties, a common expression for something that was very easy or very tiny or did not consist of anything of substance was to say it was "fly bait," so exiguous that one might set it out as bait to try to catch flies. This is common in the Cold Lake area that straddles the Alberta and Saskatchewan border.

118. SNAKES!

1. Rattlesnakes are so big here on the Bruce Peninsula, they don't have rattles; they have little bells that play "Nearer My God to Thee."

- This exaggerated and spurious welcome was given to first-time cottagers on the day they moved into their Bruce Peninsula hideaway. Central Ontario's Bruce Peninsula is the part of the Niagara Escarpment that separates Lake Huron from Georgian Bay.

A venomous and endangered pygmy rattlesnake, the Massasauga, *Sistrurus catenatus*, lives on the Bruce. The Massasauga likes moist habitat where it feeds on mice and frogs. Its zoological name does ring a bell for those who have studied Latin, Greek, or the music of ancient Egypt. The genus name means "sistrum-tailed." *Sistrum* is a Roman version of the Greek word *seistron* 'shaker.' The same Greek verbal root *seis-* appears in our shaky English adjective *seismic*. The Greek word for the tail of an animal is *oura* and it shows up here in a Latinized suffixal form *-urus*; hence *sistr- + -urus = sistrurus* 'sistrum-tailed.'

When ancient Greeks travelling in Egypt saw priests chanting a hymn to some cow-headed goddess of the sands, they stopped, intrigued by clinking noises of a small musical object that a priest held in one hand and gently struck against the other hand at caesuras in the rhythm of the religious chant. This musical percussion instrument, called a sistrum, was also shaken on the beat to emphasize the beat, to facilitate religious choreography: "Hey, man, Ra wants you to boogie like a crocodile! Keep dancing like that and you'll lay 'em in the Niles. The Blue and the White."

The sistrum was a metal frame shaped like an upended capital U. Thin metal rods hung down from the frame and jingle-jangled when the sistrum was struck.

So, picture a rattlesnake tail and you will see how apt a genus name *Sistrurus* is. The specific adjective is nifty too; *catenatus* in Latin means 'in a row like links in a chain.' So the zoological name describes the little animal's most vivid feature: a linked row of rattles for a tail. Massasauga is an Ojibwa river name and means literally 'water great mouth,' and refers to an early siting of the snake, perhaps on a wet or marshy bank of the Mississauga River in southern Ontario. A once large tribe of the Ojibwa people also bears the name *Missisauga* after the river mouth that was the centre of their territory.

119. SPEED

1. It went like salts through a widow woman.

- Leslie Duchak of the Women's Canadian Club of Calgary writes, "I love your books, and have heard you on the CBC. Canadians really do have some unique expressions. My dad was from Prince Edward Island and he had many quips, some of which you have included in your books. This one I have not heard from anyone else in Calgary. It was used by my dad when describing something moving very fast."

120. SPORTS

Hockey

1. To get tattooed onto the boards.

- To get violently checked into the boards by a real *beau coup*. So, if you were playing a Quebec team, you could say afterward, "*Merci pour le beau coup!*"

  — *Ms. Beau Gabiniewicz, New Westminster, British Columbia*

121. SPORTS FAILURE

1. The other team is unravelling like a cheap suit.

   — *Ms. Beau Gabiniewicz, New Westminster, British Columbia*

2. Those guys are folding like a cheap lawn chair.

122. SPORTS VICTORY

1. We beat them like a rented mule.

- This nasty expression implies cruelty to poor mules that do nothing but help humans carry various burdens.
  — *Ms. Beau Gabiniewicz, New Westminster, British Columbia*

123. STINGINESS

Being a cheapskate seems to be something others notice frequently, because there are many, many sayings about skinflints and pikers. It is one of the largest categories of Canadian folk sayings.

1. He'd give you the sleeves off his vest.
2. Tighter than a wet boot.
3. She's so cheap she avoids cold showers, because goosebumps are hard on soap.
4. *Lui là, y'est tellement gratteux qui parle du nez pour ne pas user son dentier.*
   - "That guy is such a cheapskate he speaks through his nose to save wear and tear on his false teeth."
5. So cheap he'd pick the pennies off a dead man's eyes, and then kick the corpse because they weren't quarters.
6. She's so cheap she'd skin a louse for the tallow.
7. He's so stingy he wouldn't pay a nickel to see Mother Teresa go over Niagara Falls on water skis.

8. She's so tight she'd squeeze a cent until the Queen cried.
9. He's so cheap when she opens her purse the Queen squints.
10. He's tighter than a crofter's lease.

- This bitter line, almost always uttered in full earnest, was brought to Canada from the Scottish Highlands in the days of skinflint lairds and massive eviction of crofters, when it proved more profitable for absentee landlords to raise sheep than to let human beings eke out a miserable subsistence.

11. He's so tight he wouldn't pay a dime to see a pismire eat a bale of hay.

- A pismire is an ant. This is cowboy Cliff Vandergrift's saying, reported by his friend Stan Gibson of Okotoks, Alberta.

12. He has his first dollar and half the arm of the man he got it off.
13. He's so tight, he squeaks when he walks.
14. Tight as a fiddle string.
15. Q: What's the difference between a Canadian and a canoe?

    A: Sometimes a canoe tips.
16. They invented copper-wire fighting over a penny.

    — *Brendan J. O'Byrne, Regina, Saskatchewan*
17. He's tighter than floor wax.

18. He would take the sleep out of your eyes.
19. He's so cheap he takes off his glasses if he's not looking at anything.

— *Bill Turner, Brandon, Manitoba*

20. Tighter than Paddy's hatband.

— *Minard Family, Nipawin, Saskatchewan*

21. So stingy she wouldn't give you last year's calendar.

— *Fredericton, New Brunswick*

22. You can't get blood out of a turnip.
23. Pay peanuts; get monkeys.

- There is however a price to be paid for constant stinginess, as Scrooge discovered.

24. He gives according to his meanness.

- A pun on giving 'according to one's means.'

— *Loretta Sherren, Fredericton, New Brunswick*

25. Tighter than a clam with lockjaw.

124. STUPIDITY

1. There isn't a neuron in the family.

— *Originator: Joe Ditsch, Dunnville, Ontario*

2. He may not be the stupidest dork alive, but he'll do until we find the real one.
3. If clues were shoes, he'd have clickers on his socks.

Clickers on shoes were something like tap bars.

(?) If you know, let me know precisely what "clickers" were.

— *Malcolm Cameron, Winnipeg, Manitoba*

4. Dumb as a post.
   - A person so described might also be called wooden-headed, since wood has never scored high on an IQ test.
5. They never finished plastering his attic.

   —Ms. Beau Gabiniewicz, New Westminster, British Columbia
6. If you put his brain in a thimble, it would roll around a lot.
7. He got those pock marks bobbing for French fries.

125. STUTTERING

1. *Mon frère bégaye tellement qu'il parait flou sur les photos.*
   - "My brother stutters so much that, when you take a picture of him, it's blurred."

126. TANNED

1. Brown as a berry.
2. Brown as a little Red Indian (politically incorrect).
   - Never mind the racism, the colours don't even match in the second saying. The racist notion that all North American native peoples had red skin began in published reports concerning explorer John Cabot's encounters in 1497 with the Beothuk tribes on the island that was later called Newfoundland. The Beothuks, victims of

systematic genocide by whites and other native peoples, were extinct by the late-eighteenth century. Beothuks ornamented their skin with red ochre for ceremonial and spiritual purposes, hence appearing red-skinned to Cabot and his men. A common error about Cabot, the man who named Canada, is that he was French. Cabot was born Giovanni Caboto in Genoa, Italy. Seeking financial backing for a voyage to find a western sea route to Asia, Caboto finally found it among merchants in Bristol, England. Before sailing, he became a naturalized British subject and Englished his name.

127. TENSE

1. She's a few turns too tight.
2. His copper is a little tight against the armature.

- This describes someone who is too tense or high-strung. The second expression refers to the copper wire wrapped around the armature of a small motor.

128. THIEF

1. He'd steal the beads off God's moccasins.

- "My dad said this all the time. He was from Whitney Pier, in Sydney, Cape Breton, Nova Scotia," writes Professor Jennifer MacLennan from the College of Engineering at the University of Saskatchewan in Saskatoon.

129. THINNESS

1. Skinny as a match with the wood scraped off
   — *Tom Cole, Toronto*

130. THREATS

1. Be good now, kids. Or, when you grow up, you'll go to Edmonton.
   - Said to misbehaving Calgary children, this Canadian saying demonstrates the playful, longstanding rivalry between the two chief cities of Alberta.
2. If I want any more lip from you, I'll rip it off your face.
3. You're looking for a bony five to the snotbox.
   - That is, I may have to punch you in the nose. This was heard at junior hockey practice.
4. Wanna play bingo? We'll start with one under the eye.
   - The result of this threat is a black eye. I collected this from a listener who phoned in while I was a guest on Bill Turner's radio show on CKLQ AM in Brandon, Manitoba.
5. I'm going to fill your pants with boots.
   - A Manitoba father said this to a son who was acting up. The boots belong to the father, and that is child abuse, so I hope the son reported him to the authorities!
6. Smell that and shiver!
   - This verbal threat accompanies a clenched fist shaken in the addressee's face.

7. You start yer mill, boy, and I'll haul yer sawdust.
• This is a central Ontario reply to someone looking for a fight.
8. I'll use a bottle-opener on your kneecaps.
9. I'll hang your hide on the fence.
• This was said to misbehaving children.
— *Donna Green, Toronto*

131. TIME

1. Time is what keeps everything from happening at once.
2. Warning: Dates in calendar are closer than they appear.

132. TIRED OUT

1. I'm so tired my hair hurts.
• This is very close to a Québec expression about having a very bad hangover, namely *avoir mal aux cheveux* 'to have a hair ache.'
— *Darrell Brown, Centre Burlington, Hants County, Nova Scotia*

133. TOUGHNESS

1. She looks as though she could chew nails and spit sparks.
— *Irene Lister, Perth, Ontario*

134. TRIP OVER YOUR OWN TONGUE DURING A SPEECH

1. Just say to the audience: Never buy your teeth from a catalogue.

- Actually there are many younger readers who will not know that false teeth were once made of wood and Canadians sent away for them by ordering false choppers from the Eaton's or Simpsons or Sears catalogues.
  — *Lyn McEachern, Thunder Bay, Ontario*

135. TRUTH

1. True as eggs.

- A saying heard in Didsbury, Alberta, this has to do with the perception that there is indeed something marvellously efficient in the structure of a chicken's egg, something devoid of excessive detail, something true. The egg is a natural design where form follows function rigorously. As a safe container made from a minimum of bodily resources, the egg is perfection.

136. UGLY

1. He's so ugly the Polaroids we took of him won't come out of the camera.

- There is a Quebec version of this put-down: *Il est tellement laid que les Polaroids qu'on fait de lui ne veulent pas sortir.*

137. UNPLEASANT

1. Uglier than a bucket of squashed worms with all the good ones picked out.

138. USELESSNESS

1. Useless as a pig on ice.
- "A bachelor neighbour used to say this. Pigs walk on their tiptoes and slide all over on a slippery surface," writes Dennis Kowal of Rossburn, Manitoba.

139. WEATHER IN CANADA

With the subcategories in alphabetical order

CLEAR NIGHT

1. The stars are as hard as diamonds.
- This describes a velvet-black, crystal-clear night in any season of the year.

COLD

1. It was so cold I could hear myself chime as I walked up the hill.
- Andy Nimmo of Edmonton reports this saying uttered by a forestry student at the University of New Brunswick, when he returned to residence after morning classes on a really frosty day.
2. Cold as a cod-fisher's knuckle.
- There's nothing worse on a cold day than handling a wet jig-line and being soaked with freezing Atlantic waves. Fisher is a synonym for fisherman.

3. Cold enough to bend the nail holding the thermometer.
4. Cold as a stepmother's breath.

• This came from England. Joseph Wright's *English Dialect Dictionary*, published between 1896 and 1905 has this entry: "Of weather, coldness, frostiness. A cold morning is said to 'have a stepmother's breath.'" Michael Traynor's *The English Dialect of Donegal* (1953) states that this is "said of a cutting north wind in December."

5. It's cold enough to freeze the arms off Golden Boy.

• The gilt statue atop the dome of the Manitoba Legislative Building in Winnipeg is a runner suggested by classical representations of Hermes or Mercury, messengers of the gods. He carries a sheaf of grain in his left hand and a burning torch in his right, and looks northward to Manitoba's future.

6. Colder than a polar bear's pyjamas on the shady side of an iceberg.
7. There's so much salt on the road, you get high blood pressure just taking out the garbage.

— *Loretta Sherren, Fredericton, New Brunswick*

8. There'll be rubber ice out there today.

• Patricia Millner of Sunderland writes about this expression of her stepfather who grew up in a lumber business north of Madoc, Ontario: "Rubber ice was mentioned in connection with driving a team of horses across ice which just held them, but bent in waves as they progressed over it."

9. It's cold enough to kill pigs.

- That is, October or November winds are blowing across a Canadian farm.

10. It's cold. But it's a dry cold.

11. It's cold as poor Willy, and he's pretty chilly; he's dead.

- Robert Marjoribanks of Ottawa writes, "I first heard that saying about poor Willy in Scotland in 1928 from my maternal grandmother, Matilda Cameron Wylie. She, however, delivered it in the Scots language: 'It's gey chilly, but no hauf as cauld as oor Willy. Willy's deid.' (Literally: 'it's pretty chilly, but not half as cold as our Willy. Willy's dead.')" The touch of cheerful morbidity and bluntness makes it likely that this saying sprang first to dour Scottish lips.

12. It's a tree-snappin' night.

- It's so cold up north that frost will get into the tree and split it. In some cases, the tree snaps or explodes, producing a long, lightninglike rip in the bark. Snappin' cold refers to the way trees snap in below-zero temperatures.

  — *Contributors: William Norman, London, Ontario, and Marjorie Andrews*

13. Not a fit day for a fence post.

- A very cold and stormy day in Prince Edward Island

14. We're takin' the mailbox in.

- There's going to be a violent ocean storm.
  — *From Port Medway, Nova Scotia*

15. Colder than a well-digger's knee.

16. The mercury's hiding this morning.

- "There's a saying used to describe a cold, cold Manitoba morning," writes Bill Turner of Brandon. "Some early thermometers were made in the US or England where their winters were milder and manufacturers there saw no need to take the scale too far below zero. Thus, on some thermometers the mercury would actually drop out of sight behind the thermometer bracket or frame."

17. Colder than a frog in a frozen pool.

18. Colder than charity and that's some chilly.

- This is an apt comment on how smug, well-to-do persons hand out scraps and tatters to the poor and then stand around congratulating themselves on their virtue.

DARKNESS

1. Darker than the inside of a black cow at midnight.
2. Darker than God's pockets.

DRY WEATHER

1. So dry last week around Virden, frogs were poundin' on the screen door, askin' for a dipper of water.

- Virden is in southern Manitoba on the

Saskatchewan border.

2. It's drier than old popcorn.
   - Said of a hot summer in Alberta, but widespread across Canada to indicate dryness.
3. It's so dry in southern Alberta, the trees go lookin' for the dogs.

Variant: So dry on the prairie that a few trees are bribing dogs.

4. It's so dry, mice have to pack a lunch to cross a field.

   — *Keith and Christie Funk-Froese, Rosenfeld, Manitoba*

5. So dry a cow's gotta graze ten miles an hour just to keep ahead of the dust.
   - This is a Saskatchewan saying.

FAIR WEATHER

1. There's enough blue sky to make a Dutchman a pair of britches.

   — *Jean Gibson, Thunder Bay, Ontario*

Québec variant: *Il y a assez de bleu dans le ciel pour faire des culottes à un irlandais.*

- There's enough blue sky to make an Irishman some britches. "My grandmother used to say this when we weren't sure if it was gonna rain or not," emails Carmen P. Joynt of Nanaimo, British Columbia. "When there was quite a bit of blue in the sky, it meant that there was a good chance it wouldn't rain."

2. We've a month on the days.

- Nova S. Bannerman, named after an aunt, Nova Scotia Sim, believes this Canadian saying is unique to Barney's River Station in Pictou County. Nova writes that "after the first hard month of winter is safely over one hears this being said, with a considerable degree of satisfaction."

3. Some day on a line of clothes.

- This Newfoundland expression suggests a warm, sunny, blowy day, perfect for drying.
  — *Jacqueline Hanrahan*

4. Let's stamp the robin.

- On seeing the first robin of spring, one licks one's right wrist with the tongue and pats the lick with the left hand, to bring good luck and fine weather. William Norman of London, Ontario, reports this innocent superstition from southern Ontario.

5. They're out today in their figures.

- That is, folks have taken off their bulky winter clothes and now in fair weather one can see what their bodies look like.

6. It's fairin' up.

- The storm is over. Clear weather is returning.

7. *Le soleil est plus beau que moi aujourd'hui.*

- The sun is more beautiful than me today. People say this when they get too much sun in their eyes and they have to squint.

FOG

1. Fog as thick as mud in a mug.

- This vivid simile is reported from Pool's Cove, Newfoundland.

FORECASTING

1. Do you know the ancient Aboriginal way of predicting a long winter? Never mind fat squirrels burying walnuts and acorns. See how much wood the white man has piled in his shed.
2. Yeah, it's gonna cloud over and be sunny with brush fires offshore.

- This is mockery of a TV weather forecaster, perhaps after a few bad calls.

HOT

1. It's so hot the hens are layin' hard-boiled eggs.
2. Hot enough to fry spit.
3. A hot July makes for a fat churchyard.
4. "Last summer, I mind, a coyote was chasing a rabbit across the prairie, and it was so hot, the both of them were walkin'."

- This saying is enclosed with quotation marks because these are the exact words of a contributor who wishes to be anonymous.

5. Hot enough to singe the bristles off a hog's back.
6. Hotter than a two-dollar pistol.

- The days of cheap revolvers, like Saturday night specials, are not gone—as current Toronto murder statistics show.

MISCELLANEOUS WEATHER CONDITIONS

1. There's water sitting on the hills.

- Said about a spell of prairie dampness and heavy rain in Saskatchewan.

2. Canadian weather? Nine months of hockey and three months of bad ice.

Variant: Nine months of winter and three months of darn hard sleddin'.

— *Gordon Dysart, Espanola, Ontario*

3. *Le diâble est aux vaches* 'the devil's in the cows.'

- In Québec, this means the weather will change soon.

4. There's a circus around the moon.

- Said of a lunar halo.

5. *Le temps a viré comme une anse de cruche.*

- 'The weather's turned like the handle on a jug.'

6. Such a pea-souper, sailors could sit on the ship's rail and lean against the fog.

- This is a Royal Canadian Navy expression from the Second World War.

— *John G. Jarvis, Calgary, Alberta*

RAIN

1. It's damper than duck dung.

- Said of Vancouver weather.

2. Q: Do you think it's going to rain?

   A: Be a helluva dry summer if it don't.

3. It's a Scotch mist to wet an Irishman to the hide.

- John Boyd of Silver City, New Mexico,

remembers his Scottish mother saying this about an all-day light rain at Oak Mountain and Peel, New Brunswick.

4. It's comin' up a bad cloud.
5. Enough rain to choke a toad.
6. It's so wet we're shooting ducks in the pantry.
7. Rain let up quick this morning. Disappeared faster than a British Columbia premier.
   - This is a reference to the precipitate resignations of several recent premiers of the province like Mike Harcourt and Glen Clark, or perhaps to the short time in power of Premier Ujjal Dosanjh.
8. *Il pleut à boire debout.*
   - The sense of this Québec expression is: It's raining so hard, you can drink standing up with your mouth open. Another *version Québécoise* is the joual: *Y mouille à boire deboutte*. Québec French has also this powerful way to describe a very hard rainfall: *Il pleut des clous* 'it's raining nails.' As well, there is the more conventional expression: *Il tombe par paquets* 'it's coming down in buckets.'
9. She's coming up to a stump-floater.
   - Heavy rain ahead.
10. When the cows lie low, tomorrow rain will show.
    - If cows are lying down in the field, it will rain tomorrow. Those who believe this old weather sign say that our bovine friends are especially sensitive

to the changes in air pressure that precede heavy rains. Why this sensitivity would make them plop down in a pasture is never explained.

—*J. Kipp, Waterloo, Ontario*

11. It's a frog-choker.
12. The devil's beating his wife.

- This is said in Guysborough County, Nova Scotia, when it rains while the sun is shining. The rain is supposedly the tears of the devil's wife.

— *Peggy Feltmate, Toronto*

13. It's pouring pitchforks and ploughshares.

SNOW

1. The old woman is pluckin' her geese today.

- Said of a fluffy snowfall. R.M. Lawson was told this one by a great-grandmother who owned a general store in Burford, Ontario. She had heard it first in 1889. But, interestingly, this is a direct translation of a Ukrainian folk saying that also shows up in Manitoba earlier in the nineteenth century.

2. Of a fluffy snowfall: She's driftin' down like dinner plates.

— *D.W. Bone, Wartime, Saskatchewan*

3. When it snows while the sun is shining: The devil's wife is fluffing her pillows.

— *From White Head, Guysborough County, Nova Scotia.*

4. Ain't but a skiff of snow to dust a gopher's behind.

- A skiff of snow in Manitoba and the Canadian West is a light snowfall, a gentle powdery dusting of snow. *Skiff* may be a British dialect variant of the noun *shift*. Skiff may be derived from Old Norse *skipta*, related to the Old English verb *sciftan* "shift."

5. It's like sticking your head in a flour sack to get away from a tornado.

- Said in Newfoundland of a heavy snowstorm with high winds.

  — *Bert Spencer, Bowmanville, Ontario*

STORMS

1. It's storming so bad the birds are walking.
2. It's a poor day to set a hen.
3. Least there's no flies out today.

WIND

1. Blowin' a gagger.
   - Ontario expression to describe a north wind blowing south off Georgian Bay.
2. That wind is strong enough to blow the nuts and the bolts off a gang plough.
   - Said of a Saskatchewan storm.
3. The wind is blowin' and it's too lazy to go around you.
4. It was so windy my hen laid the same egg twice.
5. It's windy enough to blow the horns off a bull.

Direct translation of Canadian French: *Il vente assez fort pour écorner un boeuf.*

— *Guy Charbonneau, Timmins, Ontario*

6. *Il vent tellement que les lumières de mon auto clairent dans le fossé.*
   - Wind's so strong my headlights are lighting the ditch.
7. It's horizontal weather out.
   - Heavy snow or rain with extremely high winds.
   — *Helen Burchnall, Valemount, British Columbia*

140. WELFARE & A NEW ORIGIN OF THE WORD *POGEY*

1. When a Canadian on unemployment insurance is asked by a stranger what he or she does for a living, the reply is, "Working as an artist for the government."
   Says the stranger, "An artist?"
   The person says," Yeah, I'm drawing pogey, eh."

My Own, Original Origin of the Word Pogey

- Pogey is a pure Canadian noun meaning 'welfare payment' or 'unempoyment insurance.' The *Oxford Canadian Dictionary* declares that the origin of pogey is unknown. I don't agree. I've found it. Pogey looks and sounds like a dialectical variant of "poke" especially in the phrase 'on the poke.' A poke is a small bag or little sack used by miners in the West and in the Canadian North to carry gold nuggets or gold dust. Therefore, if you were on the government's poke or pokey or pogey, that is, getting "gold" from the government coffers, you could have been said to have been receiving "pogey," in other words, financial assistance from the bag of government funds.

What About a Pig in a Poke?

The same word appears in another famous expression that many people know, but they don't know the real meaning of the expression: to buy a pig in a poke. If you purchase a something wiggling in a bag for a special low price, you can't tell if it's a fine little suckling pig, or some ribby runt, or even a wild cat tossed into the bag by some crook out to cheat you. When you buy anything sight unseen, you risk getting hornswoggled, cheated, defrauded. This is a very old scam in England. "A pig in a poke" was a familiar saying as early as *Heywood's Proverbs*, printed in 1546.

Another common expression related to "pig in a poke" is "to let the cat out of the bag." To let the cat out of bag is to reveal a secret. You bought "a pig in a poke" and didn't look inside the bag because it was a real bargain and part of the bargain was your swearing not to look inside the bag until you reached home. When you did, it wasn't a suckling pig, it was a scrawny cat that leapt out. But, if someone at the market had told you not to buy the pig in the poke, they would have been "letting the cat out of the bag."

141. WINNING IN CANADA

1. We won like Wolfe.

- Yeah, some victory. The saying is ironic. We won the battle but our leader died. On September 13, 1759, at the Battle of the Plains of Abraham, Major General James Wolfe commanded a British force that attacked the French under Lieutenant General the Marquis de Montcalm. Wolfe's troops climbed the cliffs below the Plains of Abraham and attacked. The battle was short and Quebec surrendered a few days later. Both Montcalm and Wolfe died of their wounds. We won like Wolfe and now we can stay calm like Montcalm. Or maybe not?

142. WISDOM

1. Some drink at the fountain of knowledge. Others just gargle.

143. WORK

The two categories of Canadian folk sayings that contain the most expressions are Work *and* Stupidity. *Does that tell us anything about the Canadian personality? Make of it what you will.*

1. I could jump down any shaft you ever dug, and not even break my ankle.
   - From gold-mining slang of Timmins, Ontario.
2. He works harder than a dog under a covered wagon.
   - During the settling of the prairies, homesteading drylanders drove covered wagons along trails. The wiser dogs raced alongside the wagon in the

shadow cast by the brown tarp covering the wagon. It was cooler there than in full sun, and the dog could run along farther without tiring.

3. This is not his first rodeo.

- He is competent at this job; he knows what he's doing.

  —*Vivian Hansen, Calgary, Alberta*

4. You'll soon see the rabbit.

- This Prince Edward Island folk saying implies that work is almost completed. When you cut hay beginning at the perimeter of a field, a rabbit in that field will run toward the centre. When there is no cover left, the rabbit bolts. This is T.K. Pratt's explanation in his splendid *Dictionary of Prince Edward Island English*.

5. Who will lift the cat's tail, if the cat won't?

- This is a direct translation from Finnish, and is still heard among descendants of immigrants from Finland in northern Ontario.

6. He doesn't ride the day he saddles.

- A translation from Danish, this is said of one who puts off work until tomorrow, one who procrastinates.

  — *Collected near Delta, British Columbia*

7. A fish in the punt is worth two in the water.

- The punt is a Newfoundland boat. The basic Newfoundland meaning is: keep fishing, and don't complain about how small the catch is; recognize instead what you've caught so far.

8. Of strict foremen at lumber camps: So strict, you darsn't spit on the whippletree in them days.

- James Fairfield was in Minden, Ontario, in the 1940s and remembered conditions in local lumber camps at the turn of the century.

  — *Submitted by his nephew, George Fairfield of Toronto*

A whippletree or whiffletree is the bar, of wood or steel, that swings on a pivot and to which the traces of a harness are fastened, so that a vehicle or farm implement can be pulled by horses or oxen.

9. The best fertilizer for the soil is the farmer's footprints.

10. You can't live on the wind and roost on the clothesline all of the time.

- This was said in rebuke to children who complained of doing chores on the farm.

  — *Martha Jackson, Toronto*

11. He's always puttin' things off. Why, he didn't get a birthmark until he was seven.

12. I'm sweating like a hen drawing rails.

- Chopping down cedar trees and then drawing them with a team of horses out of the bush, perhaps to make fence posts and rails, is sweaty work for a human being, and would be quite strenuous for a chicken! Domestic fowl are subject to heat stroke too.

13. Harder than pushing your truck uphill with a rope.

  — *Don Shanahan, Brighton, Ontario*

14. A new broom sweeps clean, but it takes an old one to get in the corners.

15. Might as well get a tin beak and pick corn with the hens.

- Said of any tedious chore.

  — E.C. Lougheed, Guelph, Ontario

16. As busy as a one-armed paperhanger with hives.

17. A man who watches the clock remains one of the hands.

- This is a farm pun that depends on two meanings of hand, the hands of the clock and a synonym for workers on a farm: hired hands. It suggests you will never rise above the level of hired hand if you keep watching the clock instead of doing your work.

18. *Occupé comme une queue de veau dans le temps des mouches*

- 'To be busy as a calf's tail in fly time'

19. Busier than a bee in a vacuum cleaner.

- This is a modern version of a very old saying. Thomas Jefferson left Washington at the end of his second presidential term in 1809 and never returned to the capitol. When asked about his seventeen years of retirement, he said he had been "as busy as a bee in a molasses barrel."

20. Never say "whoa" in a bad spot.

21. She's busier than a two-headed cat in a creamery.

  — From Three Hills, Alberta

22. You get paid the same for marching as you do for fighting.

- This is soldiers' slang from the Second World War.

  — *Gerry Sauvé, Gibsons, British Columbia*

23. Make yourself useful instead of ornamental.

  — *Ruth MacDonald, St. Catharines, Ontario*

24. Don't bust a gusset.

- Don't work too hard, and split the seams of your clothing, particularly a gusset, a piece of triangular cloth inserted in a seam to expand or reinforce it.

  — *Kate O'Donnell, Rainbow Lake, Alberta*

25. Fetch in the wood and water while you're resting.

- Angus McAuley of Surrey, British Columbia, recalls his grandmother's bit of Gaelic canniness when urging her grandsons to bring in water from a well and wood for the stove at noon, just before washing up for lunch.

26. Gone to fetch a basket of water.

- That is, sent on a useless errand.

27. Stuke or ride the binder.

- In other words, do something or get the hell out of the way. Steve McCabe of Oakville who was brought up on a rural Ontario farm writes, "This expression comes from lazy or tired field workers catching a ride on the binder in the earlier days of baling hay or straw. The good worker was the one stuking (piling) the bales."

28. Now we're sucking diesel.

- This modern Irish saying implies that we are making progress.

29. Cake and pie.

- Related to a piece of cake and a piece of pie, this Australian expression refers to an easy job. This brings to my mind the crafty film director Alfred Hitchcock confronted with a pompous film critic wondering about verisimilitude in Hitchcock's films. Said the portly director, almost always brighter than his interviewers, "Some people's stories are slices of life. My stories are slices of cake." This is an artist's response and is vividly valid today, when television in particular seems to have abandoned the fictional story for glum 'based on a true story' entertainments.

30. Locked and loaded.

- On the point of beginning any difficult task, the joker will twist his baseball cap ninety degrees so that the visor portion is over one ear and say, "Locked and loaded."

  — *Denis Tremblay, Ontario*

31. Hop short now!

- This Ottawa Valley expression means "wise up, move fast."

  — *Sarah Elvidge, Yarmouth, Nova Scotia*

32. Give Granny an axe for Xmas.

- The implication is you gift a person with something that will only make them work harder.

33. We pretend to work because they pretend to pay us.

- This peevish, whining complaint originated among Russian Communist factory workers in the 1950s. Since the early 1960s it's been a staple joke of English-Canadian union meetings. By the way, there will be no more cheap Russian jokes in this book. Does the name Pavlov ring a bell?

34. I'm chopping, but there ain't many chips flying.

— *Bill Turner, Brandon, Manitoba*

35. I run around the country on roller skates selling donuts.

- This response is given when one has grown tired of a proper answer to a question about one's occupation.

—*Robert H. Bilbey, Winnipeg, Manitoba*

36. *Ma mère se couche tellement tard et se lève tellement tôt qu'elle se rencontre dans l'escalier.*

- 'My mother goes to bed so late and gets up so soon that she meets herself on the stairway.' I never read a better or more rueful saying about how shiftwork, particularly the night shift, can drive you crazy and ruin your health.

37. A woman could throw more out the back door with a spoon than a man could bring in the front door with a shovel.

38. You can't make cheesecake from snow.

- Work with what you have.

39. I feel like I've been ironing in high heels.

40. Up and down like a fiddler's elbow.
- Very busy

41. I'll give it a lick and a promise.
- This indicates a quick once-over or clean up rather than a thorough job. The promise is to do the thorough job sometime later. Sharon Millie of Pilot Butte, Saskatchewan, also offers a Cape Breton Island variation: "A Scotch lick and an Irish promise."

42. There are tricks to every trade except basket making. You can see right through that!
- This jokey expression was brought to Canada from, among other places, the island of Guernsey.

43. We're cuttin' hay tomorrow.
- Work begins first thing in the morning

44. I'm busier than a one-eyed cat watching nine rat holes.

45. You better lick that calf again.
- Work poorly done must be redone.

46. You go at this like you're killing snakes with a toothpick.
- Slow down and do the job properly.

47. The hurrieder I go, the behinder I get.
- Haste makes waste even during work.

48. Okay, slaves, back to the oars!
- This is an invocation to return to drudgery still to be done, with its echo of Roman whips snapping over wretched rowers chained to the gunwales of a quinquereme bound out of Alexandria for Crete.

144. YOU CAN'T TAKE IT WITH YOU

1. There's no trailer hitch on a hearse.
   —Tim Gompf, near Oak Lake, Manitoba

Final Note to Reader

I hope you enjoyed these Canadian words and sayings. There are however many more uncollected gems of Canuck mirth and folk-saying savvy waiting to be preserved between book covers. If you know any awesome Canadian sayings from your neck of the Canadian woods that are not included here, please send them to me by email.

email: canadiansayings@mountaincable.net
website: www.billcasselman.com

B.C.

INDEX

Note to the reader: I have not indexed the Canadian sayings in Part Two of this book because they are classified reasonably by the titles of the 144 categories under which I list the sayings.

A

Abegweit: PEI name, 244-46

aboriginal medicine and first aid, 42

Acadia's favourite food (*fricot*), 131-32

Acadian kitchen recipes, 131-32

Acadian owl, 258

Acer: genus name of maple tree, 190

Adam: Hebrew origin, 68

Adam-based English surnames, 66-67

Adams: origin of surname, 65-69

Africville: destruction of African-Nova Scotian neighbourhood, 139

Agincourt, Ontario and *Hakenkurz*, 3

air bladder of cod fish, 271

Alberta chuckwagon pudding, 270

Alberta cushion cactus, 104

Alberta *rattlesnakes*, 4

alder tree: Black alder, 6;
Canadian place names, 7-8;
English surnames, 7;
etymology & word lore, 6-7;
French surnames, 8;
Sitka alder, 10;
Speckled Alder, 9;
Venice, 6;
weird quotation, 10

American wake-robin, 163

Anishnabeg 'people made from the void,' 188

Antarctica: word origin, 15

apple grunt, 138

apple paring bee, 12

apple place names in Canada, 13

apple songs, Canadian, 12

apple-drying bee, 134

apples of Canada, origin of some species' names:
Fameuse, 11;
McIntosh Red, 11;
Pacific Crab Apple, 11

Arbor vitae, Canadian origin, 13

arctic char, 14

Arctic willow tea, 15

arctic: Greek myth of Arcas, 15; origin of word, 14-15

Arctostaphylos uva-ursi: bearberry, 166-67

Aristolochia: origin of the plant family name, 90

Aristotle's lantern, 311-12

INDEX

Asarum: botanical genus name origin, 90
aspirin from willow bark, 16
Athabasca boat, 16
Athabasca 'reed beds,' 16
atungawiat: bearberry in Inuktitut, 166-67

B

bagosse (Acadian sauce), 98
bakeapple: origin of an all-Canadian berry word, 34-37
baked wind pill: comic synonym for bean, 37
bald-headed prairie, 241
Ballads of a Cheechako, 94
balm of Gilead fir tree: mistaken name, 38
balm: Bill Casselman's favourite word story, 39-41; Canadian place names, 44; surnames, 43-44
Balsam fir tree and its word lore, 37-44; tree resin, 41
bangbelly, 45-46
Bannock, Saskatchewan: origin of town's name, 250
bannock: unleavened wheat bread, 47, 249-50
Barry Callaghan, 80
bear foot: food-gathering device, 46
bear's butter (bear's grease), 46-47
bear's grape, 166-67
bedlunch of Prince Edward Island, 47
bellybuster, 47
benny (Canadian prison slang), 88
Big Dipper and the word *arctic*, 15
billy (Canadian prison slang), 88
birchbark canoe, 47-48; birchbark moose call, 47-48; birchbark rogan (container), 48
"Birdcages:" Colony of Vancouver Island buildings, 49
birl: spin a log while riding it, 176-77
biscuit-root, 242-43
Bison bison athabascae: name origin of the wood buffalo, 17
black maple, 197-98
Blackfoot mythology, 154
Blackfoot riverbed, 103
blaze-belly, 80
blé d'Inde (Indian corn): *blé indien*, 49-50
blueberries, 138
blueberry pie of Nova Scotia, 133-34
Blue-Blood Alley: Vancouver historical neighbourhood name, 50-51
bluff: origin of Canadian Prairie word, 51-52
bodewash ("cow chips") 103-4; dried buffalo dung, 103; synonyms, 103; use as fuel, 104

bog potato or groundnut, 203
boil-up, 52
bois de vache "cow wood," 103-4
bois des prairies "prairie wood," 103-4
borage: herb word origin, 56-60
Borago officinalis, 59-60
boss ribs, 52-53
botulism, 186
boucane: Quebec slang for booze, 54
boucanière (Acadian smokehouse), 53-54
boucaniers (Caribbean pirates), 53-54
bouillon d'habitant, 54-55
Bourassa: origin of Quebec surname, 57-59; Henri Bourassa, 58-59
bourdonne (Acadian sauce), 98
bourgaille (Acadian sauce), 98
bourre de laine, 56-60
bowel, 185
breadroot, 242-43
brew, 63
brewis (hard tack and fish): brewis bag, 64; brewis origin, 61-62; brewis recipe, 63-64; hard tack, 61; Newfoundland meal, 60; tacky, 61
Brollywood, British Columbia, 64-65
brue or *broue*: soapberry, 267-68
Bryan Adams: origin of surname, 65-69
buccaneer: origin of the word, 53-54
buffalo berry (*Shepherdia canadensis*), 69, 268; buffalo berry beer, 69
buffalo hunt word, 148
buffalo root, 242-43
buffalo stew, 69
bug juice, 80
bunch, 52-53
bungee: examples of Bungee words, 71; origin of word *bungee*, 70; Red River dialect of Manitoba, 70-71; word stock, 70
burgoo: English dialect word for soup in origin of Canada's rubbaboo, 253
burrito, 56-60
burro, 56-60
butte, 71-72
butter tart, 72-75; how to eat it, 72; Sheldon Posen on butter tart recipe, 73-75
buttercup family of plants, 147-48
bycatch, 17-18
Bytown: early name of Ottawa, 217

C

Cabot, John: Cabot and racist term *redskins*, 76; Cabotia, 78-79;

Latin *caput* derivatives, 77-78; name on Canadian maps, 75; origin of explorer's surname, 75-79; surname meaning, 76-77
cactus fruit in Alberta, 104
Cadillac: French fur trader and luxury car, 79-80
Calgary locale: Scotchman's Hill, 259
Calgary neighbourhood names, 252-53
Calgary Redeye, 80
Callaghan: Barry Callaghan works, 80; literary surname of Canada, 80-83; Morley Callaghan works, 81-82; surname origin, 82-83
camas plant of British Columbia (*Camassia quamash*), 84-86
Camassia cusickii, 85-86
Camosun, first name of Victoria, British Columbia, 84
camping near Pacific Rim National Park, 268-69
Canada bloodroot (*Sanguinaria canadensis*): 86-87; ceremonial face paint, 86; folklore & medical uses, 87; red dye, 86
Canada Pension Plan, 202
Canada: other names for this country, 78-79
Canada's national word: eh, 116-22
Canadian paring bee, 12
Canadian wild ginger (*Asarum canadense*): 88-90; description, 88; genus, 90; uses of plant, 89
candle fish, 216-17
Canoe birch (*Betula papyrifera*), 47
canoe routes of voyageurs, 187-88
canola: Canadian origin of word, 91; rapeseed, 90; seed, meal and oil: 90-91; turnip rape, 90; uses, 91
Cariboo Gold Rush, 92
caribou massing, 130
caribou, 91-92; Cariboo Gold Rush, 92; folk etymology, 92; *le caribou* drink, 91-92; origin of animal name, 92
carreboeuf: mistaken French, 92
catskinner, 93
CCF government of Saskatchewan under Tommy Douglas, 201-2
cedar (*Cedrus*) as plant name, 14
censitaires, 56
Central Butte, Saskatchewan, 71
Charles Dickens character and Canadian fish name, 108
Charlottetown's Dizzie Block, 78
cheechako "newcomer," 94;

origin in Chinook Jargon, 94
chiard: Canadian French term, 94-95; *chiard de goélette*, 95; *chiard du pêcheur*, 95; *chiards blancs*, 94; 'grub,' 94; 'hash,' 94-95
Chinook Jargon words: gooeyduck, 134-35; high muckamuck, 151-52; olallie and olalliechuk, 256; potlatch from Nootka language, 229; salal, 254-56; wapatoo, 110-11
Chipewyan language, 167
chuckwagon pudding of Alberta, 270
chuckwagon *tent pegs*, 4
cigarette dude, 148
cipaille (sea pie), 95-97; disputed origin of word, 96-97; at feast of *Réveillon*, 96; layered meat pie of Quebec, 95-96; recipe and preparation, 96-97
ciselette (Acadian pork & molasses dessert sauce), 97-98; other names, 98; recipe, 97-98
cod fish air bladder, 271
cohort, 3
Colcannon Night in Newfoundland, 98-102; detailed origin, 100-2; folk etymology, 100; history, 98; rituals, 99-100
combers, 158
corn words: maize and *blé*, 50
corvée, 56
coteaux of Canada (high prairie), 102; origin of word, 102
coulee (dry stream bed), 103; origin of word, 103
cowberry (*Vaccinium vitis-idaea*), 138
Cribbies, The: St. John's, Newfoundland neighbourhood, 272
crummy, 177
cushion cactus of Alberta (*Coryphantha vivipara*): 104; edible fruit, 104

D

damper boys, 105; damper cakes, 105; damper dogs of Newfoundland, 105; damper devils, 105
Davis raft, 177-78
death camas (*Zygadenus venenosus*), 85
demoiselles (French-Canadian voyageurs' term for hoodoos), 153
Digby chicken (Nova Scotian smoked herring), 106
Digby chips, 106
Dinosaur Provincial Park, Alberta: hoodoo, 152-53
dishonest use of language in Canada: *see* gobbledygook

"Dog Patch," Edmonton neighborhood, 106-7
dollar: origin of the word, 107-8
Dolly Varden trout, 108
dough gods (Alberta chuck-wagon dumplings), 109
Douglas Fir (*Pseudotsuga menziesii*), 109-10;
Blue Douglas Fir; 110
source of name, 109-10
uses, 110
Douglas maple, 198
Douglas, David: Scottish naturalist's travels in Canada, 109-10
Doukhobors in Canada, 163-65
Dragon's Blood, 86-87
Dresden: meaning of name, 173
dried buffalo dung as fuel, 103-4
drink-up, 52
duck potato (Canadian arrowhead plant, *Sagittaria*), 110-11;
alternative names, 110;
description, 111;
origin of aboriginal term (wapatoo), 111
dulse (*Palmaria palmata*, edible seaweed of our Maritimes), 111-13;
description, 111-12;
word lore, 112;
rhodophyte seaweeds, 112-13
dumb cake, 113-14
dumplings cooked on chuckwagon, 109
dunker (Canadian prison slang), 88
Dutchmess: Lunenburg cod and potatoes dish, 114
Dutchtown and Dutch Village: Halifax neighbourhoods, 138

E

East Coulee, Alberta, 103
Eau Claire: Calgary neighbourhood, 114
Edmonchuk, Alberta, 114-15
Edmonton neighbourhoods:
Knob Hill in Rutherford, 219;
Packingtown, 219;
Rat Creek, 219;
Skunk Hollow or Lavine, 219
Edmonton: "Dog Patch," city district, 106-7
eel pie: fishing for eels, 115;
eel words, 115; recipe, 115
eh? marker of Canadian speech: 800 years old, 117;
in Canadian fiction, 121;
samples from famous authors, 117-18;
use, 116, 119-20, 121-22
Elijah McCoy: African-Canadian inventor, 247-48
Etzikon Coulee, Alberta (Siksika term), 103

F

farmer's stew, 54-55
fat-back pork scrunchins, 60
FDAM, acronymic boating insult: 207

figgy duff (Newfoundland boiled pudding): history, 123; origin of *duff*, 125; recipe, 123; why fig means raisin, 124
fir tree, 38
firewater recipe, 4-5
firewater: loan translation from Cree, 125; historical spread of the term, 126; quotation from *The Last of the Mohicans*, 126; selling to aboriginal peoples, 126
fireweed of the Yukon (*Epilobium angustifolium*): Canadian and international uses of plant, 127; how to brew fireweed tea, 127; medical uses, 128; official flower of Yukon, 128; sweet pith, 127
First Meridian of Manitoba, 128-29
five-finger discount: Toronto street slang, 290
flacoons of Newfoundland, 105-6
Flats, The: Edmonton neighbourhood, 107
flèche d'eau (arrowhead plant), 110-11
flipper pie of Newfoundland: ancient Scandinavian food, 130; classic recipe, 130; flipper not a paw, 129; historic dish, 129;
flour (Robin Hood), 251
food preservation in pioneer prairie days, 135-36
Fort Whoop-Up, 4-5
Foster Hewitt, legend of Canadian hockey broadcasting: author meets Hewitt, 149-50; CBC Hockey night in Canada, 149; English surnames like Hewitt, 151; first hockey on radio, 149; surname origin, 150-51
foule: caribou migration massing, 130
foxberry (*Vaccinium vitis-idaea*), 138
freakazoid goblins in German alder trees, 8-9
Fredericton, New Brunswick landmarks: Fickle Finger of Fate, 131; The Green, 131; Little Nude Dude fountain, 131
Frenchman Butte, Saskatchewan, 71
fricot (Acadian stew), 131; *fricot à la poule*, 131-32; *fricot aux coques*, 131; *grand-pères* or dumplings, 131; rabbit stew, 132; stupid cook's stew, 132; weasel stew, 132
frolic in New Brunswick: 134; etymology of term, 134
fudge: Nova Scotia pudding, 138

"Full Nanaimo," boating insult, 207

fungy or fungee: Nova Scotia deep-dish blueberry pie, 133-34

G

geoduck (or gooeyduck): clam facts, 135; illegal trade in clams, 135; largest burrowing bivalve, 134; one of longest-lived animals on earth, 134-35; origin of word, 134; west coast clam, 134

Gimli, Manitoba, 228-29

gin pole: origin of term, 136; preserving meat in pioneer prairie days, 135

Gitchi Manitou 'Great Spirit,' 188

given names' origins, 67

gobbledygook, baloney, bafflegab Canadian-style, 17-34; in Canadian government English, 22-23; in Canadian medicine, 21-22; in Canadian school euphemisms, 22-26; definitions, 17-21; in Department of National Defence bulletin, 31-32; legitimate use of jargon, 33-34; in RCMP police reports, 26-31; in small print of banking document, 32-33

gondola: special Canadian hockey use of word, 149

gooeyduck, 134-35

gorbies of Muskoka: loud tourists, 136; origin of term, 136

gow of British Columbia: B.C. fisheries export, 137; herring roe, 137

Great Bear constellation myth, 15

grid roads, 137

grosse bosse, 52-53

grouse and prairie chickens, 236-38

grunt: blueberry and huckleberry grunt, 138; foxberry or cowberry, 138; Nova Scotia pudding or dumpling, 138; raspberry and apple, 138; recipe, 138; rhubarb grunt, 138

H

habitant: *censitaires*, 56; *corvée*, 56; habitant as insult, 56; origin of the term, 55

Halifax neighbourhoods: Africville, 139; Dutchtown, 138; Dutch Village, 138; Liquordome, 139; Slackers in Royal Canadian Navy slang, 138; Twelve Apostles, 139

Hallelujah Point, Stanley Park, 139-40

Halloween in Newfoundland, 98-102

hangover cure: prairie oyster, 241; recipe, 241

hard tack, 60-64
Harnoy: origin of surname, 140-41
Hausa language, 153
Hauskuchen: Lunenburg cod and potatoes dish, 114
Haw eaters of Manitoulin Island: etymology of haw, 142-43;
Dutch "Hague," 143;
haw in Chaucer, 143;
Manitoulin Island Ojibwe theatre group, 144-45;
origin of nickname, 142-43
hawberry, 142-43
hawthorn bush, 142-43
Hébert, Anne: her famous Quebec relatives François-Xavier Garneau and Hector Saint-Denys Garneau, 146;
her French, 145-46;
her works, 146;
origin of surname, 147
hepatica (*Hepatica acutifolia, Hepatica americana*): botanical names, 147;
buttercup family name, 147-48;
etymology of name, 147;
quotation from Catharine Parr Traill, 147;
spring flower of Canada, 147
herbe fret (voyageurs' term for fireweed), 127-28
"Here's a Ho!" Manitoba drinking toast, 148;
buffalo hunt word, 148;
cigarette dudes, 148;
sodbusters and stubble-jumpers, 148
herring: method of smoking in Maritimes, 106
herring-choker (New Brunswicker): Bay of Fundy spring herring run, 148;
fall herring run, 148;
Maritime slang, 148
high muckamuck (pompous official): Canadian origin in Chinook Jargon, 151-52
high prairie, 102
highbush cranberry or Pembina berry, 204
high-line logging, 178
hivernant 'one who spends the whole winter here,' 187-88
hoodoo (rock or earth pillar of the Canadian West): African origin of the word, 153;
in Blackfoot (Siksika) mythology, 154;
description, 152;
locations in Alberta and British Columbia, 153;
North American use, 153-54
Hoodoo Valley, British Columbia, 153
hooshum: soapberry, 267-68
hootch: all-Canadian booze word, 154-55;
Na-Dene family of languages, 155;
origin in Tlingit language, 154;
Tlingit meaning, 154-55;
Yukon's Klondike gold rush use, 154
horse mosser, 158
huckleberries, 138

human: word origin, 69
hunch, 52-53
hurt pie of the Canadian Maritime provinces: hurt cake, 155;
hurt wine, 155;
hurty pudding, 155;
Mark Twain's *Huckleberry Finn*, 155;
Newfoundland *Vaccinium* berry species, 155;
old English berry name, 155
Hydra: freshwater polyp causing "prairie itch," 241
hydro: hydro bill, hydro man, hydro power, hydro service, hydro wires, 216;
exclusively Canadian usage, 216

I

Icelandic language, 228-29
Icelandic yogourt of Manitoba (*skyr*), 264
Indian Act and banning of the potlatch, 229-30
Indian carrot, 242-43
Indian corn, 49-50
Indian cup or pitcher plant, 227
Indian tobacco, 166-67
intervale: rich alluvial bottomland soil, 156
Irish moss: Canadian Maritime dessert pudding, 156;
commercial uses, 156-57;
Irish moss products like carrageenin, 157;
Prince Edward Island Irish moss technical words, 157-58;
recipe, 156;
Stompin' Tom Connors "Song of The Irish Moss," 158-59
Irish naming conventions, 80-83

J

jack-in-the-pulpit, 162;
Iroquois name, 163;
member of *Arum* plant family, 162;
origin of Quebec name, 162-63;
plant poisonous, 163
jargon, Canadian: *see* gobbledygook
jaw-bone 'credit,' 178-79
Jewish family names in Russia and Germany, 140-41
jig, 159
jigg's dinner (Newfoundland salt beef or pork dish): letter about origin in comic strip "Maggie and Jiggs," 159-60;
"jig" place names, 159;
recipe, 159;
various "jig" words of Newfoundland, 159
jigger line, 159
jill-poke: comic insult, 160-61;
New Brunswick lumber term, 160-61
joanies, 105
jollop: kitchen leftovers on PEI, 161;
origin of term, 161
juniper berry caution, 161-62

juniper tea: First People's incense, 162; herbal remedy with toxic caution, 162; growth habit of tree, 161; from Rocky Mountain Juniper (*Juniperus scopulorum*), 161; uses of juniper berries, 162

K

kahahoosa: Iroquois name for jack-in-the-pulpit, 163

Kane, Paul: Canadian painter writes of camas, 86

kartoshnik: history of Doukhobors in Canada, 164-65; Saskatchewan Doukhobor potato cake, 163; recipe, 163; Russian-German-Italian origins of word, 164; Russian origin of the Doukhobors name, 165

keg angels, 4

kiack: Maritime insult, 166; Mi'kmaq fish, 165; Nova Scotia alewife, 165

Kid McCoy: boxer, 248-49

kinnikinnick or bearberry: *Arctostaphylos uva-ursi* plant description, 166-67; bearberry tea, 167; common names in Canada, 166; etymology of kinnikinnick in Cree and Ojibwa, 167; herbal remedy, 167; *kutai* in Russian, 167; names in other aboriginal languages, 167

Kitsch: origin in German, 169; term in art, 169-70

Kitsilano: extent, 168; German origin, 169; local history, 168; other origin of name in Squamish language, 169; pun name: Kitschilano, 169; the word *Kitsch*, 169; as a term in art criticism, 169-71; Vancouver neighbourhood, 168

Klondike gold rush, 94, 154

Krall, Diana: Canadian jazz pianist and singer, 171; career, 171; origin of surname in Sorbian, 171-73; origin of Sorbia/Serbia, 173-74

L

Labrador tea (*Ledum groenlandicum*) 174; part of "Indian tobacco" mix, 175; recipe, 174; staple hot drink of northern peoples, 174; synonym: wishakapucka, 174

Labrador: timeline of boundary dispute and history, 210-14

lacaishe: Quebec name for goldeneye, 175

Ladies' Lookout: St. John's, Newfoundland locale, 272

lad-in-a-bag (Newfoundland boiled pudding), 122-25

Lake Winnipeg goldeneye: aboriginal name *nacaish*, 175; Manitoba fish, 175; Quebec name *lacaishe*, 175; special Canadian dish, 175

lassy mogs: Newfoundland cakes or cookies; 175; origin of the word *mog*, 175-76; sweetened with molasses, 175

Latin and Greek origin of science terms, 1

Lavine: Edmonton district, 219

legend of the spooky *Erlkönig*, 8-9

Leipzig: meaning of name, 173

lek: grouse display ground, 237

lily, prairie (*Lilium philadelphicum*): 241

liquor traded to Indians, 5

logging words of British Columbia, 176; birling or log-spinning, 176-77; crummy or loggers'work bus, 177; Davis raft, 177-78; high-line logging, 178; jaw-bone 'credit,' 178-79

Lombard as source of our word *lumber*, 179-83

loup-cervier: Acadian word for lynx, 179

lowbush cranberry or mooseberry, 204

lucivee: Acadian name: *loup-cervier*, 179; New Brunswick slang for a lynx or its pelt, 179

lumber: Chaucer quotation, 182; extensive history of word, 179-83; historical British uses of term, 183; history of the Kingdom of Lombardy, 181; history of Lombards, 180; how Lombard became lumber in England, 181-83; Lombardy origin, 180; lumber in British slang, 182-83; origin of their name, 180

lumbering pole with hook (peavey), 219

Lunenburg pudding: Nova Scotia pork sausage, 184-86; origin of *poutine*, 184; origin of the word *pudding*, 184; origin of the word *botulism*, 186; origin of the word *bowel* and its connection with sausage, 185

lunettes boucanées, 54

lynx, 179

M

macadamia nuts, 66

macadamize, 66

Maggoty Cove: St. John's, Newfoundland neighbourhood, 272

Malpeque oyster: commercial oyster farms, 186-87;

Malpeque Bay, 186;
origin in Mi'kmaq language place name, 186;
Prince Edward Island's famous food, 186-87

mangeurs de lard (porkeaters): canoe routes of voyageurs, 187-88;
newcomers to Canada's North, 187-88

Manitoba drinking toast, 148

Manitoba maple, 198-99;
pollen alert, 198-99

Manitoba's First Meridian, 128-29

Manitoulin Island residents or haw eaters, 142-45

Manitoulin Island: Ojibwe creation myth, 188;
Ojibwa meaning of name, 188

Manitouwaning: Ojibwa myth & meaning of name, 188-89;
Ontario place name, 188-89

maple syrup, 191-92

maple syrup urine disease, 197

maple tree and leaf: *Acer*: origin of maple genus name, 190;
ancient Roman uses of maple wood, 190;
black maple, 197-98;
commercial uses of maple wood, 194;
Douglas maple, 198;
French maple words, 190;
history of the word *sugar*, 195-96;
Manitoba maple, 198-99;
maple bark disease, 197;
maple leaf as emblem of Canada, 193-94;
maple in other world languages, 192;
maple species,197-99;
maple syrup not unique to North America, 191-92;
my favourite maple quotation, 199-200;
new etymology of the word *maple*, 191;
nuggets of maple knowledge, 189;
Ojibwa folk story "How the Maple Got Sweet Sap," 194-95;
red maple, 199;
samara or maple key, 199;
story of the song "The Maple Leaf Forever," 194;
sugar maple, 193;
symbol of Canada, 189-201

mapping Manitoba, 128-29

Marquis wheat: exported to the world, 201;
hybridized at Agassiz, Manitoba, 201

Maverick, Congressman Maury, and coining of the word *gobbledygook*, 20

McCoy, Elijah: African-Canadian inventor, 247-48

Medicare: Saskatchewan word, 201-2;
Tommy Douglas and introduction of free hospital care, 202;
Tommy Douglas, one of my heroes' biography, 202;
universal prepaid medical care, 201-2

"Mexico North," 64-65
Mi'kmaq language place name, 186
Mi'kmaq potato (*Apios* or groundnut), 203; Nova Scotia place named after groundnut, 203; origin of botanical name, 203; sweet tubers, 203; uses, 203
Mi'kmaq word in English: *kiack*, 165-66
Mi'kmaq words: *sequbbun*, 203; Shubenacadie, 203
mina: Cree word for berry in Canadian place names, 203-4; Moosomin, Saskatchewan, 204; Pembina, 204
Minegoo: ancient name of Prince Edward Island, 244, 246
Mitchell, W.O., 238
mogs, lassy: Newfoundland cake or cookie, 175-76
monkey fur: seaweed impurity in Irish moss, 158
moose milk, 80
moose muffle soup: acquired taste, 206; dining caution, 206; Quebec French origin of the word *muffle*, 206; recipe, 205
mooseberry, 203-5; Cree origin, 204; quotation from early explorer Samuel Hearne, 205; synonym for lowbush cranberry, 204
moose-flower: trillium, 296
Moosomin, Saskatchewan, 204
Morley Callaghan, 81-82
moss horse, 158
moss money on PEI, 158
mosser: PEI term, 157
mug up: Canadian quick snack and drink on the trail, 52, 206

N

nacaish: Algonkian name for goldeneye fish, 175
Na-Dene language family: meaning of Na-Dene, 155
Nanabush: trickster god of the Ojibwe people, 144-45
Nanaimo, British Columbia: "Full Nanaimo," boating insult, 207; Nanaimo bar, a Canadian baked biscuit, 207
nettle (*Urtica dioica*): ancient uses, 209-10; cure when stung by nettles, 208; "Indian spinach" or nettle leaves, 208; protective hairs, 208; medical caution, 208; soup, 208-10; as spurious remedy, 209; stings after 200 years, 209
New Brunswick lumber term: scripture cord, 259-60

New Brunswick salted shad, 250
Newfoundland and Labrador: future squabbles, 214; history, 210-14; name change, 210-11; timeline of provincial history from 1763 to 1990, 211-14
Newfoundland berries in hurt pie, 155
Newfoundland berry wine, 272
Newfoundland Halloween traditions, 98-102
"Nokomis & The Maple Trees," Ojibwa folktale, 194-95
Northwest Company, 187
Northwest Mounted Police, 5
nuisance grounds: classic Canadian euphemism for garbage dump, 214-15; quotation from Margaret Laurence, 214-15
Nunavik: meaning in Inuktitut language, 215; Ungava peninsula territory, 215-16
Nunavut: creation of, 215-16; different from Nunavik, 215-16; meaning in Inuktitut language, 216; mid-Arctic Canadian territory, 215-16

O

office, 60
Ofra Harnoy, Canadian cellist: career, 140; Hebrew etymology of Ofra and Ofer, 141-42; Jewish family names in Russia and Germany, 140-41; surname origin, 140-41
Ojibwa mythology, 194-95
olallie: Chinook Jargon for salmonberry, 256-57
olalliechuk: salmonberry wine, 256
Ontario Hydro: Canadian uses of the word *hydro*, 216; creation and history, 216; hydro-electric, 216
oolichan (candle fish): greasy smelt, 216; medicinal oolichan oil, 217
Ottawa: brief history of city, 217; Mechanicsville, 217-18; neighbourhoods like "Happy Walk" or Gladstone Street, 217; Rideau Canal and Bytown as early names, 217; Rockcliffe Park, 218; Rooky Rockcliffe or Manor Park, 218
oyster farms of Prince Edward Island, 186-87

P

Packingtown: Edmonton district, 219
pain râpé: Acadian potato and meat pie, 247

Paul Kane and the camas plant, 86
peavey: New Brunswick lumber tool, 219
Pembina berry: highbush cranberry synonym, 204
Pembina River, Pembina Mountains, Pembina highway, 204
pemmican: berry pemmican, 221-22;
bourgeois pemmican, 222;
dog pemmican, 222;
most surprising of all Canadian words, 220;
my research into pemmican's word relatives around the world, 222-24;
origin of word, 220-21;
recipe and storage, 221
petite bosse, 52-53
petits cochons 'piggywigs' or pitcher plant, 227
phoney-baloney Canadian words, 17-34
pickerel weed (*Pontederia cordata*): growth habit, 224-25;
locale, 224;
origin of botanical name, 225
Picture Butte, Alberta, 71
pikelet: Nova Scotia drop-scone or crumpet, 225;
recipe, 225;
origin of word in Welsh, 226
piney-woods Tackies, 61
pioneer toothpaste of Canada, 89
pipe: unit of distance, 52
pipe: voyageurs' French, 52
pipsissewa (*Chimaphila umbellate*): habit, 226;
in herbal remedies, 226;
oil of wintergreen, 226;
plant locale, 226;
tastes like root beer, 226;
word origin in Abenaki language, 226
pitcher plant (*Sarracenia purpurea*): how it "eats" insects, 227;
named for Canada's first professional botanist Dr. Michel Sarrazin, 227;
official flower of Newfoundland and Labrador, 227;
other names like Indian Cup and *petits cochons* and Whip-poor-will's boots, 227
pomme de prairie (*Psoralea esculenta*): 242-43
ponask: Cree wooden spit for roasting food over fire, 228
ponnukokur: Icelandic pancakes of Manitoba, 228-29;
origin in Icelandic language, 228;
recipe & preparation, 228-29
poppy: origin of word in ancient Egyptian, 86
pork and jerk: Prince Edward Island food humour, 229
porkeaters 'newcomers to Canada's North,' 187-88
potlatch: acquired meanings of word, 230;
ban repealed in 1951, 230;

once banned gift ceremony of West Coast peoples, 229;
origin of word in Nootka language, 229;
sociology of ceremony, 229-30

pouding du chômeur: history of the word's root, 231-32;
Quebec's welfare pudding, 230-31;
in St. Jerome's Vulgate, 231

poutine: Acadian, 235-36;
complete story, 184, 233-36;
complex origin of the word, 233-34;
many meanings in Quebec and among Acadians, 233;
Quebec invention of "modern" *poutine* in 1957, 234-35;
poutine à la mélasse, 236;
poutine à la vapeur, 236;
poutine au pain, 236;
poutine en sac, 236;
poutines râpées, 235;
recipe, 234

prairie buffalo meat, 52-53

prairie chicken: British Columbia slang for prairie person, 238;
display at their lek, 237;
emblem of Saskatchewan, 237-38;
endangered grouse, 236;
greater prairie chicken (*Tympanuchus cupido*), 237;
recipe but not to be used, 237

prairie dew, 80

prairie geographic layout, 128-29

prairie potato, 242-43

prairie turnip (*Psoralea esculenta*): alternative names of this pea-family member, 242;
quote in Captain John Palliser's journal, 243;
use as flour, 242;
voyageurs' name

prairie: bald-headed prairie, 241;
etymology of *prairie*, 239;
French surnames like Dupry, 239-40;
history of the word, 238-42;
other uses of word, 240;
Prairial month, 240;
prairie itch, 241;
prairie lily, 241;
prairie oyster, 241;
prairie squint, 241;
prairie wool, 241;
pratincolous, 242;
quotation from *Who Has Seen the Wind?*, 238;
voyageurs' word, 238-39

prickly pear cactus (*Opuntia polyacantha*): cactus native to Canada, 243; Canadian locales, 243;
edible flesh of cactus, 243-44;
plant description, 243;
preparation as food, 244

Prince Edward Island of many names: Champlain's name for PEI, 246;
etymological note on Minegoo, 246;
island's ancient settlement, 244;
Mi'kmaq names like Abegqeit, 244;

Minegoo, 244, 246;
origin and meaning of its Mi'kmaq names, 245;
origin of present provincial name, 246;
quotation about PEI from *Anne of Green Gables*, 245

Prince Edward Island's Irish moss industry, 156-59

puccoon, 86-87

pudding, 184

Q

quamash plant, 84-86

quantum satis: pharmacists' Latin, 5

quilting frolic, 134

R

racist term: *redskins*, 76

rampike: dead, burnt tree, 246-47

rapeseed and its name change, 90

rappé pie: Acadian potato and meat pie, 247

raspberry grunt, 138

Rat Creek: Edmonton district, 219

real McCoy: biography, 247-48;
Elijah McCoy African-Canadian inventor, 247;
Ontario origin of catchphrase, 247-48;
other sources like MacKay Scotch whisky, 248;
story of American boxer Kid McCoy, 248-49

red alga (edible seaweed), 111-13

red lead, 4

red maple, 199

Red River bannock: alternative names for bannock, 250;
Bannock, Saskatchewan, 250;
origin of Red River name, 249-50;
origin of word *bannock*, 250;
pioneer wheat-flour and water biscuit; 249-50;
Red River colony, 249

redskins, racist term, 76

rhubarb grunt, 138

Richibucto goose: New Brunswick salted fish dish, 250

Rideau Canal: early name of Ottawa, 217

riffle, 250-51

rips: New Brunswick localism for whitewater rapids, 250-51

Robin Hood flour: origin in Moose Jaw, Saskatchewan, 251

rock tripe: exporers' edible lichen, 251-52;
lichen genera in rock tripe, 251-52;
origin of word *tripe*, 252;
quotation from explorer Samuel Hearne's *A Journey from Prince of Wales' Fort (1795)*, 252

Rockcliffe Park: exclusive section of Ottawa, 218

Rocky Mountain Maple, 198

rogan: how to make a birchbark container, 48
rotgut, 80
Rouleauville: former Calgary neighbourhood name, 252-53
rubbaboo: complex etymology of word, 253-54; English word *burgoo*, 253; explorer's journal on taste of rubbaboo and pemmican, 254; pioneers' pemmican soup, 253-54; *ruhiggan burgoo* 'beat meat soup' in Algonquian, 253-54
ruhiggan burgoo, 253-54

S

salal (*Gaultheria shallon*): food uses by Pacific coast peoples, 254-55; named after 17th-century Quebec botanist, 255; origin of word in Chinook language, 255-56; Pacific coast wintergreen shrub, 254-56
salalberry, 254-56
salicin, 15
sallow and *Salix* (willow), related words, 16
salmonberry (*Rubus spectabilis*), 256-57; aboriginal name *olallie*, 256; description of plant, 256; food uses of olallie, 256; *olalliechuk* or berry wine, 256; salmonberry charlotte dessert, 256-57
salt cod dish, 60-64
saltchuck: 'ocean' in Chinook Jargon, 267-68
samara or maple key, 199
sang dragon (Dragon's Blood—a Canadian wild plant), 86-87
Sanguinaria canadensis, 86-87
sapin de Douglas (Fr., Douglas Fir): origin of French name, 109-10
Saskatchewan grid roads, 137
Saskatoonberry (*Amelanchier alnifolia*): fruit of serviceberry tree, 257; prairie berry, 257; use in pemmican, 257
saw-off: Canadian political jargon, 257; use in Canadian sports metaphor, 257
saw-whet owl (*Aegolius acadicus*): Acadian owl named by New Brunswickers, 258
sawyer: Ontario nickname for saw-whet owl, 258
Scarborough, Ontario: extent of Toronto borough, 258; Elizabeth Simcoe, 28; name means "Harelip's Fort," 258; meaning in Old Norse language of Vikings, 259; Viking settlement in Britain, 258-59
Scotchman's Hill: Calgary locale, 259; comic origin of name, 259

scripture cord: New Brunswick lumber term, 259-60
scrunchins: Newfoundland and Labrador fat-back pork cubes, 260;
 sprinkle on fish and brewis, 260
scurvy cure from cedar bark, 13
scut: Prince Edward Island insult, 260;
 scut work, 260
sea pie, 95-97
sea urchin, 311-12
seal flipper pie, 129-30
sea-thistle, 311-12
seaweeds of Canadian waters, 112-13
seigneury, 55-56
sequbbun: Mi'kmaq word for groundnut, 203
Service, Robert W., 94
serviceberry of prairies, 257
shad, salted: New Brunswick food, 250
shank, 88
shediacs: New Brunswick oysters, 261;
 origin of name in Mi'kmaq language, 261
shoelace express: Toronto street slang, 290
shoe-string: seaweed impurity in Irish moss, 158
Shubenacadie, Nova Scotia: origin of place name in Mi'kmaq language, 203
Signal Hill: St. John's, Newfoundland locale, 272
Siksika mythology, 154
Siksika word, 103
Simcoe, Elizabeth: 259
skidroad and skid row: description of lumber camp road, 261-62;
 phrases "to hit the skids, to grease the skids, to put the skids under," 262;
 Skid Row's connection to poverty, 262;
 Viking origin of the word *skid*, 263;
 West Coast lumber slang, first Skid Road in Canada, 261
skinner, 93
skunk cabbage: author's encounter on Vancouver Island, 263;
 Eastern Skunk Cabbage (*Symplocarpus foetidus*), 264;
 meaning of botanical names, 264;
 plant described, 264;
 plant's "stink," 263-64;
 Western Skunk Cabbage (*Lysichitum americanum*), 264
skyr: food uses, 264;
 Icelandic yogourt of Manitoba, 264;
 preparation, 264;
 serving, 264
Slackers: Navy nickname for Halifax, 138

sloven: New Brunswick
cart, 265
slump: Nova Scotia
pudding, 138
smelt: etymology of smelt
words, 266-67;
poached smelt, 266;
recipe, 266;
run, 266;
storm, 266
smoked herring, 106
smoke-up, 52
Snap Apple Night in
Newfoundland, 98-102
Snotty var: Newfoundland
tree name, 38
soapberry, 267-68
soapolallie ice cream, 267-68;
origin of word in Chinook
Jargon, 267-68;
other uses of soapberries, 268
sockeye salmon: blueback
nickname, 270;
folk story about fish
name, 268-69;
origin of sockeye's scientific
name *Oncorhynchus*, 269-70;
origin of word
ichthyology, 269;
true origin in Salish
language, 269
sodbusters, 148
Songs of a Sourdough:
Canadian gold rush
poetry, 94
son-of-a-gun-in-a-sack:
Alberta chuckwagon boiled
pudding, 270;
eating anecdote, 270; recipe,
270
sonsy: Prince Edward Island
word, 270-71;
etymology of word, 271;
favourite term of Lucy
Maud Montgomery, 270-71
sounds: air bladders of a
cod fish, 271;
Newfoundland delicacy,
271;
physiological purpose, 271;
preparation, 271;
recipe and serving, 271
sourdough, 47, 94
spring tonic tea, 89
squatum: Newfoundland berry
wine, 272;
origin of word, 272;
recipe, 272;
uses, 272
St. John's, Newfoundland
neighbourhoods: The
Cribbies, 272;
Ladies' Lookout, 272;
Maggoty Cove, 272;
Signal Hill, 272
Tarahan's Town, 272;
Stanley Park, Vancouver:
origin of name, 139-40
stinging nettle, 208-10
stog your face: Prince Edward
Island and Newfoundland
slang: "eat up," 273;
etymology of term, 273;
use, 273
stubble-jumpers, 148
sugar: history of the
word, 194-96

T

tackle, 60-61

tacky, 61

tacky parties, 61

tamarin aux grillades, 98

tar sands of Fort McMurray, Alberta, 273; history of the town, 274-75; hot-water recovery process a Canadian invention, 274; life as a company town, 274-75

Tarahan's Town: St. John's, Newfoundland neighbourhood, 272

tarte à la râpure or *tarte râpée*, 247

teddy of shine: Prince Edward Island bootlegger term for homebrew bottle, 275

tetterwort, 86-87

The Backwoods of Canada by Catharine Parr Traill: famous Canadian pioneer guide book, 147

Tilley hat: famous Canadian headgear, 275; British sources of surname, 276; famous Canadians named Tilley, 276; later English source, 277; Norman sources of surname, 276-77

Tlingit language, 154-55

togue: Atlantic lake trout, 277; Algonkian source of word, 277

Tommy Douglas: premier of Saskatchewan and introduction of Medicare, 201-2; brief biography, 202

toonie: story of the birth of a Canadian coin, 278-90

toothache relief from willow bark, 16

Toronto place names: 290-94; meaning of Toronto, 291

Toronto street slang, 290

tourtière: Quebec meat pie, 294; origin of French word, 294; recipe, 294; use, 294

toutin: Newfoundland fried bread or pork cake, 295

Traill, Catharine Parr, 147

traveller's delight or groundnut, 203

tree nail: New Brunswick wooden peg, 295

trillium: origin of word, 296; other names, 296; *Trillium grandiflorum*, floral emblem of Ontario, 296

tule (edible tuber), 110-11

Tupi language, 54

turnip rape, 90

Twelve Apostles: Halifax building, 139

U

Ukrainian Canadians, 114-15

urticaria: contact skin symptoms from nettles, 208-10

urtication: former medical use of nettles, 208-10

V

Vaccinium berry species, 155

vent-view, 297

voodoo: not origin of hoodoo, 152-53

voyageurs' slang, 187-88

voyageurs' word, 103

W

wangan, wanigan, or wannigan: origin of word, 297;
wangan as New Brunswick lumber raft, 297;
wangan wooden box, 298;
wannigan as leather boot, 298;
shed on skids, 298

wapatoo (edible tuber), 110-11

weather rhymes of Canada, 298-311

western wake-robin: trillium, 296

Whip-poor-will's boots or pitcher plant, 227

whisky ranchers, 4

whoop-up: a western party, 5

whore's egg: Aristotle's lantern, 311;
Atlantic sea urchin, 311-12;
origin of term, 311-12;
sea-thistle, 311

Why I am Not a Word Cop: an essay about the author's view of language study and of attitudes to modern English, 312-19

wig, 52-53

Wikwemikong Unceded Reserve on Manitoulin Island, 144-45

wild ginger tea, 89

Winnipeg jambuster: jelly doughnut, 320

Winnipeg neighbourhoods: Crazy Corners, 319;
The Forks, 320;
Granola Belt, 319;
Portage and Pain, 319

wishakapucka (Labrador tea), 174

wood buffalo, 17

wool, prairie: sheep fodder, 241

word origins to improve school marks, 2

word stories and easier learning, 1

Y

"yesterday, today, and tomorrow" hash, 4

Yugoslavia: meaning of name, 173

Yukon holly, 166-67

Yukon official flower, 127-28

Yukon tea, 127-28

Yukon: Klondike gold rush, 154

MORE BOOKS BY BILL CASSELMAN
from McARTHUR & COMPANY

As The Canoe Tips
Comic Scenes from Canadian Life

In this first collection of funny essays, parodies, and happy nonsense just to laugh at, you will meet—

The kids at the cheap Muskoka aquarium who visit a burnt-out dolphin named Flippant. Poor Flippant just doesn't care anymore. He looks at the kiddies crowding around his tank, blows them an aquatic raspberry, and swims over to the far side of the tank.

Two summer camp counsellors discussing the parents who brought their kids to camp—

Nancy: Did you meet the Whittakers? *Primitivo!*

Joan: How primitive?

Nancy: Mrs. Whittaker carries her younger children in a fold of tissue attached to her abdomen!

Joan: My god! You mean . . .?

Nancy: Yes, Mrs. Whittaker is a marsupial. Of course, she's driving a Bentley, so we have to be nice.

Sample the comic banquet that awaits inside

As The Canoe Tips
Comic Scenes from Canadian Life

ISBN 1-55278-493-2

Canadian Sayings

62 weeks on the *National Post* Top Ten Canadian Non-Fiction List!

Samples from Bill's bestselling book:

- She's got more tongue than a Mountie's boot.
- That smell would gag a maggot on a gut wagon.
- I've seen more brains in a Manitoba sucked egg.
- He's thicker than a B.C. pine stump.
- Saskatchewan is so flat you can watch your dog run away from home for a week.
- He's so dumb he thinks Medicine Hat is a cure for head lice.
- Sign in bathroom where husband shaves: Warning—Objects in mirror are dumber than they appear.
- Of childish behaviour in a grown man: That boy never did grow up. One day, he just sorta haired over.

There is a reason this book made Canadians chuckle for more than a bestselling year. Buy it and find out why, as you laugh along with what one reviewer called "the funniest Canadian book I've ever read!"

Canadian Sayings

1,200 Folk Sayings Used by Canadians

Collected & Annotated by Bill Casselman

ISBN 1-55278-076-7

Canadian Sayings 2

61 weeks on the *National Post* Top Ten Canadian Non-Fiction List!

"Bill Casselman, bluenose among schooners on the sea of popular etymology, moors his mighty vessel, nets a-teeming with Canadian words."

—*Indigo Internet review*

Canada's funniest collector of salty sayings is back, with more than 1,000 new sayings used by Canadians, expressions not in the first volume. As usual, Bill has been careful about the limits of good taste. So you'll find gems like these:

- We were so poor we never had decorations on the Christmas tree unless Grandpa sneezed.
- Tongue-tied? That dude couldn't adlib a fart at a bean supper.
- The gene pool around here could use a little chlorine.
- You know you're out in the Ontario boondocks if you cut your front lawn and find a car.
- Dude, I'm gonna feed you a shut-up sandwich.

Canadian Sayings 2

1,000 Folk Sayings Used by Canadians

Newly Collected & Annotated by Bill Casselman

ISBN 1-55278-272-7

Canadian Sayings 3

"Bill Casselman is one of Canada's foremost lexicographers and word hounds. In addition to a career as a broadcaster and producer for CBC, he is the author of nine books on Canadian language."

—Jennifer MacLennan, *INSIDE LANGUAGE: A Canadian Language Reader*

Casselman is back with fresh bounty: hundreds and hundreds of new folk sayings not collected in the previous two volumes! Here's a favourite, sent in by a Prairie high school class:

• Why is it so windy in Saskatchewan?
Because Alberta blows and Manitoba sucks.

Hey, it's simple high school geophysics with a touch of chauvinism.

There are newly collected Canadian threats too.

• You're lookin' to spit Chiclets, Dude.

This is mock goon talk from a junior hockey arena. Chiclets are tiny pieces of gum vaguely toothlike in shape – hence the implication: I'm going to knock your teeth out.

Canadian Sayings 3

1,000 Folk Sayings Used by Canadians

Newly Collected & Annotated by Bill Casselman

ISBN: 1-55278-425-8

Casselman's Canadian Words

In this #1 bestseller, Bill Casselman delights and startles with word stories from every province and territory of Canada. Did you know that *Scarborough* means "Harelip's Fort"? The names of *Lake Huron* & *Huronia* stem from a vicious, racist insult. Huron in old French meant 'long-haired clod.' French soldiers labelled the Wendat people with this nasty misnomer in the 1600s. To *deke out* is a Canadian verb that began as hockey slang, short for 'to decoy an opponent.' Canada has a fish that ignites. On our Pacific coast, the oolichan or *candlefish* is so full of oil it can be lighted at one end and used as a candle. *"Mush! Mush!* On, you huskies!" cried Sergeant Preston of The Yukon to 1940s radio listeners, thus introducing a whole generation of Canucks to the word once widely used in the Arctic to spur on sled dogs. Although it might sound like a word from Inuktitut, early French trappers first used it, borrowing the term from the Canadian French command to a horse to go: *Marche! Marche!* Yes, it's Québécois for giddyap!

Everything from Canadian monsters to mottoes is here, and more fascinating terms from Canadian place names, politics, sports, plants and animals, clothing.

Casselman's Canadian Words

ISBN 0-7730-5515-0

All at online booksellers and bookstores across Canada.